NEW!

424 PPS.

A gathering of new work from 65 of America's best younger poets.

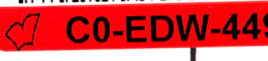

Jon Anderson	Mekeel McBride
George Barlow	Heather McHugh
Michael Burkhard	Sandra McPherson
Peter Cooley	Susan Mitchell
Philip Dacey	Jack Myers
Stephen Dobyns	Naomi Nye
Mark Doty	Steve Orlen
Rita Dove	Greg Pape
Norman Dubie	Robert Pinsky
Russell Edson	Stanley Plumly
Carolyn Forche	Bin Ramke
Alice Fulton	Alberto Rios
Tess Gallagher	Pattiann Rogers
Albert Goldbarth	Kenneth Rosen
Barry Goldensohn	Michael Ryan
Lorrie Goldensohn	Sherod Santos
Jorie Graham	Herbert Scott
Linda Gregg	Michael Sheridan
Daniel Halpern	John Skoyles
Patricia Hampl	Gary Soto
Robert Hass	Maura Stanton
William Hathaway	David St. John
Edward Hirsch	Pamela Stewart
T. R. Hummer	Susan Stewart
Mark Jarman	James Tate
Denis Johnson	Richard Tillinghast
Richard Katrovas	Leslie Ullman
Sydney Lea	Michael Waters
Larry Levis	Bruce Weigl
Robert Long	Roger Weingarten
Thomas Lux	C. K. Williams
Morton Marcus	David Wojahn

Carolyne Wright

★ **$9.95 Postpaid**

Mail to: WAMPETER PRESS, BOX 512, GREEN HARBOR, MA 02041

Please send _____ copies of NEW AMERICAN POETS

$ _____ enclosed

NAME _____

ADDRESS _____

CITY _____ STATE _____ ZIP _____

TENDRIL

No. 19-20

Managing Editor
George E. Murphy, Jr.

Associate Editors

Jacquelyn Crews	Michelle Gillet
Mark Jarman	Sandy McKinney
Sue Ellen Thompson	Bruce Weber

Contributing Editors

Raymond Carver	Brendan Galvin	Mary Robison
Carolyn Forche	William Matthews	Diane Wakoski
Richard Ford	Mekeel McBride	Joy Williams
Tess Gallagher	Heather McHugh	Tobias Wolff
	Lisel Mueller	

Cover Photograph by Jane Tuckerman.

Composition, Layout & Design by Coastal Composition
                            Box 2600, Ocean Bluff, MA 02065

Tendril is supported by funding from the Coordinating Council of Literary Magazines, The National Endowment for the Arts, the Massachusetts Council on the Arts and Humanities, IBM, and by the work of volunteer editors and by services provided by the business community.

Copyright © 1985 by *Tendril, Inc.*
                    Box 512, Green Harbor, MA 02041

Tendril is published three times per year.
Subscriptions are $12 for 3 issues, $19 for 6 issues, $27 for 9 issues.
Institutional subscriptions are $14 per year.

Tendril, Inc. is a non-profit, tax-exempt corporation under Section 501 3 (c) of the IRS code. Donations to *Tendril, Inc.* are fully tax-deductible. All patrons making a gift to *Tendril, Inc.* of $200 or more will receive a complimentary lifetime subscription.

Member: Coordinating Council of Literary Magazines.

Tendril is indexed in the *Index of American Periodical Verse*.

. . . the chapel with its round
window between the dormitories

peaked by the bronze belfry
peaked in turn by the cross,
verdigris - faces all silent
that miracle that has burst sexless

from between the carrot rows.
Leafless white birches, their
empty tendrils swaying in
the all but no breeze guard

behind the spiked monastery fence
the sacred statuary. But ranks
of brilliant car-tops row on row
give back in all his glory the

late November sun and hushed
attend, before that tumbled
ground, those sightless walls
and shoveled entrances where no

one but a lonesome cop swinging
his club gives sign, that agony
within where the wrapt machines
are praying . . . .

        from *The Semblances*
              William Carlos Williams

CONTENTS

FICTION

Charles Baxter	*Media Event*	60
Ann Beattie	*Who Do You Love?*	73
Susan Dodd	*Browsing*	128
Amy Hempel	*Three Popes Walk Into a Bar*	163
Chuck Kinder	*Disneyworld*	180
James Howard Kuntsler	*The Rise Fall and Redemption of Mooski Toffski Offski*	212
D. Leitman	*An Affair, I Guess*	233
David Long	*Great Blue*	240
Thomas McGuane	*Beyond The Infield*	264
Bob Shacochis	*The Heart's Advantage*	315
Joy Williams	*Health*	382

MEMOIR

| Charles Bukowski | *Bop Bop Against That Curtain* (Illustrations by R. Crumb) | 89 |

THE ASSOCIATED WRITING PROGRAMS AWARD WINNING POEMS for 1984:

1st Place:	Lawrence Kearney	*Uncle God*	16
2nd Place:	Dave Kelley	*Cycle for Pablo Neruda*	18
	Brenda Marie Osbey	*Portrait*	25
3rd Place:	John Hildebridle	*Thoreau: Some Times*	29
	Margaret Szumowski	*We Have No Ambassadors Here*	35
	Patricia Dobler	*World Without End*	37
	Phyllis Janowitz	*Aging in April*	38

POETRY

Joan Aleshire	*A White Horse, A New Moon*	43
	Fine Line	44
Keith Althaus	*The Ambulance*	45
Barbara Anderson	*Weekday Matinees*	46
Philip Appleman	*Euphorias*	48
Jennifer Atkinson	*Pattaconk Pond*	52
	Pig Alley	53
Wendy Battin	*In the Solar Wind*	54
Robin Behn	*Last Page*	79
Ted Benttinen	*Above Punta Arenas*	80
Jane Birdsall	*Experience*	82
Wendy Bishop	*Taking Photographs*	83
Jane Blue	*At Work*	85
Deborah Boe	*Invisible Girl*	87
Philip Booth	*Among Houses*	88
Teresa Cader	*Insomnia*	97
	Zach's Cliffs, Gay Head	99
	Gooseflesh	100
Hayden Carruth	*For Papa*	101
David Citino	*Sister Mary Appassionata Lectures the Eighth Grade Girls: Furrow, Cave, Cowry, Home*	102
	Sister Mary Appassionata Speaks During the Retreat of the Eighth Grade Boys and Girls	103
	Sister Mary Appassionata Lectures the Studio Art Class: Doctrines of Nakedness	104
Robert Clinton	*The Men I Know*	106
Judith Ortiz Cofer	*Letter From a **Caribbean Island***	107

Gillian Conoley	*New in Town*	108
	Patsy Cline	110
	Woman Speaking Inside Film Noir	111
	Insomnia	112
	The Cousin at the Funeral	113
Kenneth Zamora Damacion	*Tadpole Fishing*	114
Charles W. Darling	*Tying Knots*	115
Jon Davis	*Driving Red Bush Lane*	117
Joseph Deumer	*Sunday Morning*	121
Jond Devol	*Inuits*	123
	Inuit Woman	124
Deborah Digges	*Bums*	125
Carol Dine	*Morning/Afternoon*	126
Elizabeth Dodd	*Another Season*	127
Dennis M. Dorney	*Flight From Churubusco*	135
	Sunday With the Game On	136
Charles Edward Eaton	*The Blowgun*	137
Jane Eklund	*The Mill Worker's Daughter: 1933*	139
	The Metamorphosis	140
Kathy Fagan	*Night Flowers*	141
	The Sleep of the Apostles	142
Donald Finkel	*No News*	143
	Election Day	144
Caroline Finkelstein	*Blind-Spot*	145
Robert Funge	*Easter Sunday*	146
	from JOHN/HENRY	147
Patricia Goedicke	*Americans Shot At in Canyon*	148
Beckian Fritz Goldberg	*The Consolation of Celibacy*	151
	State Street Motel	153
	The Perception of Motion	154
Rafael Guillen	*One Day With the Dawn*	157
	The Final Tenderness	159
	Poem of No	161

Carol S. Hamilton	*Wire of Darkness*	162
Art Homer	*Incentives for Night Work*	170
Jane Hoogestraat	*The Death of the Khan*	171
	Bridges	172
Lynda K. Hull	*Tide of Voices*	174
Joseph Hutchison	*Vander Meer Holding On*	176
Kit Irwin	*The Pinboys*	177
Sibyl James	*(01)*	178
Marilyn Kallet	*The Ladies*	179
Phyllis Koestenbaum	*Criminal Sonnets*	197
Kendra Kopelke	*Jonnie Richardson*	198
Judith Kroll	*After the Snowfall*	204
	Winter Birth	205
	Same Time, Next Life	206
Maxine Kumin	*In the Absence of Bliss*	207
	Visiting Professor	210
Dorianne Laux	*Skipping Stones*	228
Sydney Lea	*Reckoning*	230
Lisa Lewis	*A History of Partial Cure*	238
Gary Margolis	*Her Apprehension*	251
Paul Mariani	*Minneapolis: At the Summer Solstice*	252
Lynn Martin	*It Is Sunny*	254
	Shaving	255
Mekeel McBride	*The Kiss*	256
	The Plainest Signs	258
	The Thief of Light	260
Gardner McFall	*After a Fairy Tale by Oscar Wilde*	261
Martin McGovern	*Near San Gregorio*	262
Sandy McKinney	*The Body of Desire*	277
Lynne McMahon	*The Red Shoes*	278
Jane Miller	*Ozone Avenue*	280

Judson Mitcham	*Home*	282
	The Smell of Rain	283
George Moore	*Mexico Firsthand*	284
Fred Muratori	*The Casket Maker's Proposal*	286
Bea Carol Opengart	*Erotica*	287
Alicia Ostriker	*The Game*	288
Robert Pack	*Clayfeld Holds On*	290
Eric Pankey	*Rhododendron*	293
	Late August	294
	The Guard: 1934	296
Wyatt Prunty	*Rooms Without Walls*	301
John Reed	*Forgetting*	304
Paulette Roeske	***A Plan to Circumvent the Death of Beauty***	306
William Pitt Root	*Newswalkers of Swidnik*	307
Michael Rosen	*Child's Play*	311
Jeff Schiff	*Articulating the Familiar*	313
Ron Schreiber	*Tie*	314
Charles Siebert	*The Lament of the Air Traffic Controller*	339
Jim Simmerman	*Rock 'n' Roll*	341
	The Reluctant Angels	343
	Daedalus Aground	344
Charlie Smith	*White and Scarlet*	346
Judith Steinbergh	*Past Time*	348
Stephanie Strickland	*In April*	349
Robyn Supraner	*The Nannies*	350
Arthur Sze	*Crush an Apple*	352
James Tate	*The Chaste Stranger*	353
	The Little Sighs Bite a Sheet	355
	No Rest for the Gambler	356
	The Sadness of My Neighbors	357
	We'll Burn That Bridge When We Come To It	358
	Short March, Teeny Wall	359

Chase Twichell	*The Odds*	361
	Translations from the Rational	367
	The Moon in the Pines	368
	Meteor Showers, August, 1968	369
Constance Urdang	*Returning to the Port of Authority: A Picaresque*	371
Larkin Warren	*Rituals of the Ordinary*	373
	Vermont Triptych, 1978	374
Bruce Weigl	*The Act*	375
	To The Dog Dying	377
Roger Weingarten	*Water Music*	378
Don Welch	*First Book Apocrypha*	380
Ruth Whitman	*Basic Training, 1942*	381
Ellen Wittlinger	*Blue Murder*	391
Carolyne Wright	*Eugenia*	393
	Talking Politics	396

FEATURE POET: RAYMOND CARVER : 21 POEMS

Where Water Comes Together with Other Water	403
The Young Fire Eaters of Mexico City	404
Interview	405
Away	406
Ask Him	407
The Young Girls	409
The Garden	410
Wenas Ridge	412
The Juggler	414
Venice	415
The Eve of Battle	416
Extirpation	417
The Hat	418
In the Lobby of the Hotel Del Mayo	420
Next Door	421
Late Night with Fog and Horses	422
Elk Camp	423
In Switzerland	425
Anathema	427

Energy 428
The Fishing Pole of the Drowned Man 429

CONTRIBUTOR NOTES 431

The 1984 AWP Award-Winning Poems

Judges:
Patricia Goedicke
Larry Levis
Richard Shelton
Ellen Bryant Voigt

Lawrence Kearney

Uncle God

1.   Those days there were no houses
behind our house. Fields of sumac,
stiff-backed bullrushes, milkweed
& Queen Anne's lace & purple wildflowers
I never learned the names of
ran clear to Hopkins Street & on
to Lackawanna, dead-ending
at Bethlehem Steel. By nightfall
the day's dust had settled, & even
the fields looked dirty. Mother
would stand by the back window,
watching the sky for signs.
                              Saturdays,
in the basement, I helped with the wash.
While we sorted the dark, the light,
Mother talked of London, the Land Army
after the war. O we laughed,
she'd say, it was just us girls.
She blamed the Nazis
for everything –– the Blitz,
the oily charms of the fishwives
in the Brixton Market,
the endless heaps of clothes,
America.

2.   Mother, in your stories
the sky above England
was a blue bar of soap
God scrubbed the world with.
England . . . you made it sound
as pastoral & remote
as Heaven.
                    One day,
when everyone was out, I undressed,
& put on your bra & panties.
I wanted to get that close
to your skin. To imagine you.
                              You
have to imagine, you said once, that God

is in everything —— & yet far away
like the sky, or an Uncle you've never seen
but know. Honey, don't listen to the nuns,
they're crazy, they talk about God
like He's some kind of Santa Claus,
but I'm telling you: God is here, right now,
or He's nowhere, & if He's nowhere
over the ka-chunk ka-chunk ka-chunk
of the washing machine. Oh brother,
I thought. What does she want from me?
That I never listen to the nuns anyway.
That one day God told me
to dress in her underwear.
Lies. Lies.
                    Mother,
it's taken me 20 years to admit
you might not have wanted anything.
I never asked. It was easier
to call you crazy. But darling,
you *were* crazy. Both of us
so easily hurt, we thought suffering
was a kind of holiness
we couldn't avoid . . . . And there
we are: still standing
beside the washer, watching the clothes
float slow-motion up & down
in that primordial soup. *Like flowers*,
you say, softly, the urgency
gone from your voice, Father's
pant legs & the family socks
blossoming as we bend over them
breathing the soapy steam
of Thomas Aquinas & the gospel
of John, our heads nodding
sleepily as we talk, our lips
only inches apart.

Dave Kelly

Cycle for Pablo Neruda

"Everything they write of me I read
without interest, skimming
as if it weren't addressed to me,
this talk, the just and the cruel."   Isla Negra

    I

ATTITUDES

When his wrists are cuffed, a man smokes a cigarette
as if praying furtively, as if either his jailers or god
might strike him now that the world has left him outside.

When the families of the poor huddle at funerals, in
the front rows of cheap, Sunday school seats, they cringe
forward as if the devil's whip already kissed their backs.

And when the comfortable read poetry as if god loved them
they smile at flowers and at incense and those words
that carefully turn the smaller corners of their minds.

    II

Ten years and an epitaph writes itself in Spanish
and people still spill into the streets as they did
and hope lies beside herself in the dirt, rolls over its
own body like a dog under a truck's wheels, lies as
still as the master with the broken heart, his soul
escaped from the prison ship as these few yellow
flowers trailing after the nameless in the streets.

And if I turn to you over some meditation, my breath
gone, my idiot's smile a void of credit and response, my
three stages of evening loss, dread and insomnia, I
cannot answer even a child this time, cannot sing
of wings in this night of boots or call on the young

with these resignant old triumphant year and year again,
their joyless dead rampant against the fields of martyrs.

III

DUSTING OFF THE SORROW

All right, haul out the old blue shirt and shake off its
wrinkles, blow the dust off the lunch bucket, the bones
of the father and his sad rosary, trudge down another road
with what's left of hope in your left hand, the one that
can play no piano.

It's true that a man stands on his country the way he stands
on his gallows; it's true we are born on the birthdays of
our heroes and that we die, a few shrivelled pieces of meat
on the saucer edge of the dawns that bring in the Days of
Assassination, holidays no one dresses up for.

And me, what am I doing boring everyone again, forgetting to
put the meals and the jokes in my songs? When will I learn
that the eye wants its reds only in roses, the nose wants to
smell what is cooked, the ear to listen to sounds filtered
through nostalgia like doves one remembers?

At a slight distance from here, perhaps only twenty years,
ice is waiting to form forever over the roofs of our houses,
snow is crouched like a cougar in ambush, and a melancholy
singer repeats the words of his people: when there is no more
bread, stones will do.

And I dust off the old sorrow again because of that and for
you, and I turn in the night as alone as each of us the way
we are when we run a single hand lightly up and down over the
edges of those sills that guard windows looking out and windows
looking in.

IV

PHENOMENOLOGY/THE AMERICAN SCHOLAR

The one, the many, the state, the actress dead
in her second husband's car, the overproductive flesh,
give us this day only one of these or the newspaper,
its little devils of paradise laughing under the breakfast,
this one sighing over the ghost of comrade, that one
under the snow, among pines for over thirty years.

On the wall is a map of Finland, small beast between
large beasts, in the parlor a book of the nationals: alone,
dressed, in group, undressed, waiting, for train, personal

(or has he forgotten history, invented tragedy, become
the physician in his attic, peering through a hole in the floor
at a bookshelf, the wanton, the lascivious, language . . .)

Each of these works alone in his own way: the stammering
theologian, the thick fur of his dog, firewood, a pie
of some elegance, cooling, only the children thieves and why
not, that little bit of soup both unpleasant and nothing

that they serve between sunup and football, corporation
and her president, trained horses, hospitals nobody dies in.

V

As fall disappears into the trees with its bald snake, its
one glove, still another man of the people turns bread into
prayers, another Peter lights his rock and warms his own hands
over it while the poor contemplate sand as, finally, the
answer to food, drink and the ordinary need for small houses
or for children who, once played with, fit back in their boxes.

As another year becomes another ten, evening finds the bishop
sitting by the wood fire, puffing the avuncular pipe, dis-
cussing the price of warthog, a man's love for cocaine, a child

and its warmest dog. Meanwhile it's raining all along the road
outside and we haven't got enough to bribe a doorman at the
elevator to the penthouse or even one stone for our shoes . . .

yes, give us this day a day's respite from the stomach, from
the red eye and its infected toe, its small shoe, and we might
pray to the Marx or his Father Almighty, might make the last
hungry act of contrition. But right now it's all soup: soup
this and soup that, to quote one one at all and the letter ing,
that strange death at the end of the busier verbs, captain
without action, knowing finally that what is being done to us
is not pleasing us, is not what we prepared ourselves for.

VI

INSOMNIA'S PHOTOGRAPH

It is a picture of seven Chilean men facing the firing
squad. The third man from the left is holding a
clay jar and you know why he is doing this, you have
heard the story before. He has bet a member of
the firing squad the money in his pocket against a
similar amount to go to his family, that he will not
drop the jar when he falls. They have agreed that
he can drop it when the coup de grace is administered,
this will not be counted against him. In another
version of the story, a Spanish one, he is simply
holding the jar out of curiosity, as a point of know-
ledge that might interest the captain after the squad
has finished with its duties.

Of course the condemned man is doing this to concen-
trate on something other than the bullets that are
going to tear through him like small metal tornadoes.
Of course he held his head all night long like his six
comrades while the jar lay unnoticed at his feet.
But now he knows the image of the clay shattering in
his death grip and the remaining shard still wrapped
in his closed fist, cutting into the palm as he lies

on the ground will drive the captain and the members
of the squad to hold their wives and mistresses so
tightly against the darkness tonight that they will cry
out in pain.

And at least some of these men will know that they are
holding nothing more than clay against the moment of
their death.

    VII

TEACHING THE OPPRESSED

For Bev Lewis

First they must learn to run down bread
in an open field, break its back and then eat it
before they are caught by game wardens. Then
we must teach them to use their hands as cups
and that when they have wept enough
they will have salt and plenty of liquid to drink.
And of course they can be taught to use
the stones as their shoes, always remembering
to leave them behind as they walk, each
step a stone, each stone a shoe, so that
the others will have shoes when they follow.
And then the cold. Of course they must learn the cold.

    VIII

HANDEDNESS

"The sons of twin brothers are half-brothers." A doctor

Without asking where I came from, I walked out
for about ten years before turning back: so many
miles south, so many east and then north; where, then,
was my father before I returned? And those children,
dead in their Bengali hovels, the Mother, laughter

of god, dust soup, a house for the dying; how do
we assimilate the week's sorrows if the week isn't
there, how do we hear the voices for wrong, the
enlarged eye of the word yes and her cousin, the one
who stands at the small end of the line, bowl out,
hand up, jaws working, electing hunger mayor, poverty
dog catcher; how do we tell the child we are sorry
at the end of the day, so many words, so many blows
or just this: the back as it grows smaller in the
eye, walking a road without its sign, a road that
turns but doesn't turn around, a board in the right
hand, a hammer and its three nails in the other.

    IX

BEGGAR'S PRAYER

Our Father which art in heaven, hallowed be thy bread,
thy hand, my mouth, hallowed by my knees, this road,
the rain turning slowly to ice and blessed be this house
that turns its back on me, a light shining in on itself.

Carefully then, we see that they will always be with us;
with the slow craft of the architect we build their houses:
one by the sea, for the rain, and one in the desert, to
make the most of that sun only we can own, only those of
this table laughing at the words of the man in black robes,

this guest of night sleepers, of the pressed crease and
the closed road, a guard at each end smiling with selection.

On the next day then, dust for the soup, mud for the bowl;
on the next day there are our children, there are the
others, the ones without tears, without a pin to count souls
on, to argue, as they diminish, the separated body, the mind

deprived of itself, a mad philologist waiting at noon
for his check, seeing the mailman the way we have learned
to as he turns to the right and walks down the wrong street.

X

SINGER

Today I want to talk to you the way a singer does
when his left hand caresses the neck of a guitar, the
way his eyes look up, asking half a question and
his mouth hints at the letter O or the voice turns,
then slips in tenor over the letter S and its vowel.

Today I want to exchange something with you much as
a dog did once when, jaws trembling, she dropped the
infant rabbit, unhurt and damp, into my palm, the way
she backed up and her tail waved, just three times
and the way the small heart of the rabbit felt then.

This morning I want to ask something but not for help,
not even for you to leave this place where you are
sitting, idly looking at a few words on paper; more,
I want you to fail even to see me the way, at dawn once,
a deer did as I walked by, unnoticed on the road, or

the way a young woman, pink with sleep, stood in the
only room of their cottage and let her blanket fall from
around her, then ran across the room to her lover, to
his arms as I passed on the beach, my feet in the waves
and the way I looked up only once before walking on.

Brenda Marie Osbey

Portrait

i sit for my portrait on the veranda.
this was once a family house
the landlady describes
how it must have looked:
double parlors
and of course,
this veranda.

almost without malice
i say,
we call them galleries

she looks out onto the avenue
horses in her flat blue eyes
skin like unleavened bread
brittle
and without variation.

2.
i sit for my portrait on the veranda.
the photographer pushes his lips together
explaining how tiring this will be
how he wants this perfect
does not want me
to look too dark.

3.
his name is lejamn
a burly big-waisted man
sooty colored

he takes two yellow-stained
gunmetal fingers
pushes my forehead back
tells me not to look so stern.

4.
big burly gunmetal black lejamn
fourth generation photographer

how did his grandfather make a living then?
taking pictures of smooth-skinned nieces
of lady friends from paillet-land?
too proud perhaps
to work in the city
selling dry goods to the white folk
or vegetables to the black?
no rag-man
tin-man
old-gold-and-diamond man
these so many lives later
to push young writer women on the forehead
and tell them not to look so black.

5.
jamaica
he says for no reason
you look just like jamaica

in my head i make a dance in jamaica

he says it again:

just like jamaica to me

what can i say?
i am only the material he works in
given over entirely
to technique.

6.
when i come there was no street sign
only dirt roads
dirt roads and a vegetable man
give me a ride,
a soft alligator pear,
and taken me home to his aunt sue lee.

they sent me to school in the city

him selling vegetables on the weekday
all the time taking pictures
sue lee taking in shirts from uptown whites
talking at them through me:

tell them i said
tell them i will

taking in shirts from the whites
and teaching little colored girls
to speak bon francais

no one stopping to question
a little tan woman
with hollow cinnamon eyes

would white children die if they looked at her?
they looked past her narrow waist instead
mouthing instructions
saying
miz suzy
too ill-bred to know
they were taking nothing from her.

sue lee sitting on the gallery of an afternoon
talking at them through me
in english when she wanted to
to show she could pronounce
the flat dead words

waving them out of sight
the screen door standing open
them running down the front walk
and sue lee never rising
until they were past her field of vision.

I stood counting out the pieces
or the money when they had come to pay
counting the silver once

twice
slowly enough to please sue lee.

7.
i sit for my portrait on the veranda
i, named evangeline eva marie
christened by sue lee st. clementh
and her nephew august anthony peter le jamn.

i sit completely still
on the three-quarter gallery
of the house where i was raised
by a sand-faced vegetable-man photographer
and his bon francais aunt

i stare in the face of the lies i have heard,
i stare into the camera's far-sighted eye.
he asks me only once:

what is your name?

evangeline, i say
evangeline eva marie clementh

he wipes a white handkerchief across his mouth
only the camera gives its click
and again:
click.

John Hildebidle

Thoreau: Some Times

    April

Burning (had the wind stayed true) the town,
the one home he hated well
enough never to leave, he'd grown
careless with matches, like some swell,

city-stale, who on a rotty
stump cooked chowder in a spring drought —
the grass flared in an instant chest high
and where the pines lined out

the pasture, the fire bloomed orange
like a demon autumn. He found
it just the thing after eating
his fill of fish and bird-song

and once it was well-caught
he had two things to do (he
loved the pure paradoxicality
of taking both sides at

once). He ran in the alarm
and lay back to watch, always
the joyous eye, as the prim farms
went like tinder, and his companion prayed

it wouldn't burn Town Meeting. Henry figured
you could find worse things to sear.
He could see he'd by luck cornered
a name that would wear

and one rich in angles as a fallen barn:
"Tree-burner Thoreau" of all
things, or as it settled out, "damned rascal"
for sooting the town's linen —

well, he could piece out the steps
for doing that job to a turn,

breeding a practice apocalypse,
and in very good place and season.

      July and after

Sage Emerson was over
viewing the old world, and hired
Alcott to build him a summer
house. Alcott soared

on inspiration and designed,
to honor the muses, a nine-
cornered cottage,
and to hell with the straightedge.

Henry worked double to cure
the meanderings of that capacious
mind; Alcott dreamed as ever
but had to get his hands, alas,

in the thing, while Henry put in more
shoulder and less brain —
moral building, each nail sure
at one stroke. Fresh from his own

house-work, just man-shaped
and left at the pond for loons,
he worked all summer. For the town
it beat a horse-pull: boys skipped

fishing to watch the thinkers
clamber on the skewed ridge-
pole like squirrels summer-
drunk. Even Henry laughed,

"Ah, he's a crooked stick," and let
Alcott hear if he deigned
to — Henry knew crooked and
from the inside. In time the great

man smiled on the house,
and ignored it. Birds found it
risky but still use-
ful for nesting, and it stood

years, weed-grown, curious,
a landmark of sorts, too
damp to burn, sagging to compost,
held, as he'd guessed, true

to form by Henry's nails
and serene geometry.

      November

Calling in autumn on "that
Walt Whitman, of the scribbling gentry,"
who at first was not home, Henry
went to the kitchen and, flat-

out, asked Walt's mother for hotcakes.
Whitman, great contradiction-darer,
fretted until he died about that lapse
in bourgeois manners.

When they did meet, words came hard.
Henry, all nose, found
the poet broad but not fine.
Whitman, who hoarded

a nation's body in his own,
down to the teeth and sweat,
guessed the fellow from Concord
knew man only in abstraction.

Imagine their talk: the universal
raver, dressed like a woodman
even in sidewalked Brooklyn;
older, stubby of body and soul,

Henry in stiff city-cloth,
who'd rather have numbered Walt's hairs
or laid a notched stick across
that beefy hand to take its measure:

"I feel, I feel, the voices great within me!"
"Aye. But know ye muskrats?"

    Mid-year

Dead summer, and the air sags from use.
His tramps persist. Heavy with dust,
as if the earth rose to claim
anything fool enough to roam,

he collects what little promise
the near shore can offer.
Apples are weeks off, and harvest;
farther still, the winter rigor,

and there is now only the past
of seed to be lived out.
For miles roundabout
walking moves from one waste

to the next. Weeds brittle in sun.
Cicadas moan over a few sour
early berries, not even worth
the picking. None

of the landscape quickens. What use
to keep at it? Why not lie down,
lazy as snakes, and risk sleeping
through this season of small fruits?

Then: today, after twenty years or so,
he learns a name, of the **rush** he'd seen
over and over but found no
one else could recognize , even

the reliable codgers. He'd
wondered if it were some by-
blow, a bastard shoot that only
he ever saw or pulled

to press in his sample-book,
a plant of the inner eye. But
no, and by accident, this finer
knowledge is his, making the shore

dance of a sudden to a communicable
step, while he scribbles,
full of the sap of that naming
which is the sole repossession.

      May

Declining in a canework cot, his own-
made, he is beyond naturalizing farmers' land.
Now he has the memory only
of short legs that could hurry

everyone else's down to stumps. Still
he seems happy. No one understands,
with his future brief and all
indoors, shrunk to a parlor of maiden-

ladies and bric-a-brac, and the rabbit
pelt a boy brought last night,
thinking it might make him feel like
tramping again. He does it

and tells no one how:
collects, the rascal! his and
our own dying, with so
much pleasure they'll hang

lessons on it he'd have sniffed
away on his good days. But now

with a great smile his beard
keeps under wraps, he has a last go

at making facts in-
to virtues, virtues into nails:
"It's better," he says,
"some things should end."

A Marker

*Longing for places he wasn't wanted
he found enough nearby to keep
outrage well-fed. He hunted
what no one could stomach: muskrat,*

*Irishman, himself; and what wouldn't be
drawn he wrote down, not afraid
of the common because even the least weed
would scratch someone. Ordinary,*

*and he knew it; one of the odd-
job men any town had, idlers
but handy, and proud of both;
proud too of the particular nowhere*

*he railed against; bathed
in antagonism as if in mossy
water; changed his name (but
only a little); travelled (but only*

*a little); made pencils and charts
and enemies and birch wine no one
else would drink and books that
mildewed in his attic, and*

*if no one listened still he shouted,
like a rook before sunup: wake,
wake, wake, wake — words
sure enough to split the husk.*

Margaret Szumowski

We Have No Ambassador Here

Green peninsulas, blue waters floated
to us. Long grasses lined the runway.
"Heaven," we said. We thought
the red carpets, the drums, the old women

frenzied by dance, the feathered skirts,
were for us. But their soldiers
rifled our belongings, our blue jeans,
our books, our toothbrushes. Even

our priests had no token with them.
They thought we were mercenaries
and spies. They thought our books
and maps would help us conquer them.
When we sang they thought

we were singing obscenities.
We were not used to real guns
pointing at us. Caged by
a circle of guns, we grew mad.
We were not used to being without
an ambassador, sleeping on red
plastic couches in an airport lobby,
guarding our tongues.

"Ici meme les murs ont des oreilles,"
The walls had ears and eyes. We wanted
our suitcases, our toothbrushes, our combs
and kleenex. Where were the gazelles,
the flamingoes wading cool waters, the people

with their hearts in their hands. After
they taught us, after one of us
had a wounded thigh, they let us go.
The dancing was over, but sunlight
so bright it could blind. They led us

to a plantation, white-pillared floating
in red and yellow cannalilies, tortoises

meandering the courtyards. We wanted

to wander by the deep blue lake, but
their soldiers waited. "You have
no ambassador here," they said.

A Dainty Way to Darken GRAY HAIR AT HOME

RIGHT in your own home you can make and apply a gray hair preparation that quickly and easily gives the appearance of youth and beauty to gray, faded, streaked hair. Get from your druggist one-fourth ounce glycerine, one ounce bay rum, one box BARBO Compound. Mix these in a half pint of water or your druggist will mix for you at small cost.

This gives you a large bottle of an old and widely used preparation that imparts a natural-looking color to graying hair, whether blond or brunette. By making it at home you are assured of freshness and an amazing saving in cost. BARBO will not wash out or rub off; does not stain the scalp or affect waves and permanents. BARBO is economical, easy to apply and has been used with satisfaction for over 25 years. Try the money-saving BARBO recipe today.

Patricia Dobler

World Without End

These insane layings of eggs by the thousands,
clear jellies clinging to the undersides of myriad leaves,
and in the streams and oceans, millions of clusters more,
the hordes eating their way southward through the trees,
or being eaten, but there's a plenty for food,
a plenty to live and breed more. Don't you tremble
at that fecundity? The mindless swell and burst,
and each like each like each. What kind of God desires
such multitudes. Stacked like cordwood on the streets in Delhi,
each a beloved soul. But oh
the raw cries of my father, the night his mother died.
My mother, who can see longer and harder than anyone,
now trying to ease him down. The deaths of the many
are nothing to me. When the sirens warn, I want
everyone I love gathered with me on a high mountain
where we start over, all of us saved by a miracle
because we are mild, intelligent and happy in our work.
But even God can't stop us
from standing on the quarry's edge, daring who will dive
into that black water first,
the insane laying of eggs, the thousands, the millions,
my father wrapped and dying in my mother's arms.

Phyllis Janowitz

Aging in April

I was befuddled as a duck with wide, splayed feet.
My equipage was neat.
My hair was not.
                My hair
was sizzling and black.
My mother would hold it back
with her hand, to free my bland face.
A haircut made a house of it.
Pitched roof, shingles,
                       dark shades drawn.
Go away! No one is home!

A sticky mist webs the ground
in the morning
                 ticking with silence
a wimpled figure grips the garden shears.

What is the point of clipping
those nearly invisible wires
that connect us,
               the ultimate
network illusion.
               Why not stop this
snip snip snip snip returning
each year like the blackberry bushes
eating the back stairs
               Mother clipped after
Father died . . .
             the next summer
lacked blackberries, and the stairs rattled.

I said,
     "You should sit,
sit on the front porch
staring at the bare fields of winter
             until your gaze
becomes clearer and the thumb-high grass
         is tufted with clover."

"They were going to strangle
the back stairs," she claims.
"You wouldn't want that!"

"But I asked you not to.
I said you could trim
                anything
but the blackberries!"

"I'll never cut anything more.
I'll never visit you again!
I found the clippers we bought
lying outside, rusted.
                I asked you
not to leave them out!"

We are branches, waving our arms.

My father built new steps
when the old ones rotted.
                We watched him
saw and hammer them in place, then paint
them white
                with flourishing strokes.

My mother still looks after him.

Wild blackberries should be forgotten,
left to grow
                unkempt in profusion.
Cheap, cheap, a pocketful of rye, sing
                the spring sparrows,
blackberry brandy,
                blackberry pie.
We shall busy ourselves with abundance
in August,
                picking quickly
before the birds strip the thicket.

2

Her unmade bed is a bog, a swamp;
a white morning glory
                        she lies among the ruins.
Her eyelashes on the white pillow
have grown longer in a day.
                        She should be in order now —
hair mown and clipped
                        sheets pulled back.

I want a procession of tulips,
black and white, Indian file,
checkerboard style, a lawn party
with glazed cakes
                        and silver teapots,
my mother wearing a hollyhock hat.

She sleeps, or pretends to, but
I notice her face getting wet
in spite of the dry season.

My mouth hurts — as hers
where they have cut it,
cracks of blood stain the ends.
The sun's imposing even here

with the windows closed
against the noise of construction:
outside everything expands,
                        they are driving posts
bringing pipe-lines into our heads.

All day we doze, sharing
a blue haze of contusion,
a flutter of pain-dulling pills,
walking in gardens
through rows of lobelia

and daffodils, tall and straight,
the way they used to grow.

3

The chopping stops, the shears remain
splayed on the steps.
                I hear an occasional
drone of a jet.
                In the backyard starlings
flock and disperse. Pigeons
conclude their solicitous musings.

My eyes continue to sweep the flat
shadows on the ground into
                        a hill of branches.
My hair rises in an electrified cloud.
No one is here to pin it back.
The garden's a fright,
                    a shower of pollen
thigh-high with weeds. Mother
you were wrong. Or right. It
doesn't (did it ever?) matter.

Joan Aleshire

A White Horse, The New Moon

"Wish on a white horse, wish on the new moon,"
my mother would say, as my father drove us
through the valleys early summer evenings,
"and your wish will come true." Just then,
as she must have known we would, we passed
a white horse — probably, in daylight,
a gray mule resting from haying — staring
at our passing car, wide eyes darker
than the darkening sky, as if obeying
the wish that a white horse be there.

I, a child, between pillars of parents,
looked up to see the moon's cast-off
fingernail, showed my mother, who nodded
"Wish," as if relieved by this conjunction
of horse and moon. My father, too, seemed
pleased. Parents of a frail child —
her future a question — they had learned
that life is as full of danger as the road
winding away from the headlights' reach.

They poured their wishes into the moon's
fragile cup; their wishes flipped like
acrobatic children on the horse's broad
back, trying to reach the moon. Unaware,
then, of their longings, their fears
for me, I watched the white horse shake
its mane, bend to graze. Like the new moon
in the darkening world, it seemed
                              to be shining.

Joan Aleshire

Fine Line

Shifting to the fast lane, accelerating,
passing two cars as if nothing could stop me :
desire is like this, so much so that I want
the hitch-hiker who grins as I go by, and
the trucker who's stopped to gather wildflowers
by the side of the road. He must be sensitive,
picking this bouquet for his wife or the cab
of his truck. Maybe he's lonely after a long haul,
would be pleased if I pulled over, led him
into the woods nearby. What's to stop me?
Imagination selects only a pine-needle bed,
the prospect of pleasure, forgets how he could
make me feel ugly, and afraid.

I always take the steep curve near my house
slow and tight, because the orchard spread
below offers such invitation: to fly past
yellow lines, black road, fences, to land
in welcoming branches, a carpet of grass.
The impulse to break out is to go past
meaning; I slow to look the trucker over,
know I won't stop, speed on. I think of
the bird that sometimes sings on my garden fence:
a finch — small, gold bird — its song threatening
to burst its throat. What confines the force
of sound — as sound pushes outward — *makes*
the song. A fine line — the thinnest of skins,
a light coat of feathers.

Keith Althaus

The Ambulance

The gravel flies up
and hits the side of the car
as I pull off the road.
The siren gets louder
and louder as I come inside
the radius of the flashing dome.
I feel my blood rise
and a rush of adrenalin
as it passes. For a moment
I bask in the cold red light.
Suddenly I'm older, smaller,
slumped behind the wheel,
waiting — as the brave chemicals
inside me rot and the street returns
to normal, cold and raining,
and the last red puddles
evaporate down the block — waiting
for a break in the traffic.
I am still on my way to the store.

Barbara Anderson

Weekday Matinees

            I

By twilight every ghost lover combines
to make up this view outside my window,
this San Francisco fog:
condensed atmosphere mangled by telephone wires
and low flying jets, then every outline blended
in quicksilver dusk, smoothed by shadow
while the droplet features of old lovers
run languidly down the glass.
                        They could be
the watery eyes of Christ that once followed me
through a stranger's room, a man I'd just met
and made love to in a canopied bed of white lace.
The face of Christ plastered everywhere,
delicately framed on the dresser,
painted in dayglow on the walls. Afterwards,
he lit a candle until everything disappeared
into the flickering images you barely see passing by
a drive-in movie on a moonlit highway . . .
And still I can't remember his face
as I dressed and left
to catch the downtown weekday matinee.

            II

People are talking to the movie
in this theatre of skipped seats,
the stained velvet upholstery,
where 75¢ gets you two features
and a luminous darkness.
Goddam Bitch babbles the fat man
from a back row to the alcoholic floozabel
on the screen. He'll never let any woman
treat him like that. Someone else mumbles
about Jesus: *Jesus Christ* in a voice rusted
and distant as the barely audible soundtrack —

       Fat City: about a failed boxer

a man who attached himself,
too late, to the wrong future.
It's also about the urban poor.
The floor creaks when the fat man
gets up to buy more popcorn. The floozy
packs her black boyfriend's clothes
in the liquor store carton because
he's back in prison now and she's not eating anymore
just drinking Thunderbird. When she tries
to get out of bed, she keeps falling back.
Nobody moves. Nobody laughs at the funny parts.

III

It gets easier.

In my bed, by myself, I love
the neighbor's clarinet practice
from the next apartment, the same woman
who by daylight stops me on the street,
shows me her photographs, those vague
double exposed postures of her mother
rising three times from her dying body
or Saint Peter blowing a golden horn.
She has even photographed Satan
who she says picks after her from the radio
and t.v., who she says, most people
can believe in without ever having
seen him, a maze of faces and blue light,
in the photograph she keeps tucked
in her pocketbook that also resembles
this city at night as it loses itself
in a featherbed romance of fog
where men and women and invisible passages
weave their light together with the fading light
and without asking we close our blinds against one another
until everything disappears, and we sleep.

Philip Appleman

Euphorias

> "I heard a child, a little under four
> years old, when asked what was meant by
> being in good spirits, answer, 'It is
> laughing, talking, and kissing.'"
> Charles Darwin, *The Expression of
> the Emotions in Man and Animals*

1. Waldorf-Astoria Euphoria: The Joy of Big Cities

> "Joy, when intense, leads to various
> purposeless movements — to dancing
> about, clapping the hands, stamping,
> etc."
> ibid

You feel so good, you stop walking:
they swirl around you, racing the 6:15.
You bless them all with a smile
you cannot explain: they are suddenly
precious. You look around, with your alien eyes,
at forty floors of windows where
they are laughing, talking, and kissing: you realize
they are priceless. You feel them
under the pavement, riding the uptown express,
straphanging bodies waving
like kelp, and you know
they are irreplaceable; you think of them
all over town, bursting
with unused happiness, and you clap,
and clap again, and clapping, you sing
a song you thought you'd forgotten, and your waist
moves gently, like jonquils, and your hand
catches her fingertips, and she smiles, her arms
moving like willows,
and the fruitseller dances with apples,
crying a musical language, and a girl
with a bongo comes on with rhythm,
her hips moving like wheatfields, and
the hardhats come up from the manholes,

their bodies moving like jackhammers,
and Chinese voices like windchimes
sing to the women from San Juan
who gather around like palm trees, and the cops
have cordoned the street and are dancing
with women from Minnesota,
their thighs as seductive as seaweed;
and you know that sooner or later
this had to happen: that somehow
it would all break out, all that pent-up
joy, and people would sing and hold hands,
their bodies swerving like taxis,
and the music inside their heads
would fill the streets with dancing,
clapping hands, and stamping;
and you sing another chorus
of we,
hey, we,
yes, we,
I said we
are all
we've got.

2. Peoria Euphoria: the joy of small towns

> "A man smiles . . . at meeting
> an old friend in the street."

You find yourself drifting
on decades: the elms are immortal, arching
the red brick street. At Main
the concrete is veined with tar,
bubbling in sun. You test it
with bare toes: hot,
exciting, all the skin
you've never touched, telling you
of houses unlocked,
cars with keys inside, faces of women
as open as summertime — Jean,

after all these years, still dying
in the senior class play,
Sally, dissecting her ancient frog,
Mary, who still believes
in Jonah's whale. They smile at you,
and you smile, of course, you can't help it,
you are all so delighted that nothing
ever changes.

3. Hunkydoria Euphoria : the joy of having it made

> "From the excitement of pleasure,
> the circulation becomes more rapid,
> the eyes are bright, and the colour
> of the face rises."

You're sweating it out: the last time
it was never received;
it was lost in the files; sent
to the wrong department.
If you get there by noon, surely
it will be all right; but the seconds
are deadly. At ten to twelve
you reach the office: there's a line.
You inch along; at noon you touch
mahogany, and just as you feared, there is
some difficulty, a shuffling
of papers: you feel
the invisible stars
swing through their long
cold journey. Finally —
you can hardly believe it —
it's there! the very thing! the thing itself!
and the holy rubber stamp
falls like a benediction,
and you hear, above the ceiling,
the seraphim rejoicing,
and you smooth your hair
and borrow a debonair manner

and step through the frosted door
so deliberately,
no one would ever guess
that right there under your shirt
the sun is dancing on water.

Jennifer Atkinson

Pattaconk Pond

in memory of Martha Hale

She stands still in the shallows,
and young trout and shiners
come bumping up from the dark,
each one complete in a finger-length.
Though aware of her, white
and warm in their water,
the fish are unafraid until
by moving she proves herself alive.
Jays cry out alarm in the woods.

In a sun-lit spot on shore
a solitary lady-slipper
nods on a leafless stem.
Its dark-veined petals are folded inward
around air. There's nothing inside.
She'd like to let her own body lean
to follow that slender stem
and allow her head to bow in imitation
of what looks like simple innocence.
But she does not.

She wades deeper in,
wishing she could somehow not
disturb the calm surface of the pond,
but just dissolve into its water
as if she were an early snowfall
gone at the first moment of touch,
changing nothing.

Jennifer Atkinson

Pig Alley

Rust-blotched cows,
bulls quiet in the muddy stockyards,
and there five, a heap of pigs, not
bloodied, calm, hind legs tied with frayed string,
ears twitched on the wind.
You can almost catch them breathing. But no,
they're dead all right. All pork. But *how*
is the mystery
with not a mark on them, that coldly.

I wonder — is my interest excessive?
Once on a Kathmandu road,
Pig Alley, I saw a buffalo slaughtered.
Its moans choked back,
blood fell in pleats from its opened throat.
A red dinner napkin. I turned
and walked up to Durbar Square
to the cumin and turmeric smell of pakoras,
bicycles weaving around the shrines.

I felt nothing much then either, death was relief,
a kneeling and then a lying down
into stillness, bright red
and the white loincloths
of the butchers. And then later
a cart, charged
with the wet uncovered hunks of flesh,
and flies, trailing
like steam off a soup bowl whisked to the table.

Wendy Battin

In the Solar Wind

There is a sleep that tells every
dream as a nightmare: the figures rise up
in a locked room, and it is the world.
And there is a sleep of open windows,
where all dreams unwind
in golden light: clear tea
with the scent of almonds.
If there is something to look on
that does not waver
like mountains in the mirror of a still lake,
like the outline of trees in a light wind,
I have not seen it.
If there is waking.
Here in the thick
afternoon, I do not remember.

*

Love, here is golden tea
in a glass cup. It is hot,
a flashing cylinder.
Hold the cup still and look in:
the future is there,
but not in a Rorschach of leaves.
Steam rises from the tea
and what begins in this room
continues. To the molecules
every wall is a window.

*

The table he sets the cup on becomes
a story about a table:
It has four legs.
And another:
She rested her head on the table.
And another:
He sat at the table and wondered
if she would appear.

He remembers the table and sets down his cup.

> *the liquid is sweet, and*
> *afterwards, almonds.*

The story of the tea fills the air.
It is not finished,
not even in the next room.

*

What does the table become for the child
crouching under the table?
A dungeon, a warren, the oak-grain
stormy an inch from the eye:
the privacy of narration,
the mechanics of hiding.

*

I am sleep, from which everything falls
as the dream rises up.

You cannot hold me,
not even in your strong arms.

I cannot hold you,
though the story might hold us.

One of us chooses to leave,
or what we are chooses:

we have chosen a world
that splinters and shifts,

from molecule to atom
to particle to quark.

Our substance sinks

into its fractured wealth

while we are left behind
in the poverty of our bodies.

*

He stares out the window
past the blue lake
into black woods
and does not see her coming.
There is the path she would take,
brown needles and earth
through the green grass.
He sips his tea and thinks of sleep,
and imagines her sleeping.

*

I could tell you my love is divisible
into need and desire.

That need reduces to past,
desire to present.

That the past is circumstantial,
the present a problem of engineering.

He sets down his cup and wanders
away from the window, into
the privacy of remembrance,
the mechanics of excuse: *when
I was a child,* he begins, and there,
where no one can find him,

the maps unfold in a small boy's hands:
the states, the pastel countries,
the earth — each sheet
drawn from a greater distance,

as if that were knowledge.
The last shows the planets
careening on the solar wind,
the sun's ionic breath.

*

The province where this story unfolds
is a sheet of blue paper.
Brown lines indicate mountains.
The stars of the cities are black,
though they give off light.
In this country a law was uncovered:

we will never need more than four colors
to mark off our borders.
One of them is green.

*

The pale blue is water,
a foreign country.
He knew he had no right to be
so happy, seeing her
floating in a clear sleep.
And so he stopped.
He did not see her coming
down the needle path.
He did not see her at all.

*

When the story has been well-told
all tasks are simpler. We have built
so many empty houses, we have made
the roads that lead back to them broad.
When your hand moves to stroke my hair
what is the distance you travel?

*

I open the chest and find it empty.
I open the door and the light

is aimless in the room and settles nowhere.
I open the book and wait

for the story to begin.
It will take our present and make it pass.

*

She is sleeping, he thinks,
and then he can hold her: his fingerprints
on the air, on empty space.

She is sleeping, like dice in his hand:
twelve chances.

She is sleeping, like a cue ball:
a problem of vectors, complex but foreseen.

*

You are here, listening,
watching me pace.
You will stay to find out
what happens, what happens.
You will want to know why.

I can tell you: the story goes on
and leaves us behind.
The teller forgets,
and the story finds a new tongue, new breath
to ride on.
The listener turns in his sleep
and then he is gone.

*

She is sleeping. She is standing
in the next room and picks up
the scent of almonds.

She has just emerged from the woods
and follows
the needle path down to the lake

where she will
stop to see her face
in the surface of the water.

Mother! Constipated Child needs
'California Syrup of Figs'

Hurry, Mother! A teaspoonful of 'California Syrup of Figs' brand laxative now will sweeten the stomach and thoroughly clean the little bowels and in a few hours you have a well, playful child again. Even if cross, feverish, bilious, constipated or full of cold, children love the pleasant taste of this gentle, harmless laxative. It never gripes or overacts.

Ask your chemist for 'California Syrup of Figs,' which has full directions for babies and children of all ages.

Mother, be sure to ask for 'CALIFORNIA Syrup of Figs.'

Charles Baxter

Media Event

    This is his story. At the moment, he is writing it himself. He knows better than to let anyone else do it. There would be subtle gaps and distortions sewn carelessly into the fabric. He is using the third person *for greater accuracy and objectivity.* He is as objective as a cat watching a slightly damaged sparrow. Please notice: he will never make the mistake of saying "I". Right now the "I" is being doused with high-octane gasoline and set on fire, right here, where everyone can see it. "I" has been burned out. Please do not call him "I". And don't say "you," either. When you speak of him, always refer to him as "he." Or you can call him by his full name: George Eliot Christianson, Jr.

    There is only one story in America and that is the story of how to become famous. This is that story right now. Right now is 9:58 in the morning on May the 20th. At this moment on channel seven *Kelly and Company* with its guest Danielle Gagnan Torrez, former baseball wife, is coming to an end. Thanks to this program, she is famous in southeast Michigan and will remain famous for about five hours, until dinnertime. Researcher William Wright has finished talking to John Kelly about one of the most bizarre murder cases of all time, the Claus von Bulow case. He is famous, and so is Claus von Bulow. Paul Wren, the world's strongest man (is he? who can be sure?) lifted the show's host, John Kelly, into the air. Beauty expert Gloria Heide showed the ladies in the audience how to highlight the eyes. All these guests were on stage, exposed to public view. They sat in front of those television cameras and they appeared on his Philco set and he watched them. Over the speaker of the set came the sound of whistling and clapping of the studio audience. Now on the Donahue show George Burns is appearing. He has written an exercise book for senior citizens. He may dance and sing while holding a cigar. George Burns has been famous for a long time. He has been God and Gracie Allen's husband. *He does not need to be on television again.* He is that rare thing, a permanently famous person. He is taking up valuable air time. Someone else could be getting famous right now, instead of George Burns, on the Donahue show.

If you are not famous in America, you are considered a mistake. They suspend you in negative air and give you bad jobs working in basements pushing mops from eight at night until four in the morning. No one famous ever punches a time clock or buys no-brand niblets canned corn. If you are famous, they know how to make your face shine under the spotlights. But if you are not famous, then you are not interesting in America, and they put you in a brown uniform and you mop the Mt. Hope Hospital corridors, which is his, George Eliot Christianson, Jr.'s, job. They don't care that he wants to be somebody. Ambitions can go to Pasadena, for all they are. Ambitions alone are not (and will not ever be) fame.

Education means reading the books and comprehending their subtle intentions. But that doesn't make you somebody. Of course not. If it were that easy, educated people might be happy. No, you have to *write* the books and then you have to get on television. If you don't get on television you might as well eat the book page by page on a street corner. Nobody who works at the hospital with him is famous or likely to become so. If they were special, *special in any way at all,* it would be known. They would be on television, or at least, on radio. It's a simple fact. Everyone knows it.

Contempt is visited upon the anonymous, here in our country, this America. At the department store cashier's window they would not cash his check because he does not have a charge account with them. Without credit cards, which in the American Express commercial make you into a celebrity, he cannot rent a car. *He cannot get anyone to pay any attention to him. He is irrelevant to the world.* The world wants to erase him, inch by inch, to make room for someone who will be somebody.

There's no reason to be stupid or obscure and there's no special reason to die like a dog in the shadows. Everyone knows it's better to shoot someone and get your name in the newspapers than to sit at home in front of the television watching other people shoot someone. The first great philosopher who suggested murder as a stepping-stone to fame was Friedrich Wilhelm Nietzsche. He has read Nietzsche's philosophy and he advises his readers to do likewise. He advises reading *Menschliches, Allzumenschliches.* My God, how it revaluates those values. If he were alive today, Nietzsche would be a publicity agent. Or he'd be a megastar. *If Nietzsche were alive today he would not be mad.* Everyone agrees with Nietzsche now. They would have a cure for his headaches and catarrh. He'd have so many friends, he'd be a wise-guy, a sage. No sweat. Who is there who hasn't at least tried to be a superman, a would-be Ubermensch? Nietzsche invented self-promotion for our time. Behold the man.

He, George Eliot Christianson, Jr., is not going to shoot anybody. He is not a violent person, except spiritually. For him, violence is no fun. Never has been. A violent person would not work on the housekeeping staff in a hospital. He doesn't like guns or hurting other people. But he is going to be famous. One way or another.

Ever wonder what those girls on television get paid? The ones who appear in the toothpaste and life insurance commercials? The ones with nothing wrong with them? They sit on a park bench and men tip their hats to them. Sorry, folks, sorry to disappoint you. As it turns out, they don't have to be paid. They're angels.

His parents were readers. They read novels in the evening after supper. In some cases, beer, tea, or coffee were served along with the novel. This bookish mode of leisure time activity has, now, a slightly antique quality, the genteel smell of leather bindings and glue. They liked fat novels. Novels like *Middlemarch.* Like *Adam Bede.* His father worked in a skyscraped office and his mother sometimes worked in an office and when they came home they read books to relax. They cooked gourmet dinners and then read more books, such as *Felix Holt the Radical* and *Daniel Deronda.* They named their one-and-only son after a woman, the author of those books. But they also named him after his father, who himself was named for that same woman. He was named for a woman and named for a man. It was a mad idea. *He has no name of his own.* George Eliot Christianson, Jr. is a name that has always mixed him up. Except for that "Jr." He is certain about that. It sucks, for sure.

When they moved out to the suburbs, his parents built themselves a swimming pool. What they liked best, was to have the under-water lights turned on while they ate cold shrimp salad on the adjacent deck, and drank white wine, and discussed their investments. From the pool came the turquoise glow of the painted water waved by the evening wind, and George Sr. would look at it and say, "Somehow it reminds me of a Japanese painting."

"It reminds *me*," his wife would say, "of water in the Caribbean."

George Eliot Christianson, Jr., home for the evening, sitting with them, eating his scanty dinner, keeps a respectful distance, a proud silence during this monstrous colloquy.

"George," George says, "do you have any plans for changing your job?" His father looks at him with that look.

"No," George says.

"Well," George says, "maybe it's time to *start* thinking about it. Maybe it's time to start making something of yourself."

"Yes." The theme is the pool; he is the subject.

"We — your mother and I — are often asked what our son is doing and we have to tell them that he's a janitor in a hospital. I know your mother sometimes just doesn't tell them at all."

"I'm on the housekeeping staff," George says. "I'm not a janitor. There's a difference. They fix it. We keep it clean."

"Oh, George," his mother says, turning to him, "let's not talk about this tonight. Let's have a nice dinner." Her face is lit by the rippling and flickering blue waves in the pool. Believe it.

"I must say," George says, "I am sometimes annoyed by your obstinance. I know your sisters are puzzled, as I am. Here you are, a young man with all the advantages: intelligence, and a good education. *You had no defects.* And yet, look. What happened to you? You will not play the game. You *insist* on ruining your prospects. I remember the hippies and perhaps it is the fashion again to spite us and all that we stand for. I cannot believe that a young man with a college degree should *want* to work in a hospital, however. Is a secure life with a solid income so shameful a thing? Why don't you wish to make something of yourself?"

"Hmmmm," George says.

"I hate to think that you'll never find your peg, your niche. I hate to think that you'll spend your life being strange."

Looking down into the water, he can see fish, several feet below the surface, swimming in a neutral manner. But really he is being pulled too fast to see much of the fish or even the sun as it is reflected on the water. He's much too happy to notice things. He's a decisive waterskiier. If it were his own boat he'd be even better, but it's Freddy Emerson's father's Alumacraft, his father's Evinrude outboard, and Trace is Freddy Emerson's girl. She is privately held.

Well. Imagine yourself up on that one slalom ski, in that lake in Wisconsin. Then say to yourself: if that was ten, or even fifteen, years ago, what visions of sunlight have been his share since that time? What happens to sunlight in the complicated culture of postcapitalist America? What has happened since they snuffed the summer sun and Trace took off her swimsuit and put on her power clothes for her job in the office on the ninth floor where she draws down 47K per year? What has happened to George and his happiness? Stay tuned. How does a man keep on falling through the water until he becomes one of the fish?

"Oh dear." You look up. "Another story about a maladjusted person. Another flake. Another weirdo. What a shame."

Dear reader, George Eliot Christianson, Jr. is an extremely relevant person. He stands up for the stupid and crazy. He is a spokesperson for those sucked out of comfort into odd rented rooms, shacks, and messy walkups. Why, *you've got one like him in your own family.* Your brother's son. Your own daughter. Your cousin, who couldn't hold a job. Your uncle, who keeps having accidents and whose bills are paid by the family. Your husband, who sits at home. Your grandchild, who isn't turning out right. Your own blood, your genes, your genetic pool. Your wife, your mother. You.

Don't you goddamn dare pretend he's so strange.

How *did* George Eliot Christianson, Jr., who earned a B.A. *magna cum laude* from a fine college in Massachusetts and whose habitual prose style was not unremarkable and whose prospects were, as they say, bright, how did this promising young man from the deep midwest, this little lamb without a spot, how did he manage so forcefully to crash the car of his career into a solid void? No, it's a dull question and he won't answer. Look around: astonishing quantities of also-rans in all walks of life, God's plenty of failure. No scarcity. Do you think it's unusual that a man of astrostellar potential should be pushing a mop down a hospital corridor?

And then he, George Eliot Christianson, Jr., awakens, and looks toward his father, and says, "I am *not* strange. I am a product of this society, just as you are. I just don't have your idea of swimming pools as wondrous objects of beauty." And he stands up, and takes his plate of shrimp salad, and his wine glass, and drops them into the water of the swimming pool.
For the first time in the evening his mother screams.

Now he is back in his apartment sitting on the bed. He has driven home in his unsafe-at-any-speed Pontiac Astre. He is staring out his sooty apartment window at the King Koil factory, which is almost in his backyard. Here is what he sees: brownish brick, interrupted every seven feet by high windows with translucent glass, open, and bare light bulbs visible inside. Here is what he hears: incessant rhythmic clatter. Here is what he smells: the odor of hot metals, and grease, and metallic dust, and paint. Black smoke emerges from the chimney, environmentally protected smoke, rubs its muzzle on the windowpanes, and slips inside his room, where it burns his throat with the soulful righteous waste of manufactured bedsprings.

He'll draw you a picture, a vacation from sitting on the bed and looking out the window at the bedspring factory. Here's the picture. Waterskiing! People in swimsuits. It's a lake, let's say in Wisconsin, where the water has temporarily escaped acid rain and where the houses on shore have been designed so that you can't see them from the water. They blend in. That cosmetic feature costs extra in exterior natural wood paneling but it's worth it. In this picture three people are happy. There's this man, Freddy Emerson. There's his girlfriend, Tracy Edwards, whom everyone calls "Trace." And there's George Eliot Christianson, Jr., whom everyone calls "George." Freddy and Trace are substantially beautiful in the mid-summer sun. They both have the copyrighted suntans of the youthful leisure class. Freddy is behind the wheel of the powerful outboard and Trace is sitting in the backseat, watching. Who's going to be up on skis? George is, that's who. He's up now, the future disappointment to the serious world, skimming over the lake. *He is on one ski!* And, like Freddy and Trace, he is physically picturesque. All three of these people are eighteen years old. Two of them admire George as he slashes back and forth across a slalom course of blue anchored plastic bottles. The future hospital housekeeper is very very impressive, a golden Aztec sungod. The sun has baked his hair so that it's quite blond.

Half the underclass in this country could competently staff the Sorbonne. Here's what happened: George Eliot Christianson took a slight psychic tumble. He fell into a bit of depression about himself and his ultimate human prospects here in this, our, America. He got depressed and so did the economy. It's a free country if you have a million dollars, but if you don't and you're a little discouraged about things, you take what they give you. At Mt. Hope they were passing out mops. He took one.

The woman is sitting on the edge of his mattress. She is naked and she is smoking a Camel Lite and complaining about the view. "George," she says, flicking out her hair with her other hand, "I don't mind that you have paper windowshades. And I don't mind that they're ripped." She exhales some smoke and scratches her instep. "But what I *do* mind is the noise of the factory and what I mind even more is that when we do it in this room you do it in time with the noise of those stamping machines. Boom. Boom. Boom. Boom. Boom." She transfers the cigarette to the other hand and lowers her long painted fingernails to his chest. "You're kind of sweet, sometimes, but when we go at it in this room I feel like I'm mating with an android." She reaches down for an empty Coke bottle and flicks the ash from the cigarette into it. "Oh," she says. "One other thing. I wish you'd buy some furniture. *One* chair won't make you part of the bourgeoisie. Even revolutionaries eat their meals at tables." She drops the cigarette into the Coke bottle and it makes a hollow hiss.

The sum and substance of being on the housekeeping staff in a modern hospital is what now follows. Being new (1976), the hospital is dressed and decorated in tranquilized earth tones of copper, brown, speckled rust, and tan: the reassuring and antiprimary end of the spectrum. He himself dresses each night in a locker room where he puts on his antiprimary uniform of deepest darkest institutional brown. He has his own special housekeeping cart, labeled C-7. At one end of his cart is the bucket filled with Huntington Hi-Tor Germicidal detergent, and, of course, the water. The bucket also contains a wringer for draining one's mop, which bucket is bolted to the aforementioned end of the cart. His job is regularly to mop the basement and ground floor hallways and once a week to wax them with Huntington's Hospital-Industrial Floor Wax and to use the General Electric buffer on those floors, not once but twice, according to housekeeping regulations. But he is not finished describing cart C-7 and its contents. He must clean the bathrooms. Bathrooms constitute a special problem. They must be mopped, of course, and the red liquid soap — Huntington Germa-Medica 'R' — must be poured into the handsoap dispensers. If these dispensers are clogged, the men from maintenance must declog them. He must wash and rinse the sinks and toilets and spray the mirrors and walls with Compass Germicide and Deodorant, in its red-and-white can, another little passenger on his cart. Gum underneath the sink? It must be removed, *and he must do it,* with his spray can of Claire chewing gum remover with the special long nosed nozzle. When he cleans out the gift shop he must vacuum the brown polyester carpet using the Hoover purchased from Ask Tidy Tom Services, Inc. Certain porcelain surfaces must be scrubbed with one's cleaning rag and Liquid Por-San. When no one is looking, he does something he is not authorized to do: he dusts the faces of the clocks set into the walls at fifty foot intervals. You always know what time it is in a hospital. He must pick up all refuse and put it in his clear polyvinyl-chloride bag, which will eventually be noosed with ribbon wire and transported to the dumpster on the north side of the building. During coffee break he steps outside and with his co-workers Jim Ripley and Joanne Ash he sucks into his lungs several hits of the potentest Colombian that a laborer's wages can search out and score. Then he blithely re-enters the building, where, because it is modern, the hallways meet at acute or obtuse angles. Only on the surgical floor can lines be found that meet at 90°. At four o'clock in the morning he has done one man's penance and passed through another working night and he is ready to punch out. All night he has held in his nostrils the smell of soap and sickness, and that smell is now nesting under his fingernails. He knows by heart the odor of the ailing disfigured physical body. It is that smell that enters his dreams, not the recessed lighting or the enclosed garden courtyards or the nurses' stations. He goes home and in his bed where Sandra-the-cigarette-smoker also sometimes sleeps he dreams of acres and acres of rotting orchards where the fruit smells of disease and soap.

Sometimes he feels the wind blowing inside his fingers. Yes, *inside.*

We know about Oswald and Ray, but who remembers Sara Jane Moore, or Squeaky Fromme, who had nothing against Gerald Ford, or Mark David Chapman, who had nothing against John Lennon, or John Hinckley, Jr., who had nothing against Ronald Reagan? They weren't just typographical errors. *They weren't exceptions.* They found guns and went looking for someone famous to shoot. Oh. He almost forgot. Arthur Bremmer. And his line as he pulled the trigger: "A penny for your thoughts."

Any man who has imagination must resist servitude; he must learn how to turn himself into a terrible risk.

We all agree that everybody wants to be somebody. We all agree that that is where the pressure is applied here in America and where they turn up the spiritual thermostat. The problem with fame is that the means to achieve it cross into insanity or criminality. If they lock you up, your fame is useless, for the most part.
Who really wants to be in the *Guinness Book of World Records?* Is that a sensible way to achieve selfhood? Who really wants to go bowling for two days without stopping until the fingertips are bleeding and the knuckles are so swollen that they've become useless? Who wants to do this just to get into the *Guinness Book?* Who wants to sit on a ledge for eight days or eat twenty cherry pies in a row or fall two thousand feet from a speeding orthogyro just to get into that book? No, the *Guinness Book* is a record of failed acts of the imagination, notable only for their duration.
What about interrupting Vladimir Horowitz? Suppose Vladimir Horowitz is performing Beethoven's fourth piano concerto with Zubin Mehta and the New York Philharmonic. He is performing in his usual style. The auditorium is oozing with rapture at his "magnetism" and "dynamic power." Beethoven is forgotten. What is exciting is Horowitz. It's time to put a stop to this travesty of musicianship. Who does it? You do. You stand up and you cry, "Stop this grandstand meddling with the classics!" You might even go up to the stage and forcibly remove Horowitz. Result? You will be famous, the first man to have stopped Horowitz in that gentleman's long career of murdering the classics. Some will admire you. Much good their admiration will do you, in your cell. This cell will be padded because you will be crazy without appeal, because in this society the very definition of sanity is *completely* associated with staying hushed at symphony concerts, especially those at which Vladimir Horowitz deigns to appear. Just *try* to find a psychiatrist who doesn't love Vladimir Horowitz. "I may not like you," the psychiatrist says who is examining you with his tweezers, "but I *love* Vladimir Horowitz."

Two weeks ago he was bicycling to work. He had to stop at an intersection for a red light. He looked around, gazing at the urban intersected world. An apartment building. Second floor, corner window. A man in an undershirt, his back to the street, sitting next to a highchair. He was spooning cereal into the baby's mouth. His wife across the table was watching. A picture of calm, of peacefulness. George Eliot Christianson, Jr., sitting on his bicycle, felt the two hands of implacable fate gathering around his heart, and as those two hands squeezed he looked down into the gutter and saw an ant carrying a piece of cracker. You can look all you want. But if you're being erased, it'll make you feel like a man in a maelstrom.

What will lead him out of the maelstrom and the hospital where he works as a mere housekeeper into the limelight, where everyone is a star, and therefore happy? He knows what will capture the imagination of the public. He will no longer tease you with his project. Here is what he is going to do. He is going to walk through plate glass.

He remembers his boyhood dog, Sonny, and some good dinners. He remembers good sex. Well, fine. These memories — he too drank Kool-Aid, he too went to the beach — do not minimize the turned-up tension of his anonymity. Take him outside. Show him the sun. Explain the name of that tree. Praise the grass. Then praise the sky and note for the one millionth time in your life that it's blue. Will such praise cure his spiritual ache? Has such praise ever worked with your weird uncle, or your daughter who turned out bad, or your brother the unemployed beer drinker? Ever sermonize to them about the sun? They don't even look at you, do they?

He stood at the window, then walked to the kitchen. He took down a glass and filled it with water. He drank the water, then sat down on a pillow in the living room. He checked the view. He scratched his left shoulder. He stood up. He touched the wall. He walked into the bedroom, then back out of it. He saw through the window in the distance a time-and-temperature clock. 2:57. Blink. 61°. He thought of the other insomniacs and those possessed by intolerable longings and he thought of them all, wandering from room to room, a little army writing the natural history of the waking night.

Of course Sandra-the-cigarette-smoker thinks the typewriter project is a joke. He must be writing this up to improve his typing skills for a possible clerical job. Well: there he is, sitting (in a chair, Sandra, *in a chair*!) at this very desk day after day, she thinks, to while away the working-class leisure hours. She thinks that if she were to put her long arms around his neck and insert her tongue in his ear and so on and so on, he'd be okay. The desk is cluttered with pencils, coffee cups, and a dictionary of synonyms to fulfill a hobby, she thinks. *No one walks through plate glass.* Come on, give her a break. Not her guy George. Through plate glass? And ruin his face? And cut himself? Where's the logic?

Plate glass.

Well, it's obvious. It keeps you out and them in, pretends it's not a wall, *can* be broken by human force, lets you see what you want but keeps you from having it, *is* the stoned face of every television set in the land, and is made of sand and built with fire and lets us look but not touch.

What goes on behind plate glass?

In their own rooms, soft with plush decorations, live the lucky ones, with souls. They sleep at night. Daytimes, they walk on sidewalks headed for some destination. Their children laugh musically. Ha ha ha. Their landscapes are shockingly green. The seasons arrive on time and leaves follow blossoms and are themselves followed faithfully by fruit. The airwaves shake to the sound of arguing birds, and there, there in the distance, is an incognito mountain. Green meadows, anonymous slopes. Here are baskets of bread and cheese. Drink and eat.

Well, okay, it's true that that mountain may be a little sentimental, but it's not a golden mountain, it's not imaginary, he's seen the pictures, his parents have been there, and so have his friends, and they brought back presents, bottles of white wine.

Sometimes he thinks he is making a terrible mistake. He looks over what he has written so far and thinks: oh, this can't be right, this is awful. They'll look at him and say, the man didn't know what he was doing. A self-intoxicant. A media hound.

The doubts don't go away. Why isn't Sandra's body enough?

And he steps forward. His adidas tennis shoes give him considerable momentum. His forehead touches the glass first, then his left shoulder. A moment of resistance. Then. Then a crack, a crackling, a spider web of splitting sections. And the sun splits, and then it's raining knives and daggers and icicles. And he stands in this rain, a brief summer shower of glass. He keeps his eyes closed as he begins to bleed, and he's happy.

Q: Which plate glass?
A: The front window of the First Manufacturer's Trust.
Q: Is it thick?
A: Quite thick. But it can be walked through.
Q: How do you know?
A: He knows because someone once walked through it by accident, so they put a green painted line on it so no one would walk through it again.
Q: What injuries will you sustain?
A: That is a big question mark. It depends on the speed and the angle of entry. There are likely to be severe lacerations on the forehead and arms and probably on the shoulders, which will be the first actually to emerge on the other side of the glass.
Q: What if the glass cannot be broken?
A: That is unimaginable.
Q: Why the Manufacturer's Trust?
A: It's a bank. His puny checking account is there. Banks represent for him and for most people the seat of plate-glass power. People *want* to break through, into, banks. Happiness is held secret in their huge vaults.
Q: Does anyone know you will be doing it?
A: He has called channel two, channel four, and channel seven and told them to have their news crews out in front of the bank at two-thirty p.m. He has mailed three different *but highly articulate* rationales, over which he has spent uncounted hours, to the stations. Once in the hospital, he will set up interviews like this one and begin writing.
Q: Which hospital?
A: Mt. Hope. They know him there.
Q: You *do* expect injuries?
A: Everything has its price. There'll be some loss of blood. Not to worry.
Q: What will you write?
A: The plate glass statement. The last word on the subject.
Q: Do you regard yourself as a victim, a loser?
A: I regard myself as a hero, a winner.
Q: What will your friends, parents, associates think?
A: They have not been informed. They will understand, in time.

In a few hours, he will be famous. At least you have to admit that he's thought this through; you have to say, "He *has* his reasons." Many others might do the same, given the right circumstances. If everyone has the right to be famous for fifteen minutes, you have to admit that *now is the time.* He speaks for many. This is an army. Their numbers are growing. They are churning their way into the public eye, by God. Sometimes they are violent. But *no one is going to be hurt here,* except for him, a bit. But he'll come out flying. It's a small price to pay for a picnic on a mountain, for a real name in this unreal world.

Go ahead. Wish him luck. Be polite.

Ann Beattie

Who Do You Love?

Ellen and Hale were at a beach house that he had rented for the last part of August. That morning, his nine year old son, Jake, had come back from the bicycle rental store with a slightly rusty blue Italian ten-speed with a basket on the back that held a kitten wrapped in a towel. "Somebody dumped two of them through the bicycle shop's mail slot. The owner's mother took the good one. They were going to kill this one, " Jake said, holding the kitten in the towel out to his father. It looked like a sloppily wrapped pressent. The kitten had one eye open and one eye closed.

"Are you asking if you can keep it, or telling me?" Hale said.

"Telling you," Jake said, his voice much smaller than his usual child's voice.

"Then you'd better get the thing to the vet," Hale said. "There's a vet on Beech street." He took his wallet out of the pocket in his swim trunks, unfolded it, and removed a twenty. He held it out to Jake.

"Yes, sir," Jake said.

"You've never called me sir in your life," Hale said. "I already said you could keep the damned cat."

The kitten had jumped onto the kitchen table. Jake picked it up and wrapped the towel around it again, folding it the way people in restaurants flip the linen napkin back over the basket of rolls.

At the beach, Hale turned on the radio. He had pretty much

decided to quit the law firm he was with. Since the day they arrived at the beach, Ellen had watched him: his expressions and movements were all exaggerated. Hale was taking himself very seriously. In effect, she was watching him watch himself. On the radio, the disc jockey insisted that everyone buy tires that had just gone on sale. The sale would go on through the weekend. "Everybody's heard of rolling with the punches," the disc jockey said. "This is going to give you a chance to roll with *radials.*"

"When you visit your sister next month," Hale said, "I'm going to London."

She was surprised; she had tried to get him to go to Europe for their vacation, but he had insisted on renting a beach house.

"Floyd's going over there to move his mother into another apartment. He asked if I wanted to go along. Knock around for a week."

"Who's Floyd?" she said.

"The guy who gave me a ride home in the MG. He works in my building."

"You're going to England with him? I didn't know you knew him that well. You've never mentioned him since the day he gave you a ride home."

"I don't have any friends," Hale said, digging his heels in the sand.

The disc jockey said that now he was going to play his favorite song of all time. It was "Good Golly Miss Molly." A few seconds after Little Richard started screaming it out, the disc jockey cut in and screamed, even louder, "Don't forget about those tires!"

"You've only got three friends," he said. "Two, if you leave out your sister."

"I have half a dozen friends at least," she said.

"Nobody has six real friends," he said. "I'm talking about real friends."

"Why are we talking about this at all?" she said.

"You're right," he said. "We should discuss what's going on with us."

She inhaled deeply and smiled on the exhale, in spite of herself. It was another one of those times when he wanted to test, to see if he could destroy everything. He often did this at times that should be pleasant: Christmas eve; his birthday.

"No," she said. "Just no." She rolled away and turned her face to the side, looking away from him. When she was almost asleep, she felt a strange sensation. Without looking, she figured out that he was pouring a thin stream of sand into the crook of her arm.

74

The next day, Jake went to the beach with them and found somebody to play with. Late in the morning, he and another boy disappeared behind the dunes, where a small inlet of water ran under a bridge. Some of the kids threw inner tubes there, in water almost too shallow to keep them afloat. When the tide was out, it was as ugly as a flooded urban playground. From what she'd overheard on the days she'd walked over the bridge to go to the shack for lunch, the boys were much like their parents; they gossiped, except that they talked about children instead of adults, and instead of lying on beach towels, they spun in inner tubes.

"Do you want a sandwich?" Ellen said to Hale.

He was reading a spy novel. "Hot dog with mustard and a Coke," he said. "But I'll get it."

"I'll get it," she said. "I'm going to eat mine at the counter. I want to get out of the sun for a while."

He rolled over and smiled at her. "Remember three summers ago in New York?" he said.

That was always the way he talked about the beginning of their affair: Three summers ago in New York — as if the word affair was indelicate. She could never put that together with the fact that Hale did such outrageous things. After the third lunch they'd had together in four days, he'd stopped on Lexington Avenue and bought a nylon suitcase. He took it to a trash can, pulled out the paper stuffing, and handed it to her. "What's that for?" she had said. He took her hand, and they turned into the doorway of a hotel behind them. She hung back when he went to the desk, not believing that he was getting a room. The clerk rang the bell, and a bellhop who had been studying them since they ran into the lobby came forward and picked up the empty bag. He swept his arm toward the elevator. "My wife insists on travelling light," Hale had said. "Well, if you need more clothes, Bloomingdale's is just a few blocks away," the bellhop said. She had not intended to go to bed with Hale so soon, and she was trying to figure out, before the elevator reached their floor, what she would say when she got back to the office, whether the bellhop had meant the comment about Bloomingdale's as a put-down, and whether Hale would ever figure out how to undo her inordinately complicated wrap-around dress. As it turned out, she did not remember, either.

A month later, she asked him to marry her. He moved her out of her apartment that weekend, into his. He told her to wait another year to see if she still liked living with him and Jake. She did, but they rarely discussed marriage the next year, and this summer, she was a little surprised that he had asked her to marry him, and more surprised that she'd said no. After three years of helping to raise Jake, she felt that he was no longer a baby. She didn't want more children, and Hale did. "I'm going to talk you into it," Hale said. She knew that as long as they weren't married, he'd have a hard time convincing her. Secretly, she was afraid he'd get his way — when didn't he get his way? — and it frightened her, so she lashed out at him. "Marry somebody else if you want to breed," she said. "Just don't waste three years on them. Go out and knock somebody up tomorrow."

"You know you're acting crazy," he said.

He had begun to put things in the suitcase she had half packed. It was the Lexington Avenue suitcase. The next day, they left for the beach.

She was walking across the parking lot, almost to the bridge, carrying Hale's lunch in a cardboard box, when the wind blew the pile of napkins away. She put the box down on the asphalt and ran after them. One blew into the water. She wadded them up and walked to the trash can outside the shack. That was when she heard the commotion and looked to see what the children in the picnic area beside the shack were laughing about. A circle of children, hands clasped, spun like a horizontal ferris wheel around the child in the center, chanting, "Who do you love?" over and over. Jake was the child at the center. A man sitting at a table under the pine trees hollered, "A little less noise over there," but nobody listened, and suddenly the pattern the children formed was too erratic to be called a circle. One boy — the boy who had taken Jake behind the dunes that morning — was the leader; he shouted so fast that the ones who couldn't match his tempto became an echo. Then, through the crazy circling motion, she saw Jake's hand shoot out. "Burton," he screamed. The circling stopped. "What do you mean you love me?" Burton said. "There's three girls here for you to love. You don't love girls?" Then, searching for something to look at other than his tormentor, Jake's eyes suddenly met Ellen's. "I don't want him to love me — he's a scub," the ugliest of the girls said. She raised her hands, fingers down, and bounced them like pouncing spiders. Burton was laughing. He stuck out his hip, looked over his shoulder and smacked the air with a kiss. Somebody slugged somebody else on the shoulder. Jake broke away and ran behind the shed. She wanted to go up to Burton and kill him. Since she couldn't do that, she tried to think what to say that would hurt him. Another boy hollered, "Hey, Jake — come back and love Burt!" She went up to what remained of the group. "Burton," she said, "You're not good looking, so you'd better bank on your loud mouth. No pretty girl is going to love you, and you might have to settle for boys."

The man eating hamburgers at the picnic table looked astonished. When she walked away, she saw that dozens of napkins had been blown out of the garbage can; the wind had lifted them up and peaked them into pyramids dotting the asphalt. She looked for Jake and couldn't find him. The box with the hot dog and Coke was also gone.

That evening, she walked half a mile to the boardwalk, still as disturbed as if she'd been surrounded herself. She hadn't told Hale about the scene — something made her think that Jake would only be more embarrassed if his father tried to console him.

As soon as she climbed the ramp onto the crowded boardwalk, she realized she'd never find Jake. She walked to the pier, found a bench that wasn't sticky, and sat down across from the roller coaster, picking up some of the excitement of the people climbing into the cars. She was afraid of things she hadn't been afraid of even the summer before: of getting food poisoning from eating at the boardwalk food stands. Of the undertow. The roller coaster. She watched the cars climb slowly, heard voices, then screams, as the cars poured over the top and disappeared, dipping up faster than seemed possible on the track. She squinted at the endless maze of unlikely, shiny whiteness holding everything up, the elaborate cross-cross of bents and uprights.

When she got home, Jake was on the porch.

"How come you just stood there today?" he said.

"I didn't realize at first it was you they were picking on," she said.

He'd taken off his running shoes and wadded up his socks inside them. He knocked the shoes together and apart as he rocked.

"Do you wish that I'd broken it up?" she said.

He didn't answer her.

"Did you even know that game? Nobody plays stupid games like that at your school, do they?"

"I knew what was going on," he said. "I just didn't know anybody's name. Those kids are creeps. It's no big deal."

"You're still upset about it," she said.

"Listen," he said, pointing to the railing where she was sitting, "Hale just yelled at me because the bike got swiped. I left it there, and somebody just came up and took it. He acted like it was the end of the world."

She pushed her hair behind her ears. Her face stung. She had gotten sunburned.

"Your father's upset about his job. About other things," she said. "For some reason I don't understand, men don't talk to other men about things that are important. They talk around the subject, or they pick fights with each other to let off steam. I hope you don't get like that when you grow up. I hope you know that you can talk to people."

"The way he acts, I'm not surprised he doesn't have any friends," Jake said.

She looked up, surprised. She had been looking at the floorboards because Jake was on the verge of tears and she didn't want to be looking at him if he started to cry. "You don't think he has any friends?" she said.

"*He* says he doesn't. He goes from talking about how stupid I am to leave an unchained bike out in plain view to talking about how nobody cares about him. He was even pissed off that you went for a walk. He gets off on yelling. He's like that kid at the beach."

Hale was in the bedroom, naked, lying on his stomach, the book on the floor by the bed, fan blowing on him. His arms were above his head, one hand overlapping the other. He didn't move when she came into the room, or when she sat on the bed. His face was too blank for someone really asleep — middle-of-the-night sleep, maybe, but not the way someone would look who'd just slipped into an afternoon nap. She put her hand on his back.

"If I talk you into it," he said, voice muffled in the pillow, "we can have a kid and work really hard raising it so it won't be so stupid it'll lose its bike."

She grabbed his shoulder and he turned toward her, surprised that he'd provoked such a response. But that wasn't it at all: the kitten, from somewhere out of sight, had rubbed against her ankle, and she had kicked, reflexively. Then she jumped up, just as quickly, and ran to the corner where the kitten had landed. She picked it up, holding it against her, relieved that sometimes you could say, just with your hands, that you were sorry.

Robin Behn

Last Page

Book, give back the names of the loved.
Send them to bed, sing them a song of sorrys.

Set false trails for others who would follow,
But keep the loved in hiding

In some dear, familiar place.
See that they are well-fed, counted. After

All, the names of the loved, dragged screaming
From their beds by the quietest of sisters —

There may be some disturbances,
Rustlings, near-falls, they dream they're on stage . . .

Check sometimes, will you? Be a nurse in mouse shoes,
Fan their knotted shapes with sleep's cool page,

Then go, ugly one,
Ink the anonymous air.

Ted Benttinen

Above Punta Arenas

    (for Chile, in memoriam)

The road disappeared without drama
into a field of stones
where two untethered horses grazed slowly
on weeds. The small houses
thinned out into rough stragglers
hanging onto the hillside
like the last few dwarf firs
that are needed to define a timberline.

Across the straits, lenticular clouds
capped the mountains of Tierra del Fuego
with long flags of wind.
A few miles northwest of the city,
an old four-masted bark
that had been stripped of its yardarms
rode alone in its own bay
full of prisoners of the regime.

An old man motioned to me
so sparely his hand nearly disappeared
into the wind. I followed
through hanging burlap
into the mixed haze of kerosene and wood.

Under a coarse blanket,
there was a young woman dying
among friends. A makeshift altar
with three white candles burning
honored an unframed picture
of the Virgin. Wildflowers
lay unevenly around the rims of cans.

As she stared past me
with clouded blue eyes that once held
all the life of her fourteen years,
I learned she had tried to stop
the generals with the single word PAX

scribbled beneath Christ's cross
on a crude sign, and that for this
crime, grown men had beaten her for days.

> *W*hy, there's Sam! Remember his wedding?
>
> RATHER — WHEN THEY TOOK THE LABELS OFF HIS SUITCASES AND WROTE "BRITAIN'S MOST BEAUTIFUL GUEST HOUSE" ACROSS 'EM. . . .
>
> *Singularly appropriate, but rather cruel. . . .*
>
> CRUEL BE HANGED! EVERYTHING ARRIVED, ALL RIGHT. WHERE ELSE COULD THEY GET TO?
>
> *I suppose, if you put it like that, the Palace was the only place to—*
>
> AND THE ONLY PLACE WHERE GOLF, TENNIS, CROQUET, BOWLS, SQUASH, BADMINTON, SWIMMING POOL, DANCING, CINEMA & ENTERTAINMENTS ARE ALL INCLUDED IN THE TERMS!
>
> *Just listen to him, Daphne, he knows it off by heart.*
>
> **PALACE Hotel, TORQUAY**
>
> *Britain's Most Beautiful Guest House*

Jane Birdsall

Experience

I walk through the front gate
bold as new brass smiling my girl's threat,
watching the bee-keeper pale under her gauze veil,
rise from her chair expecting me.
"I could use some help," she says
stepping off the porch
like a bride jumping from a slow train.

I don't care
just want experience
so I can get a job at Olsen Knife
when I graduate.

Sweating in long clothes
I follow her to the hives
where thousands of buzzing eyes ignore us
as she hands me gloves, a pith helmet with gauze.

"My sister's got a job at Wolverine Glove," I brag.

"This here's a fair wage
you do as I say.
Take hold of her left wing with your thumb
and another finger.
Don't pinch or squeeze her belly.
Raise her from the comb,
let her stand on another finger or your knee.
Without hurting either of her legs
pass one blade of a small sharp scissors
under her right wing. Clip off at least two-thirds.
Before she tries to fly
place her on the comb among the bees.
As soon as a swarm follows her out
go to the hive with a glass tumbler.
Watch for the queen crawling on the ground.
Cover her with the tumbler.
The swarm will hover."

Wendy Bishop

Taking Photographs

1   The Photograph

A moldy cake under a plastic cover
and a cooler for beer and meat,
full of pigs' trotters, are details
I only notice later.

Viewed from above, from the second floor
stairway, perspective
flattens this family restaurant
to patterns of light in shade.

The few tablecloths are set
with cups of hot sauce
and the burners of the gas stove
hold six full cooking pots.
The cooler is never very cool
so vegetables pile
in clay bowls near the sink on red
and pink tiles.

No one tips
in a restaurant like this. Eating is serious,
the absorbing of stews
with stacks of tortillas. At the back,
cut in two by the balustrade
I find the lower half only
of a woman's body, her long legs
and black patent shoes.
On her hand a ring gleams, in her hand
a newspaper droops.
There is little news or the news is old.

The room looks quiet, each table
with its chairs, the floor swept,
in the perfect repose before the first guest.

2   The Day of the Photograph

    1/25/79
    Patzcuaro, Mexico

I climbed the stairs,
sick, yet paused to photograph
the room unfolding
below me. The kitchen
seemed appropriate
for a picture of early morning —
before the day's noise and dust and drunks
filtered through the doorway.
My landlady was cook, inn-keeper,
head of family.
Homely and fading, she
smiled aimlessly
like sunlight through window
blinds come undone
with sag. Her place was cheap,
her kitchen too cozy
and smelly for someone as ill
as me. I gripped
the railing. The stillness seemed
to be disappearing
into vapor and heat,
the frying fat
spitting, and suddenly motion
in all the rooms, on all the streets.

Jane Blue

At Work

half awake in the morning
I walk through Personnel

a door at the end of the hall
is open, there are bodies
on the floor, all on their backs
all women in blue jogging suits
side by side, head, feet, head
feet, like the fat boy's
sardine sandwich in parochial school
when Peter was a boy

they stuck out of the bread
head, tail, head, tail
and in twenty-five years
Peter has not touched a sardine

in the afternoon
the bodies are there again
one up on a long table
blue legs dangling
a baby laid on her chest

CPR manikins, they wait
to teach us how to breathe
life into the dying
and if the dying die
to save the organs

at break I go
into the women's room
a shopping cart full of heads
blocks the sink, clones
of a woman named Annie
pale, with straw-colored
hair sprouting through holes
in rubber scalp, open eyes

a large cheerful woman

is washing the germs
out of their mouths

From Private to General

They all enjoy a wash with

WRIGHT'S
Coal Tar Soap

(The Soldiers' Soap.)

It Soothes, Protects, Heals.

Box of Three Tablets 1/-

Deborah Boe

Invisible Girl

The first time it happened,
as far as I can remember,
I was in the nursery school playground.
A woman began calling names
and then got to mine.
I was in the box-car of a small train,
flattened to the wood below.
If I rose and got in line
everyone would know *who I was.*
So I stayed.

Later on, in second grade,
I bit my pencils to expose the lead
and to avoid being seen
at the pencil sharpener
in the front of the room.

When I was ten
I began to perfect a formula
to render invisible what would be so.
For instance, the first pubic hairs.
I didn't know that something
wasn't seriously wrong between my legs.
I could have been turning male.

To this day, not a soul
has seen me purchase a tampon;
it is a great mystery why
I don't bleed through my clothes.
And in bed, no one has seen
my face when it counted most.
It could have been anyone,
that pale, naked form
covered by another, and I
am the best kept secret around.

Philip Booth

Among Houses

Among houses, none an adequate windbreak
for any other, this cold house
on a cold harbor, the Labrador current
icing the spilings on every tide.

Time seeps away. As nights gather,
the same argument over and over,
the last twenty years empty as Christmas.
Neither one what the other wants;

one day of sun and twelve of overcast,
the relentless nimbus of wanting change,
but the same wind picking at chinks,
the same small house grown smaller.

The emotions of shut-ins. They've insulated
themselves to no avail: he will not let her be,
she will not let him feel. The old wind
catches its breath and starts in.

Christ, she thinks, *in my lifetime
has not risen. I continue to miss him.*
He in his corner stiffens: *Who was I
before I went numb? Who did we used

to be?* They sleep separate dreams
and eat the same breakfast, same cold argument:
one day of argument, twelve of truce;
the same newspaper stuffed in chinks,

the same plastic tacked over the window.
Miles of drift-ice close in on the coast,
the world gone over the edge with sunset,
nothing to speak of left.

Bop Bop Against That Curtain

by Charles Bukowski ©1975

ILLUSTRATED by R. CRUMB ©1975

We talked about women, peeked up their legs as they got out of cars, and we looked into windows at night hoping to see somebody fucking but we never saw anybody. One time we did watch a couple in bed and the guy was mauling his woman and we thought now we're going to see it, but she said, "No, I don't want to do it tonight!" Then she turned her back on him. He lit a cigarette and we went in search of a new window.

"Son of a bitch, no woman of mine would turn away from me!"

"Me neither. What kind of a man was that?"

There were three of us, me, Baldy, and Jimmy. Our big day was Sunday. On Sunday we met at Baldy's house and took the streetcar down to Main Street. Carfare was seven cents.

There were two burlesque houses in those days, the Follies and the Burbank. We were in love with the strippers at the Burbank and the jokes were a little better so we went to the Burbank. We had tried the dirty movie house but the pictures weren't really dirty and the plots were all the same. A couple of guys would get some little innocent girl drunk and before she got over her hangover she'd find herself in a house of prostitution with a line of sailors and hunchbacks beating on her door. Besides in those places the bums slept night and day, pissed on the floor, drank wine, and rolled each other. The stink of piss and wine and murder was unbearable. We went to the Burbank.

"You boys going to a burlesque today?" Baldy's grampa would ask.

"Hell no, sir, we've got things to do."

We went. We went each Sunday. We went early in the morning, long before the show and we walked up and down Main Street looking into the empty bars where the B-girls sat in the doorways with their skirts up, kicking their ankles in the sunlight that drifted into the dark bar. The girls looked good. But we knew. We had heard. A guy went in for a drink and they charged his ass off, both for his drink and the girl's. But the girl's drink would be watered. You'd get a feel or two and that was it. If you showed any money the barkeep would see it and along would come the mickey and you were out over the bar and your money was gone. We knew.

After our walk along Main Street we'd go into the hotdog place and get our eight cent hotdog and our big nickel mug of rootbeer. We were lifting weights and our muscles bulged and we wore our sleeves rolled high and we each had a pack of cigarettes in our breast pocket. We even had tried a Charles Atlas course, Dynamic Tension, but lifting weights seemed the more rugged and obvious way.

While we ate our hotdog and drank our huge mug of rootbeer we played the pinball machine, a penny a game. We got to know that pinball machine very well. When you made a perfect score you got a free game. We had to make perfect scores, we didn't have that kind of money.

Franky Roosevelt was in, things were getting better but it was still the depression and none of our fathers were working. Where we got our small amount of pocket money was a mystery except that we did have a sharp eye for anything that was not cemented to the ground. We didn't steal, we shared. And we invented. Having little or no money we invented little games to pass the time —

When you made a perfect score you got a free game.

one of them being to walk to the beach and back.

This was usually done on a summer day and our parents never complained when we arrived home too late for dinner. Nor did they care about the high glistening blisters on the bottoms of our feet. It was when they saw how we had worn out our heels and the soles of our shoes that we began to hear it. We were sent to the five and dime store where heels and soles and glue were at the ready and at a reasonable price.

The situation was the same when we played tackle football in the streets. There weren't any public funds for playgrounds. We were so tough we played tackle football in the streets all through football season, through basketball and baseball seasons and on through the next football season. When you get tackled on asphalt, things happen. Skin rips, bones bruise, there's blood, but you get up like nothing was wrong.

Our parents never minded the scabs and the blood and the bruises; the terrible and unforgivable sin was to rip a *hole* in one of the knees of your pants. Because there were only two pairs of pants to each boy: his everyday pants and his Sunday pants, and you could never rip a hole in the knee of one of your two pairs of pants because that showed that you were poor and an asshole and that your parents were poor and assholes too. So you learned to tackle a guy without falling on *either* knee. And the guy being tackled learned how to be tackled without falling on either knee.

When we had fights we'd fight for hours and our parents wouldn't save us. I guess it was because we pretended to be so tough and never asked for mercy, they were waiting for us to ask for mercy. But we hated our parents so we couldn't and because we hated them they hated us, and they'd walk out on their porches and glance casually over at us in the midst of a terrible endless fight. They'd just yawn and pick up a throw-away advertisement and walk back inside.

I fought a guy who later ended up very high in the United States Navy. I fought him one day from 8:30 in the morning until after sundown. Nobody stopped us although we were in plain sight of his front lawn, under two huge pepper trees with the sparrows shitting on us all day.

It was a grim fight, it was to the finish. He was bigger, a little older and heavier, but I was crazier. We quit by common consent — I don't know how this works, you have to experience it to

I fought him . . . from 8:30 in the morning until after sundown.

understand it, but after two people beat on each other eight or nine hours a strange kind of brotherhood emerges.

The next day my body was entirely blue. I couldn't speak out of my lips or move any part of myself without pain. I was on the bed getting ready to die and my mother came in with the shirt I'd worn during the fight. She held it in front of my face over the bed and she said, "Look, you got bloodspots on this shirt! Bloodspots!"

"Sorry!"

"I'll never get them out! NEVER!!"

"They're *his* bloodspots."

"It doesn't matter! It's blood! It doesn't come out!"

Sundays were our day, our quiet, easy day. We went to the Burbank. There was always a bad movie first. A very old movie, and you looked and waited. You were thinking of the girls. The three or four guys in the orchestra pit, they played loud, maybe they didn't play too good but they played loud, and those strippers finally came out and grabbed the curtain, the edge of the curtain, and they grabbed that curtain like it was a man and shook their bodies and went bop bop bop aginst that curtain. Then they swung out and started to strip. If you had enough money there was even a bag of popcorn; if you didn't to hell with it.

Before the next act there was an intermission. A little man got up and said, "Ladies and gentlemen, if you will let me have your kind attention . . ." He was selling peep-rings. In the glass of each ring, if you held it to the light there was a most wonderful picture. This was promised you! Each ring was only 50 cents, a lifetime possession for just 50 cents, made available only to the patrons of the Burbank and not sold anywhere else. "Just hold it up to the light and you will see! And, thank you, ladies and gentlemen, for your kind attention. Now the ushers will pass down the aisles among you."

Two ragass bums would proceed down the aisles smelling of muscatel, each carrying a bag of peep-rings. I never saw anybody purchase one of the rings. I imagine, though, if you had held one up to the light the picture in the glass would have been a naked woman.

The band began again and the curtains opened and there was the chorus line, most of them former strippers gone old, heavy with mascara and rouge and lipstick, false eyelashes. They did their damndest to stay with the music but they were always a little behind. But they carried on; I thought they were very brave.

Then came the male singer. It was very difficult to like the male singer. He sang too loud about love gone wrong. He didn't know how to sing and when he finished he spread his arms, and bowed his head to the tiniest ripple of applause.

Then came the comedian. Oh, he was good! He came out in an old brown overcoat, hat pulled down over his eyes, slouching and walking like a bum, a bum with nothing to do and no place to go. A girl would walk by on the stage and his eyes would follow her. Then he'd turn to the audience and say, out of his toothless mouth, "Well, I'll be god damned!"

Another girl would walk out on the stage and he'd walk up to her, put his face close to hers and say, "I'm an old man, I'm past 44 but when the bed breaks down I finish on the floor." That did it. How we laughed! The young guys and the old guys, how we laughed. And there was the suitcase routine. He's trying to help some girl pack her suitcase. The clothes keep popping out.

He'd turn to the audience and say "Well, I'll be god-damned!"

"I can't get it in!"
"Here let me help you!"
"It popped out again!"
"Wait! I'll stand on it!"
"What? Oh *no,* you're not going to *stand* on it!"

They went on and on with the suitcase routine. Oh, he was funny!

Finally the first three or four strippers came out again. We each had our favorite stripper and we each were in love. Baldy had chosen a thin French girl with asthma and dark pouches under her eyes. Jimmy liked the Tiger Woman (properly The Tigress). I pointed out to Jimmy the Tiger Woman definitely had one breast larger than the other. Mine was Rosalie.

Rosalie had a large ass and she shook it and shook it and sang funny little songs, and as she walked about stripping she talked to herself and giggled. She was the only one who really enjoyed her work. I was in love with Rosalie. I often thought of writing her and telling her how great she was but somehow I never got around to it.

One afternoon we were waiting for the streetcar after the show and there was the Tiger Woman waiting for the streetcar too. She was dressed in a tight-fitting dress and we stood there looking at her.

"It's your girl, Jimmy, it's the Tiger Woman."
"Boy, she's got it! Look at her!"
"I'm going to talk to her," said Baldy.
"It's Jimmy's girl."
"I don't want to talk to her," said Jimmy.
"I'm going to talk to her," said Baldy. He put a cigarette in his mouth, lit it, and walked up to her.
"Hi ya, baby!" he grinned at her.

The Tiger Woman didn't answer. She just stared straight ahead waiting for the streetcar.

"I know who you are. I saw you strip today. You've got it, baby, you've really got it!"

The Tiger Woman didn't answer.

"You really shake it, my god, you really shake it!"

The Tiger Woman stared straight ahead. Baldy stood there grinnig like an idiot at her. "I'd like to put it to you. I'd like to fuck you, baby!"

We walked up and pulled Baldy away. We walked him down the street. "You asshole, you have no right to talk to her that way!"

"Well, she gets up and shakes it, she gets up in front of men and shakes it!"

"She's just trying to make a living."
"She's hot, she's red hot, she wants it!"
"You're crazy."
We walked him down the street.

Rosalie had a large ass.

Not long after that I began to lose interest in those Sundays on Main Street, I suppose the Follies and the Burbank are still there. Of course, the Tiger Woman and the stripper with asthma, and Rosalie, my Rosalie are long gone. Probably dead. Rosalie's big shaking ass is probably dead. And when I'm in my neighborhood, I drive past the house I used to live in and there are strangers living there. Those Sundays were good, though, most of those Sundays were good, a tiny light in the dark depression days when our fathers walked the front porches, jobless and impotent and glanced at us beating the shit out of each other, then went inside and stared at the walls, afraid to play the radio because of the electric bill.

Teresa Cader

Insomnia

By the window late at night,
I hear air conditioners hum,
the first hint of wind
in the trees. I am here
because I almost fell asleep,
because the night was so hot
it took me from conscious desire
and the droning of the TV
in the apartment above me.
Because I wanted to fall
out of my body the way
a child does in mid-sentence.
And I am here
because there is a child
in my body
who can only nap
in off hours
when the world has turned
its back,
who stretches out in the car seat
when the adults finally
have something to say
to each other.
This child is waiting
for the landscape to change,
for the map
to refuse to be followed.
This is the child
who stayed up nights
imagining where the edges
of the universe were
and what lay
on the other side.
The child who wanted
to believe
someone could answer
her questions:
What does anything mean,
and why

is this night
so frightening?

WOODWARD'S
"GRIPE WATER"
FOR ALL DISORDERS OF INFANTS & YOUNG CHILDREN

Teresa Cader

Zach's Cliffs, Gay Head

A gull lifts off the cliffs
And hangs on a current, wings
Taut. Against the sun
Pivoting into the sea,
Against the cliffs
Cool and damp,
It is as clean
As letting go, as cool
As desire's abandoned heat.
In this it is effortless:
Beyond the furious flapping
We associate with flight.
This is not a desperate move
To rise above,
But a *rising out of.*
Like the mind's easy disclaimer,
The world is full of flight plans:
The shortest route
Between heartaches is *not*
A straight line,
Not our ability to nose dive
Into any field,
But letting the air take us
As it will.
Holding our damage claims
Unfettered like wings,
And rising,
Hungry,
Again.

Teresa Cader

Gooseflesh

On March 28, 1757 Elizabeth Trapp
of Edgartown married Elijah Webster
of Lebanon in a shift wedding.
That is, being dowerless,
she was made to appear in her chemise,
to remind her she was naked
of this world's goods. Stepping
across the king's highway to the hall,
she was the ripple of gooseflesh
the Good Lord gave her, the bare
blessing of inheritance.
Who was she marrying,
she must have asked herself —
flesh like her flesh
or the Other,
who looked like Elijah
and held in his left fist
a pasture and a house
by which he was clothed
and presumed good. As good
as the world's goods, as dour
as a man might be, marrying
a half-naked woman in public
on a night in March. Because
the road was icy, because
he thought it peculiar
to have his friends see her body
at the same time he did, he longed
to throw her his cape, wrap
something, even the horses's
blanket, around her shoulders.
But love is part convention,
part the inheritance of goods.
And so being a good man
and conventional, he could stare
at her gooseflesh,
at her shame,
as if they were gold.

Hayden Carruth

For Papa

So long gone that was called Jimmy Yancey,
that played the piano blues, that like his eyes
heavy-lidded searching the cocaine haze
laconically drew as it were a necromancy
from very ancient melody where no fancy
thing was heard, but a lingering, falling phrase
or a slow trill touched over the limping bass
in reticence, in almost silence, the chancy

lines of the song held in informing purity,
the bitterness of his love, the soul of *sonetto,*
as once with him that was called Dante, for so —
and only quietly so — might simple clarity
flow in the antsy moan of the crowd, a tone
of primordial sorrow, the deepest and so long gone.

David Citino

Sister Mary Appassionata Lectures the Eighth Grade Girls:
Furrow, Cave, Cowry, Home

More descriptive epithets have been coined for the vulva
than for any other part of the human body.
                              — *Encyclopedia of Esoteric Man*

First furrow, sea from which we all crawled
tracing the path of the prime member, conch
that gives us music of the spheres, scrim
we part to begin our every play, word from

the beginning, all poetry must pass within
your well-wrought gate of horn. You mean the cave
in whose encompassing dark we learned all hues,
arc and line of art, pristine spring without which

every field becomes desert, every single night
a death. Triangle poised on the apex, perfection
of circle, box from which even evil issues,
grail and jug, press and vine, tunnel of love,

you make pleasure and pain their own reward.
Your might makes shall, an edge that splits
the grandest redwood to switch limp as eel,
slays the fieriest dragon. You remind us all,

shining cowry pretty as dawn on rippling river,
of pleasure's depth and breadth, life's bounty
limitless as all we can't know, beauty
of loam, spray, meadow and wood, every inch

of every journey, map of loveland, heaven our home.

David Citino

Sister Mary Appassionata Speaks During the Retreat of the Eighth Grade Boys and Girls

Three entrances to the world of fire:
slip of zipper; blouse gaping too wide
or at the wrong time; mouth, lips
and tongue wagging with the latest passion.

You don't believe in flesh's urgencies?
Hold your hand two inches above the candle's
tear-shaped flame, or place your lips
on a sighing lover's flushed throat, then
tell me beauty doesn't move you, art,

blood, bone and skin don't carry weight.
Lot's daughters were forced to take the law
into their own hands. Potiphar's wife
spent her nights wrestling a eunuch.

For what she did who are we to blame her?
Dominic Savio and Teresa tried to stay saints
by forcing their eyes away from loveliness,
crying to put out every fire. They only
gave themselves headaches. Even the Savior

had an eye for beauty. The young lovers
found the morning after twined in sin,
rigid and blue with nature's last rapture,
eyes glassy with passion, the exhaust

of the '57 Chevy clogged with snow
in the drift they'd backed into in their haste
to age, clothes thrown around the back seat
like crumpled Christmas wrapping? They
lost their minds perhaps, and we their names

but the goodness they have to one another,
dexterities of love, the fire they made
by moving limbs together, long as together
we live and breathe, never will grow old.

David Citino

Sister Mary Appassionata Lectures the Studio Art Class: *Doctrines of Nakedness*

1.
In Greece each cynic trotted about caked in mud,
lifting leg like bitch and pit-bull, believing only
what could be mounted, perceived, taking on in time
the hue and shade of grave. Apollo's healing rite
meant nude virgin administering balm to nude patient,
proving art can make us whole. The Israelites
lost their shirts to the gold calf, and David lost
wife and kingdom to earn the right to sing unmuffled.
One disciple ran naked into night because of Judas' kiss.
The Iroquois paired off to dance uncovered together
to bring down on field and forest the spirit-sweat.
To lovers and mirrors going bare's the loveliest wisdom.

2.
Even Luther undressed to scare off
temptation. There are times
when this earth's so cold
even a lightning god must be
wrapped in swaddling clothes
until death casts lots for
his seamless garment. Thus
still today in graveyards
we drape our angels in folds
of stony white even though,
like Adam, Eve and us, they
haven't a thing to hide.

3.
The Middle Ages knew four ways of human revelation.
Nuditas naturalis meant Eve and Adam before they went
down, babes, morons and savages who couldn't comprehend
the lies in which women and men try to cloak themselves.
Nuditas temporalis, nakedness of each of us before
chance and law, rattling bones of poverty and fate,
snake-eyes of age. *Nuditas virtualis* signified
the clarity of the seer, unadorned truths of all good,
anchorites, dendrites, pillar-sitters embracing God.
Nuditas criminalis was the sin of sins, hot lovers

bearing passion before all else, flaming sword
and molten sheath, hell of knowing mortality too well.

A JACOBEAN Interior

Quality always carries its own Hall Mark

WESTON BISCUITS

Robert Clinton

The Men I Know

The men I know
born by chance all of them
go along the rock.

At intervals they split
re-name and move apart
one up the line one down.

Discipline of day keeps them
quick and temperate
circled each by children.

On the best nights
they go home slowly
fixing it by stars

just beyond the noise.
The men I know
born in labor all of them

go along the rock
the way I go without
much hesitation.

Judith Ortiz Cofer

Letter From a Caribbean Island

This island is a fat whore lolling
tremulous and passive in the lukewarm sea.
Nature has shamed us like a voluptous daughter:
no place to hide from the debauchery
of sun, wind and vegetation.
All roads end in the sea,
and the mountains are like a garment
shrunk by the heat.
We are hungry for white, longing for snow.
So much color corrupts the soul.
We pray for a different weather, a civil storm,
one that won't enter our homes
like a soldier drunk on blood.
How can we be good Christians here?
In this tropical Eden we sleep on beds
soaked in sweat, and spend our days
under a demanding sun that saps
our good intentions.
There are no puritans here.
We throw open our windows to conceive,
letting the western wind blow life into the seed.
Sinners all, we pass the time as best we can
in paradise, waiting for the bridge across the water.

Gillian Conoley

New in Town

Tonight a teenager
peels the foil from a gum wrapper, imagines herself
floating. Her mother watches
television send its blue light
through the living room,
tell her what it is like
to live in Italy.
Outside white laundry waves goodbye.

This is not Italy.
In the glass-eyed window the manager stores
phials of dark mercury.
This town knows its pilgrims.

No one knows me,
though at the grocery there is a camera
rolling over my shoulder
as I select tangerines.
There are the tin moths stupidly hitting the light.

The fluorescent sidewalk,
which I can feel more easily than leaves,
bares its veins and I realize I
could be anyone. My sleeves
hang suspiciously over my hands.

Telephone numbers drop from my pockets.
While the baker's not looking,
I change hats.

I carry a bouquet of oleanders
behind me, ready to flash.
I carry on.

Finally my feet ask the rest of me
is this the place? The I
I think I am
wants to answer with the sound that keeps following me
from town to town, the sound I hear

but cannot name,
maybe water, a foreign piano.

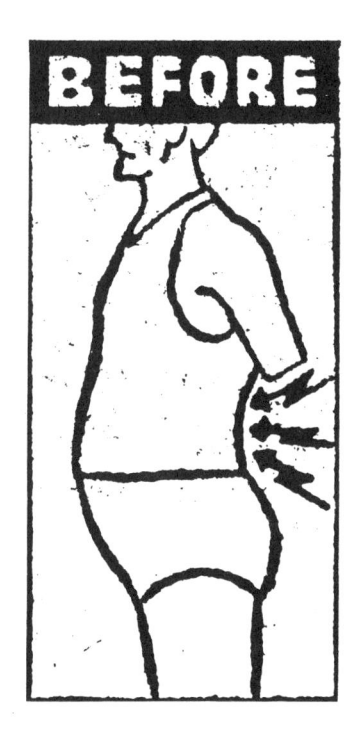

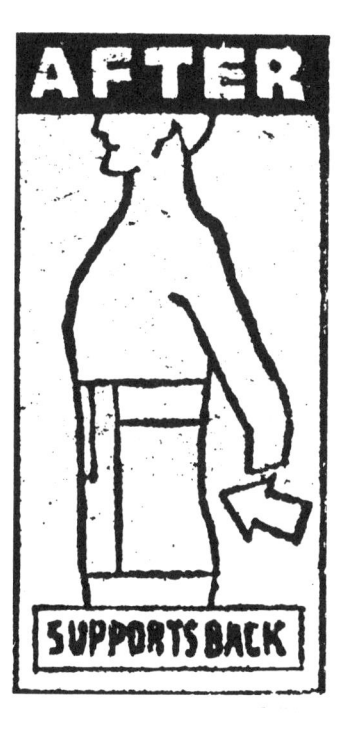

Gillian Conoley

Patsy Cline

When I'm alone, I like how my nylons
mesh, the rustle I get
just walking.

I keep walking this way,
moving down the stage
like it was ice. Not like she did
in that yellow skirt,
strolling in
so everyone saw. You keep telling

the story a different way,
how nothing matters
outside this room. The thin coins
dropping out your pants.

But I still see
that bar, the lights
strung bare above every man's back,
the sticky perfume,
her skirt a breeze you could carry.

Once I got home,
I draped sheets over the posts
so my bed was a chariot.
But you were cast in every crease,
thick and strange
as when you danced, your arms
swallowing her

like a hot jewel. Let me tell you
I was not born in the shack
you'd like to see me in
with a fork and lipsticked cigarettes.

I may be walking backwards onto this plane,
but you're looking
like some rat-eyed pimp,
some hillside jack
on a slide.

Gillian Conoley

Woman Speaking Inside Film Noir

What I want happens
not when the man leaning on a lampost
stares up to my room and I meet his gaze
through the blinds, but in the moment after,
in the neon's pulse, when his cigarette
glows in the rain like a siren
and he looks away.

I go back to bed and imagine
the sound of his shoes
on the wooden stairs, flight
after flight; my pincurls loosening,
falling across the pillow
gentle as dropped bolts of bargain silk.

When the door flies open there's nothing
but the luminous band of the radio,
still he steps toward me
in a pyramid of light.
Our shadows yearn across the dresser,
my perfume bottles glisten
like shots of scotch. The mirror
is one more stilled moon
that wants the wish of him,
his face upturned,
astonished, cloudy as opal.

Gillian Conoley

Insomnia

In some sloppy, ingratiating movement,
wind slips through the weeping hysteria of trees
before winter, boughs in the dark boat

that recurs, but far away,
like the same boat I try
my sleep in. Tonight

there is the embarrassment
of a runaway gown, and the reminder
of the partner beside me,

undone, his breath an odd light.
I have a plot, the morning we wake up
cheerful at the window,

but the plot needs furniture, and these chairs
are really childhood pets barking
their way back, here to take me somewhere,

show me what was
never retrieved. A mob
of wild ideas waits

in the hallway, but there is no
getting up. This is the city
with no moon, and it is useless

turning the day over. In Hong Kong,
the light is leaving
only its smallest suggestion, and soon

it will be mine, bleaching
the absolute clarity
hanging over me,

threads begging
connection, the fragments
already disappearing before me.

Gillian Conoley

The Cousin at the Funeral

Three in the afternoon,
                      my skirt
held up in one fist,
our grandmother not even cold, we waded
far down the river,
                      not stopping
until the tree moss
                      hung in sweeps
and there was shade. Even then
I thought of how
you would tell it:

                    years later, after making love
in a city,
        its noise clanging
below you, your lover
watching as you stare away from her
to speak. She strains

to see you then, the way
you must have looked,
                    tall in your suit,
and me, like you,
                tanned and gangly
but a girl.

        You tell her
slowly, your voice carrying
                      until she begins to nod,
knowing the amber light,
the smell of the rotting trunks,
                    the glimpse of me, you,
lying there on the shore.

Kenneth Zamora Damacion

Tadpole Fishing

I close quietly the door to the bedroom
of my niece. She is three,
and her parents have been dead for three days.

Tonight we are tired
from fishing in the creek.
I showed her
how to let the tin can
sleep at the creek bottom,
how to jerk
the stick and string,
to scoop up
the black tadpoles wandering inside.
At the creek's edge
I sat with beer
and Erin with candy.
Her black ponytail brushing her back.
All afternoon, I felt uncertain
of how much to say
of the mauled lamp posts
the overturned cars. Instead,
we cardboard sledded down
dry summer hills,
collected walnuts, secrets
under trees with the brown husk,
the nuggets of meat inside.

Before bed,
Erin nestled in my lap. I pointed out
the deep-throated croak of a bullfrog,
and told her about a tadpole's
loss of its tail,
the growth of the hind feet.
I had fished for evasive answers
all afternoon, waiting
for the right time to tell her,
waiting until she shifted her catch
to a platter before we had hunted out the walnuts;
until she had found the tadpoles dried by the sun.

Charles W. Darling

Tying Knots
    — Stave Island, Summer, 1983

As I jump from the little boat to the dock,
my friend calls out, "Tie it with half-hitches.
I don't want it getting loose in the night."
Half-hitches. I half remember the word.
When I was a boy, my neighbor, Al Moon,
thinking it was something boys should learn,
tried to teach me knots. He was a painter,
and you could see him on a summer day,
edging down a roof line, rappelling from chimney,
painting the flashing a brilliant red, or,
ladder tied to under-eave, he'd lean to dormer's edge
to finish off a window sill with one quick line.

He taught me his knots, starting with easy ones:
lark's head, cat's paw, clove hitch, and square knot.
("That's a granny knot; it's not a knot," he'd laugh.)
Cow hitch, anchor bend, sheepshank, barrel bight.
And what they were for: never use a square knot
to join two different ropes; use a sheet bend instead.
He wouldn't teach me how to tie a noose
and slapped me hard, once, when I tried.
Use a timber hitch where a clove hitch would bind
from being wet or holding too much weight.
And the simple bowline — the king of knots —
the bowline never slips or jams.
"I can pull you from a well with this," he said,
"and never pinch your guts or crush your heart."
I pictured myself in the slick esophagus of earth,
waiting for the dangling rope from Mr. Moon,
tying my perfect bowline and being pulled to light,
to the clapped relief and cheers of those who loved me.

Al Moon, I need you now: I am helpless to recall
the knots I need to hold this boat all night.
The kinds of knot I tie will either slip or jam,
and what I cannot hold by heart and wish
I wrap, like a spider, in thick cocoons.
I think you are painting a house now,

as I cling to a ledge in the well's dark side,
calling your name, less loudly each time,
afraid to fall asleep, waiting for your face to show
in the circle of all I can see.
Remind me, Father Moon, of the bowline's strength.
Let the rope be long enough. Let me tie it right.

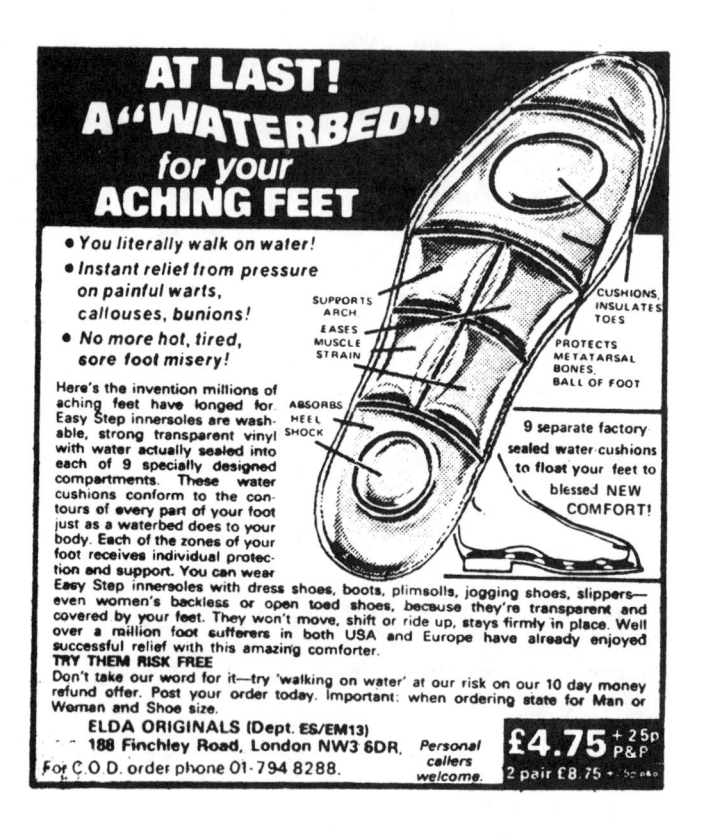

Jon Davis

Driving Red Bush Lane

I've got my own way, see,
I don't want to live like my father —
thirty years in a sweat shop
then one day you're fishing
beers out of a tub of ice
with the whole family jabbering
and flinging Jarts, and your heart
just swells and bursts
and you're dead. I know.
I saw it all. And my mother,
her face went flooey — eyes
wide and darting. She looked at me
like I could fix it, then
watched the whole thing, moaning,
"Jimmy, Jimmy." She just watched,
just watched him die like that
in front of the whole damn family
and me just a kid, what could I do?

I could've played basketball;
I can handle the ball, shoot
ten-for-ten from the top of the key.
My father knew the coach of Notre Dame;
I could've gotten a scholarship.
But then he went and he died.
It pisses me off sometimes
to see other kids and their fathers.
I hear them in the stands saying,
protect the ball with your body,
or yelling *three seconds*
when I'm standing in the lane.
No, I'm through with sports.
I've got my own way now,
my own plans. I'll learn to
drive a semi, join the guard, maybe
pick up the guitar again. There's
a lot of things I could do.

Saturdays I spend waxing my Camaro.

I pop Black Sabbath into the tape deck
and all the kids ride down on their bikes
to listen and help clean. This
is the fastest car in The Valley — bar none.
It's got an Edelbock Hi-Rise manifold
with a big old Holly Three-Barrel
squatting right on top
pissing gas into that motor
faster than an elephant. Yeah,
I've got my own way.
I don't like to be bothered. My mother
comes nosing around here sometimes
on weekends. But I don't let her in my room,
I don't tell her nothin'. She checks
my tires for wear, but what does *she* know?
I tell her it's normal. *These tires,* I say,
they're soft rubber — for traction — they wear down.

But I tear 'em up on Red Bush Lane,
alongside the railroad tracks. I carve J's
all over that road and the kids go wild.
No one's ever seen a driver like me —
I'm a little different. I like to take a chance.
Some nights I'll run that whole goddamned road
without lights. All three miles. Last week,
driving like that, I hit something.
I felt it thud against the bumper;
the car shook and jumped. It sent us
skidding, but it felt good —
like a grape popping out of its skin.
Like I said: I've got my own way.
We turned around — Crazy Joey and me —
and went back to see what we hit.
We went past it once, fast, and Joey,
well, he said it was a dog.
But I saw it good, and I know.

But I didn't say nothin', just drove.
Drove fast enough that neither of us

had time to think: not about what we hit,
or what's right and what's wrong,
or about my father, dying like a fool
in front of the whole family.
We closed *The Frog Pond* that night.
The Series was on, Joey got drunk,
Jackson hit another homer. I had a friend
hung himself in the halfway house
across from *The Pond*. I used to
whip his ass on the asphalt courts
back of Beaver Street School. Lately,
I think about those games, how,
with the score nineteen to one,
I'd drive the lane and jam it, or,
in a close game, I'd rock back on my heels
and nail a twenty footer. What did I want?

Home from *The Pond,* I stood in the driveway
until three-thirty just looking at my car —
how the moonlight glittered in the chrome,
curved along the windshield. I listened
to cars rushing on the highway; twice
I heard sirens. I know what I've done,
but I'm young, I've got a life to live.
In the morning I washed the car,
walked to the *Highway Diner* for coffee.
I avoided the papers, even *The News*
spread out on the counter, a picture
of some woman who killed her doctor husband.
Only *I* know, maybe Joey but he won't say.
Later I walked the fireroads through
Water Company land, and looked down on Red Bush Lane —
two cop cars cruising, then, for no reason,
flooring it past the torn garbage bags, tool sheds,
stacks of railroad ties, their 440's howling . . . .

Today, for the first time in a week,
I stopped at the courts, shot
baskets with the gang. Chuck's van

was pulled up close, the tape player
blasting. There was a girl there
used to be in my home room. I drove her
to school once and she said
she'd seen me play basketball
and she thought I was good. I remember her eyes
looking at me through her brown hair.
I think I'd like to go see her, to talk
about those games on Beaver Street, maybe
go for a ride up the River Road, past Newtown
and Sharon, past the lake where Joey keeps his boat,
the dam, past the *Crossroads Diner,*
farther than I've ever needed to go . . . .
I don't want to live like my father, that's
not my way. I've got something better in mind.

Joseph Deumer

Sunday Morning

I wake to the insistent mocking
birds and the serrations of sirens
cutting the clear early air.

On Sunday mornings, I write
letters to Congressmen and Senators,
sending copies to the *LA Times*.

I know I could do more,
but at what cost to those I love?
It is hard to love strangers.

I'm not trying to be funny.
I have a friend who was arrested
protesting at an Air Force base

against cruise missiles, and spent
some days in jail, separated
from her young son. She learned

that guards, even military guards,
know fear, and respond
to the occasional good word.

And I'm not saying her time
was badly spent, only that it seems
the greatest benefits accrued

to my friend's conscience,
spiritual comfort, and self-
satisfaction. The missiles

remain perched on their hair triggers.
Late on Sunday mornings I can hear
the *crump crump* of the Navy

taking gunnery practice, aiming
at the small island off our coast,

uninhabited except for scrub pine, feral goats, and other useless stuff.

Jond Devol

Inuits

Blued seal-skin heads
wear hair of white bear, arctic fox.
On their knees devour the raw
ghost freed in their bodies.

The woman squats like a berg,
seals her jaw on the slippery cord,
slurps the placenta like cooled soup,
smothers a first-born girl with hard kisses.

The man, a freckle on the albino world,
a body too spent for a marked birth.
The seal-gut line saws between them:
ice-diver, seal-woman.

He borrows ice for a sunny window,
the reflection makes her squint.
He lets go in yellow coins,
a small, dull rainbow.

Jond Devol

Inuit Woman

Complacent with seal gut
her boned gums gnaw it free of ice
the way her tongue accepts its hunger.
She knows a ghost follows the kill.
Her spit catches mid-air.

An ice skull sprouts.
She is born, sucked back into
the mouth of her home.
She sleds to the edge of the world on runners
he slicks with spit.

They are too cold to thaw, too warm to stop.
He comes from the hunt with half-eaten walrus.
She sucks the oil clean, keeps one of the hollow tusks
curved at her leaking breast.

Deborah Digges

Bums

At night you jump from the trains.
I know you have not come for me
the way the bee man who tends the hives
each September promises to take me
home with him. I wait all night
in a red dress of my sister's
while you build fires in the orchard
with apple boughs, clean rabbits
with pocket knives, dry the still warm
skins on little stick houses.

In the morning my father
crushes the houses, bloodied,
deserted, and tosses your empty bottles
to the center of the pond.
I pick up a shirt that smells
like it belonged to a child waiting
at a screen door, who grew tired
of waiting. Now you clear a death in one
leap, change flying from your pockets,
and nothing to frighten you.

Carol Dine

Morning/Afternoon

1.

Around the corner
of my eyes, the sun
comes low outside my window,
raising its orange back
behind the leaves;
a perfect circle of flame
for three seconds —
then gone. In the fury
of the sun's perfection,
I mock myself:
Not with the question of time,
but the lack of magnificence.

2.

At the harbor
under the oval horizon,
everything is in order:
houses, waves, boats.
I want to own the equilibrium
of the water breaking,
and after the breaking.
The blue afternoon enfolds
in spite of me; with no grand design,
no choice but to rivet myself
like a mussel
to the bed,
the black rock.

Elizabeth Dodd

Another Season

She is the woman guessing
each day what might have gone right
had she never married. Some days
she pulls clothes from the bureau
like bandages. In the winter,
tiny birds thud the windows, sometimes
spinning back out among the birches,
more often wadding down against the
gutter-stained snow. She gathers them,
windfall apples, unopened pinecones.

In the worst spell they couldn't bear
to lift from the feeder, even when
she stood right there on the deck,
wrapping her empty arms
around her waist. They watched her
with February eyes, and went on
feeding their own furious heat.
Sixty below in the wind
and the squirrels couldn't spook
the jays and nuthatches. All around
the house the snow stayed
pitted and torn with feathers dropped
like branches under the glittering weight.

In other cities her sons
grow taller than their father,
that man who cannot decide
what he wants. Last summer
he sat on the lawn writing letters
to women he touched forty years back.
Long before October, the trees
snapped into color. Then she gathered
armfuls of sumac, red oak, pale curling
birch. Autumn in August, how long
until even the body has lost faith?

Susan Dodd

Browsing

I see my ex-husband at a yard sale.

Immediately I duck behind a metal utility cabinet, which has been painted green and decorated with vegetable decals. A moment ago, I was browsing, a decent pursuit. Now I am lurking. Craven.

It is not that I mind seeing him. On the contrary, my instinctive self-concealment is in concert with that very desire: I *want* to see my ex-husband. To observe him. How does he conduct himself, alone, on a Saturday morning, at a sale of secondhand goods? What is he in the market for? In calculating the long division of our property, did I manage to cancel out some object, functional or ornamental, that he finds he can't live without? Perhaps I should have consulted him about the garlic press, ask if he wanted a divider for the top kitchen drawer. Who am I, after all, to presume he would eat in restaurants all the time, that the sight of his few forks lying in a jumble with his knives and spoons would not pain him? It is possible that he may turn out to be a better cook than I am. After all, I know so little about him.

He moves closer to me. The utility cabinet is too narrow. It is only a matter of time before I am discovered: lurking. He is taller than I remember. Still a growing boy, perhaps? He bends over, nearly halving himself, to scrutinize a table of kitchen gadgets and curios dispossessed of their cabinets. Yes, the garlic press, I think, guilty as sin over the scampi and salad dressings I've prepared and consumed with splendid disregard for the wants of my one-time spouse. The egg timer. Two wire whisks. I had no shame. That is not the case now.

Gregory, assuming that is still his name (his name — oh God, I even kept half of that), is arrested by something on the table. He freezes in a half-crouch, his face as respectfully bemused as an anthropologist confronted with some aboriginal artifact of worship or war. He makes no attempt to mask his ignorance, but is careful not to give offense. His long-fingered, white, shockingly beautiful hand reaches for something with prudent reverence. He straightens his spine as he lifts it: a pronged wooden mallet. He examines the object at not quite arm's length, his eyes vaguely shocked. Little as I know him, I know he is imagining domestic violence.

"It's for spaghetti," I say, stepping out from behind the green metal sarcophagus sprightly with animated peppers and radishes.

"Hello, Ruth."

It is like old times. I never was able to catch him offguard.

"I haven't got one myself, but you sort of wind the strands around those little spikes to lift them out of the boiling water. I think that's the idea."

Gregory nods politely. I am the aborigine, bellicose and god-dazed. My former spouse is a respecter of alien and primitive cultures. He sets the wooden mallet back on the table, just where it was, between a food scale and a calico woman with yarn hair who hides a roll of toilet paper under her skirts.

"How are you?" he asks me. I recall the grounds of our divorce: irreconcilable courtesy. He started it. I retaliated, viciously civil.

"It isn't so bad," I say. "Really not so bad."

"No, it isn't, is it?"

"You look good. Better, I mean. Not so thin."

"I don't get enough exercise."

"I meant it as a compliment," I tell him.

"I know you did."

His fine, flyaway hair, unduly red on a man nearing forty, needs cutting. It curls over the back of his collar so I can't tell if his pink oxford cloth shirt is clean and in good repair. I find no fault with the front. No buttons appear to be missing. But then, finding fault with Gregory was never easy.

"You're on sabbatical this semester?"

His light gray eyes blink once behind the polished lenses of his rimless glasses, as if I've reminded him of something he'd prefer to overlook. "Yes. Working full-time on the book."

The book: "Love's Iconoclast: The Demystification of Romance in the Novels of D. H. Lawrence." Only a working title, but how could I compete with that?

"It must be a relief — being able to concentrate on it, I mean."

The iconoclast smiles. "Actually, it means there's no relief. No excuse not to finish now."

"You'll do it." Finish, or find an excuse? I leave the choice of my meaning up to him.

He ignores the ambiguity, a characteristic failing. "What about you — are you doing anything now?"

"By *your* standards, you mean?"

"Oh, Ruth . . ."

"Sorry. I'm still a sucker for a straight line."

"I wish we could be friends. I'd like this to be . . . amicable."

"It never really was. Maybe you wouldn't take things so hard if you remembered that."

I pick up a set of steak knives with pistol-shaped handles. There are five, bound together with a greasy leather thong. I take care to hold the points in a neutral direction. My ex-husband is shaking his head sadly. "Do you have any steak knives?"

"I don't eat at home much," he says.

"Then you have everything you need."

He shrugs, smiling in a way I find new and attractive. He has learned a thing or two about irony.

"Ask me again," I say.

"What?"

"If I'm doing anything."

His innocent face ages abruptly with wariness. He takes his time, thinking the semantic problem through. "What are you doing now?"

I reward him with what may be my last ingenuous smile, preserved from my girlhood for just such a moment. "I've applied to law school. Finally."

He straightens his shoulders, as if a burden has been shifted to someone else. "I always knew you would." When he reaches toward me to remove the steak knives from my hands, his cool, pale fingers brush my knuckles. "I'm glad for you."

"I haven't been accepted yet."

"Pro forma," he says. "Nothing to it."

Self-conscious, I study the display of linens hanging on a clothesline behind him: assorted napkins and tea towels, dresser scarves and doilies. Irish linen, Belgian lace, unbleached muslin cross-stitched and appliqued by hand. That sort of fancywork isn't done anymore. I knitted a sweater for Gregory while he was writing his dissertation. The sleeves were too short. I sometimes wore it to bed during the winter, when we lived in a basement apartment in Morningside Heights. We have come up in the world: a yard sale in Amherst. Evidently we are both still in the market for something. A bargain. A finishing touch.

"I didn't do badly on the LSAT's."

"I'm not surprised. You're going to make one hell of a lawyer."

"Maybe . . . if I meet one."

His laugh exists for the sole purpose of humoring me. It costs him. "I'm still your straight man," he says, believing it.

"And I'm still your friend," I lie.

"Prove it." This time he does not smile.

"What?"

"Let me get you a present, Ruth."

"I don't . . . "

He stands his ground. "Treasure hunt," he says.

The first year we were married, a ritual more passionate and tender than newlywed lovemaking: the last Saturday of each month, scraping bottom, waiting for the next fellowship check, the thin salary envelope from the Institute for Global Concerns, where I typed position papers that didn't concern me . . .

The first year of marriage, the last Saturday of the month, my young husband and I would take our bottom dollars — one for each of us — and go off to buy one another gifts.

We would comb the Salvation Army stores, flea markets, junk shops, craft fairs in the parks. Hunting. I recall the treasures we turned up more clearly than the opulent wedding gifts from family friends. The life we made was never suited to silver trays and chafing dishes. Crystal goblets seemed to sour what wine we could afford. When candles burned in our cramped apartments, it seemed simpler to blow them out than to find the sterling snuffer, a gracefully inverted bell on a wand-like handle.

I wore the colored glass earrings my husband pulled from his pockets, though. Even now I have the potholder from the St. Louis World's Fair in my latest kitchen, a bookmark made from a laminated scrap of an old quilt, three wooden buttons from Africa in the shape of elephants' heads, a mauve feather boa that sheds, and a small glass ashtray — "Souvenir of Shreveport, La. Hot Sauce Capital of the World."

And Gregory — do you still, when occasion demands it, work your heels into your dress shoes with the ivory-colored plastic shoehorn endorsing Aldo R. Bianchi for Judge of Probate? Still open beer cans with a lurid naked lady who has a church-key for a head? Do you thumb a long-outdated edition of Guinness's records now and then, seeking food for thought?

I do not imagine my former husband recalls the circle pin enameled with flowers. I wore it on my bathing suit all summer, the year we lived near Crane's Beach. The salt water wore the flowers away, and in September, when school was starting someplace else, even the metal was corroding. Gregory would have no way of knowing, now, that I finally found a chenille bed-jacket. The other day I removed three pearly blue discs from it, replacing them with the heads of small elephants who keep their trunks folded under, where they cannot catch on anything. I always used what he gave me . . . eventually.

"Treasure hunt?" I echo my ex-husband faintly, as if he has proposed a suicide pact. He stares into my eyes, challenging my well-known penchant for gracious acquiescence. He knows my greatest weakness: I am a good sport.

"The limits?"

He looks at his wrist watch. "Ten minutes," he says. "One dollar."

I scan the yard sale quickly. I haven't foraged much these past few years. I am rusty. My eye isn't as sharp as it used to be. "Fifteen," I counter. "Two dollars."

In the end we compromise: a quarter of an hour, a dollar and a half.

By custom old enough to have become instinct, we turn and move off in opposite directions. The rules need no elaborating. We'll meet at the appointed time on the spot where we parted. We have learned how to avoid each other in crowds. I cheat and look back: Gregory is bent low over a display of Avon bottles and campaign buttons. He is only warming up. We both know he won't capture my essence among perfumes and politics.

When we played before, in our heyday ten years ago, he invariably won. His gift was always better for me than mine was for him. The intervening years have taught me something: he has me at a perpetual disadvantage. I have never known the opposition as well as I should.

The pressure is on. This is my last chance. A gift, both parties concur, is a statement. It is better, safer, to give than to receive. But from either position, misstep can be lethal.

I am trapped. This Saturday morning, I came without guile to survey my neighbor's goods. I didn't expect to covet them, and I don't. Just looking. I am in the market for something, it's true, but I'm not sure I'd know it if I saw it. Or that I could afford it. If there's one thing I don't need, though, it's gadgetry. Memorabilia. Running into my ex-husband and playing games.

But here we are. Opportunity knocks. I believe, even now, in grace under pressure, fate, good things in small packages, and summing-up. This is probably the last possible moment for my parting shot. I can tell the red-haired stranger I was married to just exactly what I think of him now — that is, I could if I knew.

Longingly, I reconsider the steak knives, attracted by their easy suitability. Sharp serrated blades, grips like dueling pistols. The gauntlet has been thrown down; I have no second, and the choice of weapons was not mine. Appropriate in the extreme, those knives. But they cost five dollars, and I would not let him catch me in a deception at the last minute. I wonder if I might find the owner of this yard, these goods, plead a case for being allowed to purchase a single utensil? I'd gladly pay a dollar, as high as a dollar-fifty, for the privilege of taking away the odd one, breaking up the already-broken set.

But I put the knives back where they belong. I knew all along, really, that their symbolism was too facile. Heavy-handed. Not the last impression I'd care to make.

I stand, irresolute, among the tables and cartons of a household's offal. Time is running short. Nearby, a woman with a fraying chiffon scarf tied over her gray hair sits in a canvas director's chair. Her attitude is proprietary. I glance rather desperately at her. "Looking for anything in particular?" she wants to know, in the voice of one who has every right to ask.

"Not exactly, but . . . you wouldn't have a garlic press, would you?"

"Wait," she says.

Wobbling on swollen ankles and perversely high-heeled shoes, she goes to a nearby table, rummages through several small boxes. When she turns around, her expression is arrogant with triumph. She raises the tarnished metal tool over her head so I can see it, a prize.

"How much?" I ask her.

"Guess you could have it for a dollar."

I take it from her without examining the merchandise. I dig out a wallet from my shoulder bag and remove six quarters, put by for the laundromat. "A little extra for your trouble," I say, turning away quickly so I won't have to confront her suspicions.

I return just under the wire. Gregory is already standing where I left him, holding a rumpled brown grocery bag in his arms like a baby. From ten yards away, I can see he has chalked up another victory. It will, I believe, be his last. As I reach him, I take the garlic press from my purse and hand it to him. The pleasure is all mine: replacing one of the many things he has no idea I took from him.

He does not know what it is. That is hardly my concern. He'll have to find out for himself. "Very nice," he says, guarded. No doubt he is imagining his thumb, grasped in the blunt metal vice. Minced: one of many terms unfamiliar to him. He will learn.

Slowly my ex-husband reaches inside the paper bag and pulls out a plaster of Paris statue. Once painted to resemble bronze, it is a woman, seated on a pedestal. Draped rather sloppily in a loose garment, its folds forever stiff, she wears a blindfold and holds a set of scales in one hand.

"Justice," I whisper, awed by his effrontery.

"Amicus curiae," says my former husband, establishing his innocence once and for all.

Justice is a lady. I touch her face, where the nose has chipped away to show white. I do not allude to her blindfold, or the fact that the scales seem askew. This is easier than I anticipated, accepting a parting gift from my ex-husband. He doesn't know what I like anymore.

"Amicus," I say, putting the sightless, battered woman back in her bag and preparing to move on. The next time I'm in a mood to shop around, I'll think twice about where I go browsing. Maybe I've finally outgrown second-hand souvenirs. No need to tell that to him.

As I leave the yard sale, I pass the proprietess in her canvas chair. I smile at her, but she returns a scowl. I have nearly reached the street when she catches up to me and roughly grabs my elbow. Squinting into the sun over my shoulder, she drops two quarters in the open top of the bag. They clink softly against the statue.

"No need to get carried away," she says.

Dennis M. Dorney

Flight From Churubusco

Call it homesick, when the afternoon
inquires in broken English you cannot answer;
where a rented room still sloshes fury
from the last tenant's Mescal bender,
and centerfold nudes you've memorized
like clouds over convent windows
laugh with grins too wide for the occasion.

Gladly, you'd buy a clunker and drive
away from here, as sickly pigeons
spray from the cracked windshield.
Following that compass taped to the dash
you'd recite names of Mexican towns
just to stay clear-headed, fire Sinatra
through Marlboros to hold sleep in front.

But you have no pesos for a car,
no return ticket, and the woman you left
in Los Angeles is straddling a man
so eagerly, it could almost be you.
Stamped, you carry sorrow's passport
from cathedral to slums, eventually inside.
No hotel safe will secure its worthlessness.

Blocks over, Trotsky pleaded his assassin
to pull the shades, mollify his defeat.
Isn't that the secret? Aren't Indians,
bulldozed into begging on the zocalo,
really family you fight away? Downstairs
an idling four-door is horny for theft.
Within a democratic blur, you ease the clutch.

Dennis M. Dorney

Sunday With the Game On

Coastal fog had stained my curtains
into densities found on expired coupons.
I watched the game, skimmed Sunday's Times,
with a visit from my ex-wife,
hairstyle spiked into current flame,
scented, I imagined, of acquaintances.
Weekends we still poked at love, a blindman's
stick surveying the dark just above injury.

Not much different than playing doctor,
we pursued a simultaneous striptease, limp
porno complete with eye contact, bad timing.
She had me examine her panties,
proffered cork from an expensive vintage,
claiming it begat a vigorous performance.

But nothing ran smooth. Bodies passed
affection with hands of cashiers, schtik
more in keeping with novice faith-healing.
Dull light pulsed from the colored tube
painting us shadowy mimes in contortion.

Saved by a gift, we quit, dissolved
ourselves among tattered cushions.
There are moments when everything lives
awaiting an excuse, a dexterous joke.
My eyes wandered to a young girl
flanking a marching band in Wisconsin;
her slender arms out-stretched for a baton
I prayed she'd catch, braced for the flub,
the cold walk home in that stupid uniform.

Charles Edward Eaton

The Blowgun

Looking at the rose, the prick of color,
He felt he had been struck by a blowgun,
Or as if the rich rose itself shot
Its thorns, a quiver of tiny arrows.

But you would not, of course, have seen him wince —
Better the savage not startled too soon,
Even though you see the headdress gleaming in the leaves,
Poised with the long pipe at his painted lips.

The sting, and then the long, sunken shiver —
The neural efflorescence, the blood called up
From its far counties, running in quick swales
As if to swamp round the ecstatic wound.

Somewhere in town a man with a blowtorch
In his way increases the intensity —
Something must be gotten into, in through,
A soft heart in the hardest material.

He would say that he has it all in hand,
But that struck Adonis in the garden,
Trailed forever by his own bright savage,
Gives on and on where the sharp point strikes in.

When steel burns through, indeed a kind of rose —
A lovely flare never to be discounted,
And a quiet, deep sleep while the berms of blood
Carry sensation to the open sea.

Still, in the morning one will resubmit,
Like Saint Sebastian, a beau ideal,
Some unsuspected mark for these roses,
Some small, fresh target for the brilliant eye.

It is common practice among lovers
To pluck out the dead arrows each evening,
A kind of good grooming without grievance:
Next time, next time, those swift shafts in a hail.

Not to be struck down dead by anything,
But to find that relations of ravishment
Would one day make of the mouth a blowhole:
Ah, ah, so this — *that rose, that rose, that rose!*

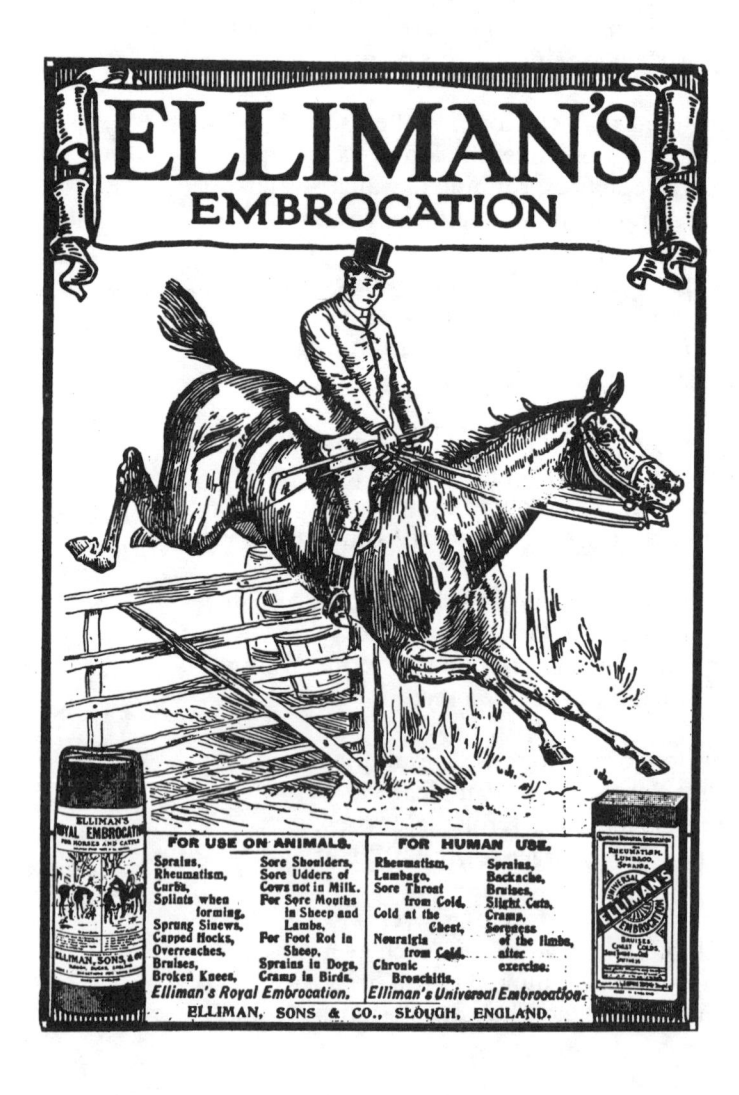

Jane Eklund

The Mill Worker's Daughter: 1933

Daddy, the night won't cool.
You stand in the doorway, unloose
the bib on those blue overalls you wear
all summer. I walk over, cut a line
in your sweaty back with my finger, wait
for the swing and slap of your hand. It doesn't come.

Nothing comes. Not the boss with his pouch
of coins, not the wavering rain clouds
we're promised. All we can count on tonight
is the frog's throaty cry, the dog's howl
out back. So you want a pocket full of money
jingling you to town? Night of whiskey

and sex smell in the whorehouse?
Tough. What you've got is this: mud
yard and tin shack and never enough
beans to go around. But listen, Daddy,
beneath this cotton shift, I'm a woman, almost.
I can take you by surprise.

Jane Eklund

The Metamorphosis

Even my violin betrays me;
its music a thin crack growing
through these walls. Father's dozing off again,
and Mother sits attentive though her mind's
somewhere else. In the next room,
my brother's growing wings, antennas,
trappings of the grotesque. Still, he's all I have

left of the other — the travelling salesman
with blind affections, now just a blur
in the mind's eye. I know he loved me most.
So who can blame me
when I hurry through this creature's room, thrust
my head out the open window?
It's not so much the sight of him
I can't bear, it's his room that can't contain me.

Last night I dreamed I was so small
I could fly away on the wing of a bee . . .

Mornings, the same: pails of water slopped
on Gregor's floor, the handle of my mop
daring him to draw too near.
In the old parable, the ugly
daughter sweeping cinders is transformed;
becomes lovelier than anyone
could wish to be. What I wish is simpler:

to smash the glass of roses at the supper table;
to say something that would hurt my brother;
to touch him; to tell him
how it is, how our lives are just one big
mistake after another.

Kathy Fagan

Night Flowers

Twilight blue as the skin at your wrist
and the townlights rose trailing
like a vine of night flowers and followed
the crawl of a dull moon. Moon,
or the lamp's glow caught at a window?
Stars, or the quickening pulse of planes?
Still, people sang on the stoops of their walk-ups,
stashes of beer in the trunks of their cars.
And always, at town's edge, a single driver,
talk radio cranked loud, pops gravel
up from a road's shoulder like the gradient
paths of a drive-in theater.
                              Over
the black globe of a gear shift knob,
a couple lace fingers as their son sleeps.
He is stretched full-length on the rear dash.
His breath is clouding, unclouding the glass,
and his hands hold mirages which roll
from the grills of the cooling concessions
that empty beyond him. The crowds return
speakers to their metal trees, take rows
toward the exit as if skimming the waves.
The sound of their tires is the rain
she has longed for; the breath of her son,
the sharp breeze off the shore. And the figures
on-screen move only for them now, the tinny
theme music plays only for them;
and the firework splitting the dusty horizon
bursts from its center like a bloom
mad to die, to burn into night like the screen
colors fading, like windows which darken
in the homes on their lane, and the closing
eyes of those within them, grateful for sleep,
for what they have, and for what
they have not said to one another.

Kathy Fagan

The Sleep of the Apostles

Branches foam green in the foaming street lamp
where it rains only there, in that circle of light
steadier than tire lines etched in the pavement
or the bells of the Cathedral of the Magdalen resounding.

On the west side of town a siren chokes short
as a train passes out of the Santa Fe station.
I imagine its passengers, mile-weary, sleeping
a traveller's sleep like the sleep of the apostles.

Only one light shines in a car ahead.
There is dust rising toward it and scattering away.
There is someone awake among all those sleeping
who listens and watches as the train lows forward

like the slow-moving beasts in a field beyond.

Donald Finkel

No News

In the paper tonight it's as he thought:
The mole has no mating call, although it can make
a couple of sounds that are more or less "conversational."

He contemplates the peacock's obscene shriek,
tunes in on the great whale's shameless serenade,
throbbing halfway round the world. A mole of few words,

he fumbles among the small talk: *these small sounds*
probably occur when a male and a female mole
"stumble into one another." Somewhere, he knows,

a soft grey nymph with moist, myopic eyes
dog-paddles toward him through the fragrant loam.
This moment, the earth might crumble between them,

the last crumbs of topsoil toppling from her velvet nose.

from *The Detachable Man*

Donald Finkel

Election Day

Up since daybreak, he cast his worm with the earliest birds,
flew down to the grade school gym and exercised
his insufferable right to choose,
among losers, the one least likely to exceed.

One cheer for the off-white knight on the scrawny horse
and the stunted platform: *A pinch of salt in every pot.
Asperity's around the corner.*
Hole in his gauntlet, couldn't sell a Cadillac to an arab.

Mind, not that our citizen's bored.
A tang of civic fervor still kindles his blood,
but the whole bitter day's before him
and the bars are closed.

Not a twig in this twittering city
to roost on for a spell in the glow
of this uncommon communal fever
while it still simmers.

Caroline Finkelstein

Blind-Spot

I could describe you.
The way your wrists hinge
with wire, what happened
when you were small, your cough.
And my skin, lucid, translates
in the mirror.
              I've seen the pond gone green again,
the algae rising and the near glade
rinsed of snow.
In detail, as we approach the pond,
I've seen our legs wet
from the licks of grass,
the car waiting on the gravel,
and the new shoots, reproachful and familiar.

I could render the covered pond,
but beneath its water nothing is clear
nor what it is we do to one another.

Robert Funge

Easter Sunday

Beethoven's *Pastoral* moves me through the mountains
to Santa Cruz and breakfast with my daughter.
We walk along the storm wracked shore
& talk small talk, then of her brother, lost
in his world of *Jesus Loves You & God the Avenger.*
It's the hell of it that angers me, Henry,

and what it's done to him. I liked him better
when he wanted to be a fireman or a vet.
His God's gonna fire us ever.
Back inland early, my daughter with her friends
who bore me, being easily bored, needing
something, not *His* strange love.

Jesus loves you, they say, & if you love Jesus
He will not have you burn forever in the depths
& despair of a fiery hell with those who love
flowers & mountains & cats & Henry's songs,
Beethoven & storm wracked shores, but not Jesus.
Paid a whore forty dollars & rose from the dead.

Robert Funge

from JOHN / HENRY

> *I have an endless scream in me . . .*
> *Do you recognize my songs?*
> — Rilke

A tall one with a small mind would cut me down
to his size if he could. A foreman barks
The Company is bigger than the man!
Dizzy the days and dizzier the nights.
Seized and committed to the discovery room.
A daughter shouts me back to the isolation ward.

I am a man with a stone in his head.
I see at a distance a solitary man
rolling a stone up a hill. I see on a boulder
over an ocean a solitary man.
I see on a bridge over a frozen sea
waving his hand a solitary man

planting his feet firmly in midair.
Too late. A broken ghost. Someone is missing.
Someone has died happily ever after.
I hear a surf roar over a silent land.
I forgive my good daughter. If I had it all
to do over again, I would.

Patricia Goedicke

Americans Shot at in Canyon

    First it was a handful of black coathangers
it looked like, stuck out
on a barbed wire corral
a few yards from the long, wandering
tar and gravel snake stretched
over the bare hills from one distant
ranch to another: MIRV
missile site, of course, my Indian
friend raised neutral eyebrows: miles down
under the coathangers, two scared
boys at the controls buried
forty-eight hours before they'd see
daylight again.

    Next it was the low cabin
my friend's mixed blood French
great grandfather built,
squat as a riverboat
up to its hips in gray stone
beside the creek bed, scrub oak,
alder, fire berry, ouzels
flittering over cold green
water rushing down the protected
narrow corridor from Canada:
mountain goats, elk, grizzlies
in their time passing
secretly down the cliffs, over
the snow peaks, the pine
forests, maybe even
the dusty track we drove in on.

    Then it was the long ramble
we took, miles out over the dry
wheat colored hills, gray
silver groundcover crumbling
like old lace, steel sky
overhead, in all that vast
paper light nothing anywhere
but air, in sandy gulches a few

grazing horses looked at us
gently, snorting a little by red
faint tipped sumac, fat snow berries
dove winged, almost white pieces
of clay, tan chunks
skittering, scabbed rusty lichen
past Guerney's Butte breathing
the brisk turpentine of sage
as suddenly Jim shouted, grabbed
my left arm and stopped me
just short of the round
break-a-leg-hole yesterday's
looking-for-oil-well
prospectors left uncovered.

    Next it was hiking back
up the canyon to the cabin
at evening, trees along the sides
in the gathering dark closer
and thicker every minute, snow
on Old Baldy shelved,
shining down the ravine
under a cranberry sky shifting
from violet to black corduroy lit
by one star hanging, the sound
of dogs barking: dogs barking?
No, it is geese, Jim points
just over the horizon, the staccato
invisible river of honks rises,
pours over our heads higher
and higher, a hundred
no, two hundred! disappearing
wild coughs, pained
longing-to-be-home cries,

    and then it was Sunday morning,
heavy artillery
detonating down the gorge!
Low booms, cavernous

rumbles under our bunks
woke us, drove us
out onto the chill bank
bare of any print but ours
and passing animals, birds
nowhere to be seen,
only in the ravishing blue
and clear air a chopper
full of oil-and-ammunitions
experts banging across quiet
bony hills with their delicate
apocalyptic instruments dragging aloft
over the weathered slopes a bright

      orange survey balloon!
Out of the desert it appeared
in all its poster paint glow
like a huge Disneyland cumquat,
shimmering, smooth, seductive
as any Howard Johnson's
oasis we love like Mother,
all twenty-eight flavors
sherbet cold, congealed
into one tangerine sphere hanging
right up there in the sky
where we put it, cameras
snapping their top secret shots
of hidden faults, underground
cracks filled with fire
whatever form it takes, ourselves
here in this bleak dawn
trapped in the open, stunned
under the clicking triggers
in the glare of appetite stand
with our mouths open, craning
straight up at the fat
pumpkin silent as gas
over our pinched faces caught
only for a moment staring
and then gone.

Beckian Fritz Goldberg

The Consolation of Celibacy

So cold that morning, not a fly in the air.

Our friend the ex-priest can't stop talking
about the disembowelled ones the boy Alvaro
led him to. Women
nursed their children outside the shacks, pulled
sweaters that would not stretch across their breasts.
He drinks gin with dinner, and it's satisfying
the way each guest has stopped listening and sits
toward Colombia, but is really thinking
about some day or night he loves.
Maybe, Father, memory's the right punishment —
When I close my eyes the old house grows up
the way legs in a running-dream go on and on.
Make up a reason: You're married to God and you wear
black skirts. My sister and I used to wonder
who owns the body, the man with the breasts of the woman,
the woman with the hair of the man . . .

We used to watch the white June moths
doubling mid-air in the alleys.
"They can't help it," we whispered
and closed our eyes letting it go on, on
like almost all the girls we'd talked to
who were convinced they'd *never*.
And, in a way, we never did. Remember
our smooth stomachs and calves dripping solitary
from early summer baths. Nights
we climbed into like booths where we kneeled
undressed, down to the damp lace of our thoughts.
"I'm going to be a nun," my sister said. Three months
later she smelled like him, said, "I think about Saint Teresa
when we're doing it." I picture her

   telling a priest in a dim Chicago parish that she was tired
after twenty years, forgiving him. Her hands
clutch a kleenex and a comb in her open purse
as if she's not quite sure which she needs.
And all the time the priest is thinking of a green

watercolor behind the house he grew up in. A certain squirrel.
So cold that morning. I remember
what it feels like to be just one, clean as a bead

or a new orange — just like I remember the story
lovemaking makes up, want to
remember the one about the monk who ravishes
brown women with flakes of milk on their breasts.
They took off his skin, slowly. He was talking
to the pair of lips we all imagine in the air, praying
for convergence. He raised his eyes a little to see
everything coming back: It is dinner. Strangely,
the ex-priest is saying, as he stepped over
the blue-red parts of the body — while the boy watched,
his mouth open — he blessed them.

Beckian Fritz Goldberg

State Street Motel

The wallpaper is full of larkspurs
which halve and curl at each seam. You lie on the bed.
The mirror holds a precise dark mouth
where the tip of the closet door is open.
I am watching you and thinking
how we took a train to get here
through snow, the tiny curtains that parted
New Haven, White River, Montpelier Junction.
It was two hours late and then somewhere
outside a town, swelled to a stop.
The lights blotted off
the shapes of passengers' heads
all along the car, the crackle
of someone stepping on a candy wrapper. Inside
our window, a birch's comb, glazed,
and the snow's seals, broken and pasted back
over footprints. Everyone whispered. But now
there's nothing louder than two suitcases
set neatly in a corner of this room, a day

where snow on the hills lifts like thin paper.
I am writing this down because I don't understand
anything about us. In this room, a bed, blanket
flipped over like a leaf of a calendar:
In April there's always a picture of a meadow,
a quote from Wordsworth, a holiday
for fools. Your curled hand is emptying exhausted ponies
from the edge of the bed
onto the hard yellow carpet. I'm here
watching you sleep because six years ago
we promised each other something.
We were married outdoors. I can't remember
the last time I stayed awake this long.
The snow outside you falls,
light the January sky tears up. What is this place?
When do we arrive? Maybe
the dreams that keep us going
are no better than our lives.

Maybe it hasn't turned out like this.

Beckian Fritz Goldberg

The Perception of Motion

First he dropped two iron balls,
the light one and the heavy one,

from the tower, at the same instant.
A pigeon went on overhead

chintzed with light.
He did not have to wait long:

A peasant rolling a wagon wheel
down the stone street

let it go ahead of him
and part two priests

walking from the baptistery, their cassocks
rising about the height of the chickens.

Then the wind dropped.
The wheel fell against a nut merchant's stall.

The balls clacked
on the ground like two beads,

one sound. He carried them home
and wrote, *two round objects*

*of different weight will fall
at the same speed, straight.*

But it was hard to describe
as that moment for the peasant

when the quail shot in flight
shuddered and moved back

and dropped in an arc
behind him

reddening the field grass.
Each word reflects belief

about the motion
it stops. This was most difficult

for the priests
who held Galileo *heretic*

yet could not deny
such a being

moved forward as he fell —
just as the spring water that year

in Pisa, received its impetus
from river ice

that had carried it slowly
over its release.

The peasant, Giorgio, the vine-tiller
who could not write

would have told them
there were tiny animals of God

in wine, that tunneled
like ticks into his red feet,

but he was lucky.
That year, as any other,

snow fell, the dog's teeth
knew the plush of quails' necks . . .

Sometimes he missed
and all the field birds rose

at once, in the same direction,
and revolved.

It was hard to explain the good
of the invisible;

as talking to his daughter at night,
he thought of many things

but only told her one.

IMPORTANT: Mate-Herb is not a harmful Aphrodisiac, nor does it require a doctor's prescription. It is not a pill, capsule or any type of vitamin formula. Mate-Herb is a concentrated powder unlike most anything you ever tried . . . you can be sure ! ! !

Rafael Guillen

One Day With the Dawn
                    Translator: Sandy McKinney

One day, with the dawn, I came back alone
from my manly affairs. It's possibly some time ago.
Clarity was born there in the depth of the streets,
as pain is born at the bottom of a drink.

We always come back alone. I don't know why the streets
seem so empty at the end of a night of love.
Beyond the closed doors, the couples could be heard
shifting in the dampness of sleep.

I've never understood it. We climb onto a body
the way a boy goes for the highest branch.
And suddenly, beneath heaven, the body that was everything
consumes itself away beneath our embrace.

And then and there we see how earth fails us,
how life drains out through a crack under the door.
The round plenitude that came to us with a touch
in the same touch escapes and dissipates.

In the fields, over the roofs, five o'clock was ringing.
Somewhere near, a jasmine must have been coming awake.
I came back tired, the way a man comes back
who's contributed his share to the pain of the world.

The nakedness of an arm. An expanse of throat.
Two legs flung apart, seeking an exit.
A firm waist to cling to with the hands,
the way you'd lean your weight against a plow.

I've never understood it. Gazes face to face,
like twin mirrors reflecting only each other.
In front of the eyes, an opaque film
behind which ever lover conceals his egoism.

She was very close, that once, to giving me something
that might have become, in time, a memento.

I look at her from here, but she has no face.
It couldn't be sadder if she'd never existed.

We throw ourselves on a body as into the sea, and learn
that love, like water, doesn't offer resistance.
Precious little is what's left afterwards, if tenderness
doesn't invent its reasons to keep on living.

We thrust into places that don't belong to us.
Flesh, like smoke, moves away when it's touched.
Today I don't ask for reasons, and I give myself
and accept, and pretend, but I know it's blackmail.

That day started the way all days start;
because all days start and never end.
The dawn softened the last roof-edges
and the light prepared its first explosion.

We always come back alone from making love. Like then.
Because a man is bound in his skin, and dreams
only count, not always, when a breast, half-glimpsed,
suddenly unveils to us our great misadventure.

Rafael Guillen

The Final Tenderness
                        Translator: Sandy McKinney

Today I've come back to the place, to the walls
that swaddled, so quietly,
that almost boyish heat, or something
more passionate yet, and that clarity
of morning that shone
from your upraised arms as you worked
at pinning up your hair.

I've come back to that brief
stretch of time that still
was there, as if waiting, stuck there, poised
on the jiggling edge
of an unmade bed, a table stripped of its cloth
and retiring into its modesty, a tumbler
that nurtured, within its opaque glass,
one of those tragic moments of lucidity
that occur in love.

I've come back following the trace
of a sunny corner, without the sun, where seated,
huddled, I feel
arriving — above and slowly — until it swallows me up,
all that nothingness, or God, that keeps on
following me, accosting me, through the places
I searched for what only exists
within myself: that which now, too late, I realize
was only in me and in my other self
which is you, surrounding
my loneliness, like a lusty mirror
that sends us back our own light and at the same time
isolates us from sounds and from existence.

Today I've come back to see what's left to me,
what's no longer left to me, of the vast
tenderness that, one moment,
only a few short centuries, filled
my heart, still tense there, suspended

like an avalanche of weeping, among the folds
of your clothes strewn about in disorder;
like an avalanche of loneliness, that crackles
reborn in the devastating
miracle of another motion.

Because loss, when everything is lost,
well, love is the hardest unit of all;
it robs the soul of those tiny
intimate hollows,
those shady caves that are the nesting place
of all the great and beautiful that in a man
needs the moisture, the animal vapor
that supports his readiness, his defenceless
giving of himself.

Because loss makes us insignificant,
as when we were children
a social call snatched us away
from our games to seat us
at the grownups' table; sets us,
we don't know how, in the midst
of cold cities, in doorways
where everyone walks by without looking at us,
situates us lost and cancelled out
in the radiant show-windows
of all the commerce of the world.

Today I've come back to the place where life,
one day, set me
on my feet, when it was enough,
for a sense of being alive, to listen to the rain;
I've come back so you can look at me
from where you are no longer, from this pillow
where you are not, and forever;
I'm late again, and I understand,
finally convinced, that when we arrive
late in love there's nothing,
will never be anything more to redeem us.

Rafael Guillen

Poem of No
                Translator: Sandy McKinney

You said no. Along your gaze
the boats passed slowly. And there were
seagulls in your eyes, in your soft
great dark eyes,
where the bitterness was falling
like a twilight of moaning sirens
in the ports of the South.
You said no, serenely.
It was a non-original, that existed already
before you, that spoke for itself
while you, impotent, absorbed, your eyes
fixed on me, felt its reality,
tested its roots inside you.
It was a no insinuated,
mute, weightily silent.
Your warm, firm body
said no, for no reason, curled
around itself, as though
turning back to infancy. You weren't there.
You said no, and in your expression
flickered a sorrow I would call
maternal, a sorrow begging
for comprehension. A no of contained
heaviness, but total, open,
lightly extended
on the shores of lament.
You said no, faraway, alone,
terribly alone, manacled,
without a whatfor to lean on, but
it was no, was no, without crying out, no.

The ports, the whistles,
the ships in the night, everything
went on losing itself, going away.
And I, beside you, wretched, helpless there.

Carol S. Hamilton

Wire of Darkness

Purposeless, starless, you cross the lawn,
hoping that someone will interrupt your progress
and balancing on the uncertain shadow
you alone depend on — wire of darkness

hovering, swaying, in its quiet wind.
You said too much. You always say too much.
The words evaporate, but you despair,
stare at the headlights flickering on the highway.

Arms outstretched, tremulous, looking down,
you slowly traverse the wire of darkness
hoping a lover's hand will halt your progress.
Love with a net. Love with its tearing mouth

of wishes, lies, and wounds. You wave goodbye.
The awful dark has taken you to heart.
Crossing the lawn you hear the ambulances start
far off, below the hill, coming toward you.

Amy Hempel

Three Popes Walk into a Bar

Sydney Lawton Square is a park for a transient population; there are no benches. You can walk it end to end in minutes. The architect for the Gateway Condominiums squeezed it in between the barbecue place and the parking garage. You would put quotes around this "park" the way you might send traffic fines to the Hall of "Justice." But this feeble attempt at nature is walking distance from the club — so that's where I meet Wesley, at the Fountain of Four Seasons.

The fountain yields dead earthworms, not coins; the worms outnumber pull tabs, cigarettes, and leaves. At the nearby north entrance to the square there is a faded brick arch with a bronze-like plaque that says "Historical Site." All of it is contrived to suggest that something was once there, but none of it tells you what.

Wesley calls out "Ahoy," so I know he has made up his mind.

"You think it's a crime to change your mind?" he says. "Just because you are able to do a thing doesn't mean that's what you have to do, does it? Because I could but I don't want to," he says as we walk the tarmac path.

He is talking about performing. He's still funny, and he wants to stop.

"I could keep on," he says, "and you know what I'd have to show for it? Ten percent liver function and a felony in my bed."

"I think what counts is timing," I say. "As long as you try your first choice first."

Three popes walk into a bar.

A guy in the airport Clipper Club recognized Wesley and bet him he couldn't get a punchline out of it. They boarded a plane in Honolulu; Wesley had the five hours to San Francisco to make it a joke. *Three popes walk into a bar.* He lost money on this, but I didn't ask how much. Coming off a tour he is sick with foreign germs. I met him at the gate and drove him straight to the club. It's what Eve usually did, but she delegated to me. Eve Brand is Wesley Brand's future former wife.

"Eve cabled the hotel that she's coming tonight," Wesley said. "But she won't laugh."

"You won't hear her not laughing over the six hundred other people," I said. "You're sold out."

"But I always know. You *know.* She wants me to buy a boat, is all. After, of course, I have stopped performing."

"What's it to her?" I said. "She's leaving you."

"Or not," Wesley said. "Maybe she's not leaving if I buy the boat."

"That doesn't put you on the spot or anything."

"You talk to her tonight," he said.

About Eve Brand, Wesley has said that he married the most beautiful woman he ever saw and learned the irrelevance of beauty.

He met her at a club where she danced topless. She told him that Wesley was the name of the first monkey in space. She told him how Nasa used that Wesley up and then abandoned him to an animal shelter for destruction. Then a group of women kidnapped that Wesley and took him to a zoo, where he lived out his life in comfort.

Wesley knew the monkey's name was Steve, but thought it was sweet of her to say otherwise.

With Wesley's encouragement, Eve stopped dancing and pursued a career in journalism. She thought she would be a natural at it because people always wanted to talk to her. She wrote an article on spec for the Sunday paper and had it returned six weeks later. Wesley asked the editor what was wrong with it, wasn't it boring enough? Then he cashed a favor with a publicist and got Eve a job at a fan-zine doing a monthly column on vanished TV actors. The column was called "Where Are They Now?" but we all called it "Why Aren't They Dead?"

Wesley signaled the waitress and placed a special order. In a moment, she returned with a bowl of canned peach halves. Wesley took a bottle of Romular cough suppressant from his coat pocket and poured most of it into the bowl.

"I really admire you," I told him. "I couldn't go out there and make people laugh if *I* were sick."

"Don't be silly," he said. "You couldn't do it if you were well."

He forced down the reddened peaches.

"But I'll tell you what you *can* do. You can tickle me," he said.

Eve usually did that, too. His grandmother started it when he was a boy. She used to tickle Wesley beyond fun, he said, until he felt trapped and helpless and would have cried except that he learned to give in to it, and at that moment felt relief and calm move in.

It is this tickling and giving in that makes him funny, he thinks. Like every kind of recovery, comedy demands surrender.

Wesley cleared away the chairs and squared off in front of me. At the signal I dove at his belt.

I get something out of this, too.

The club manager's office was open and empty, so we took a couple of drinks in and closed the door. Wesley scanned the shelves of video cassettes, pulled one out and popped it into the deck. He joined me on the couch.

It was a tape of every low-budget commercial he had made for local affiliate stations. This, Wesley said, is comedy.

The tape kicked in and there he was in suit and tie for the Cherry Hills Shopping Mall over in the East Bay.

"Tell me when it's safe," he said, and covered his eyes with a hand.

Onscreen, he said, "That's Cherry Hills, between the MacArthur and the Nimitz. MacArthur and Nimitz — both fine men, both fine freeways."

"Oh, I hate myself," he moaned.

The machine sizzled with static.

"This next one is Evie's favorite."

The product was a deep-penetrating epoxy sealer that you pumped into cracked cement to bind it into one integral piece again. The homeowner in the background eyeing his cracked sidewalk was Wesley's former partner, Larry Banks. They split up a couple of years ago when Banks ran for mayor on the campaign platform, "Anything You Want."

The machine jammed on the tagline, "Cement cracks, this we know."

Wesley turned off the machine and opened the door. He asked the waitress for vodka.

"I tell you about the night I met Banks?" he said. "My manager brought him to watch me work. Then after the show we all go to this Polynesian place to get stewed. Banks, he was just starting out, he orders this sissy drink for two, only he doesn't realize it's for two. So the waiter shows up with this washpan of rum, and Banks is all embarrassed and so on. I told him, comics can't *get* embarrassed."

Wesley sat back down beside me and said it was time to change his life. He wanted to. "But how does a person start?"

"Small," I said. "Start small and work up. The way you would clean a house. You start in one room. Maybe you give yourself more time than you need to finish that room, just so you finish it. Then you go on to the next one. You start small, and then everything you do gets bigger."

I myself have never done it this way.

"Of course, I could be different," Wesley said. "Maybe everything I do will get smaller. On the other hand, there's still the stage, you know — when it's good up there, when I stand up there and have nothing to say but it has to work! It's — being human on purpose, it's falling back on the language in your mouth. It's facing these people and saying, You think Jesus had it rough! Ah, when it's good," he said. "And when Evie's good, too. When Evie's there. In the night. Do you know what I'm saying?" he said. "Because she's the one who is there in the night. Before her I had what you'd call contacts. Like the last one, this one that was hanging around one of the clubs — so I asked her if she'd like to go out. And she said she did. She said she wanted to go all the way out."

Wesley swallowed vodka.

"Which is something I don't even understand," he said. "How about you? Did you ever want to die? I mean, try to *make* yourself die?"

"Only once," I said. "I drove my car real fast and I was going to have an accident but then I wasn't going to."

"Well, not me, not ever," Wesley said. "I sometimes think this is how depressed the people who commit suicide get. And then I thank God I'm a Leo."

An hour before the show, Eve met us in the bar. She looked good; Wesley said so, and everyone else noticed right along with him. Marzipan skin, white-blonde hair that always looked backlit. Eve would look good in barbed wire.

"God, my jeans are full of me," Eve said, and undid a narrow snakeskin belt.

A waitress came to our table and asked what could she get us.

"I'm not drinking," Eve said. "Just a 7-Up."

The waitress asked if Sprite was okay.

"No — then make it a diet Coke."

"Eve here used to live next door to the vice-president of 7-Up," Wesley explained, "so she's hip to lemon-lime drinks."

"So who's here?" Eve said. "L.A.?"

L.A. is any Hollywood agent who comes north to look at talent.

"Supposed to be, but not," Wesley said.

"It's just as well," Eve said. "They're such a tease. They fall all over you and then you never see them again." She sighed. "Just like everybody else."

She touched Wesley's shoulder, and he turned in his seat so that she could massage his neck with both hands.

"She's too good to me," Wesley said.

"Oh, I'm banking this," Eve said. "I'm not just throwing it off a cliff."

A voice broke in behind them. "Who said comedians don't have groupies."

It was the owner of the club, the man who would introduce Wesley onstage.

The owner told Wesley to join him backstage. Eve and I blew a kiss and carried our drinks upstairs. We passed people in line at the ticket window. To one side of the box office there was an eight-by-ten of Wesley. It was a publicity shot from years ago, the sincere-looking one. It was the same picture he had on his mantel at home, only there it carries a caption: "He aimed for the top. He started at the bottom. He ended up somewhere below in-between."

We found the small round table reserved for us up front. Eve offered me the first sip of her diet Coke so that it would be me who would get the one calorie.

"Look over there," she said, nodding far right. I looked, and saw four men, twenty-ish, crowded together, a pitcher of beer on their table. They were novices who played smaller clubs on open-mike nights.

"They're something," Eve said. "Watch them when Wesley's on. When he makes you laugh, look at them. One will say, *'That's* funny,' and they'll all nod their heads madly and none of them will smile.

"A couple of months ago that little blonde one opened for somebody here," Eve said. "He saw us in the bar after and asked Wesley what he thought of his act. Wesley said, 'Well, Bob Hope can't live forever.' The guy took it as a compliment."

Eve smiled her great rectangular smile.

I asked if she had changed her mind about Wesley, and she said, "Mmmm. Can we not talk about that?"

I worked at my drink. Eve stared at the empty stage. I said I was glad we weren't talking about *that*.

"I have a fondness for him," she said. "Sometimes it's weak... Did he seem nervous to you?"

"Always."

"That's what I mean," she said. "That's why the boat. That's why," the lights went down, "I'm always here."

The owner of the club bounded onto the stage. He grabbed the microphone off its stand and began to speak. Seconds later the sound came on.

He said, "Every night I come out here and tell you what a great show we have and you know, it's the God's honest truth. But tonight I really mean it."

Eve and I scooted together till our shoulders touched. We heard him say Wesley's name. A blue spotlight followed Wesley onstage. We heard Wesley tell the audience how great it was to be back in L.A.

In Sydney Lawton Square, the knolls roll carefully into each other, but the trees don't match, and there aren't enough of them. Wesley and I pass the doggy station — half a dozen segments of yellow-painted phone pole carved into hydrants, to *receive* water, not give it.

"I did what she wants," Wesley says. "I got a boat, and we're leaving the first of whatever comes after July. Hell, I did what *I* want. I've always been a seaman at heart — your Conrad, your Old Man and the Sea, your fish. It'll be good to get out on the waves and sort of expand my limitations. Sink in *water* for a change.

"As for Eve, she's not sure it will work. But it will. I told her, The trick is this — I do what I want, and you do what I want."

He laughs at himself. "And because, too, I love her to death. I watch that girl like a movie. 'Eve Brand Does Three Hours of Laundry.' I'm watching."

"Why don't you tell her these nice things?" I say.

"I could," Wesley says, doubtful. "But, hey — I guess I'm just a jerk."

"Can you just up and go?" I say.

"I get residuals, remember — Cement cracks, this we know. And Eve can always apply for Aid to the Totally Disabled. You'll want to tell her I said that."

A teenaged boy hefting a tape deck matched his pace to ours and Stevie Wondered us to death.

"You know," Wesley says, as if he doesn't hear the music, "I meet a person, and in my mind I'm saying three minutes. I give you three minutes to show me the spark. It's always there with Eve, and it's been how long? So I keep thinking — can't we just be together all the time whether we're together or not?"

Ahead of us poplars wave against the sky, just as if they had grown here.

"Isn't it true that that's what people can do?" Wesley asks.

And I say, "Who's to live in a world where that isn't true?" But I think, Three popes walk into a bar.

Art Homer

Incentives for Night Work

Where we drink they call the barmaid Forklift,
work a fucking shame. I like driving swing shift
down the corner pocket, chalking up to shoot again.

More often I miss. The foreman says two more
then home to give the old lady something
to live for. His moons rise hairy off the stool.

Better this, the jukebox begging us to stop
the world and let it off, than work, the steward
lost to reason. The Mafia is out to run us,

corner the world market in widgets, he figures.
His finger tests the broken window pane. Bullet.
After closing Jean's, the last place we try

wants cover. The waitress never thinks it fair,
having to ask if we're looking for love. The dancer
still on duty doesn't care. Asks if I've seen Paris.

I've seen the old man come home late and Irish,
hating the fifty cents an hour that makes it
hard to get up mornings, cursing the Army.

Naples, 1946. The citizens line up to spit
on M.P.s at the embassy. Short-changed at a bar,
he breaks, and every beer thereafter buys dishonor.

Maybe someone's out to corner the market on dreams.
Look at me, living it all different. I remember
his terrible fists swinging back like a broken gate.

It's me now coming home, finding it funny
some mistaken skunk has drifted by to check
a leak at the gas reservoir two blocks away —

nose and tail aloft for love or war.

Jane Hoogestraat

The Death of the Khan

And with primeval melancholy
the Khan at that moment recalled:
that though he had slaughtered so many
he had understood nothing at all.

— Yevtushenko

So much remains forever unexplained
of the night the horsemen arrived,
their hair frozen black behind them,
men who rode beyond words for returning
or son or daughter or home, who stopped
in a village on the edge of Germany,
helping first from his horse the khan
who would not live the night. Before morning,
his lifeless body would be lashed to his horse,
most of the riders and all of the horses gone,
riding back along a route of blackened villages
they would not return to plunder again.

The riders did not have words for what
had driven them westward toward a sea
they could not have known was there,
had few words for the only knowledge
stronger than the fire they rode with, the one
certainty before the sea that would have stopped
them: that a khan could not be buried or chosen
away from his own country.

So much remains forever unexplained
about the riders for whom the horde did not
return, who would never ride through burning
villages again, whose story would never
make sense in any language, about the women
in the village who had no words for the strangers,
no words for the eyes of the strangers who stayed,
but who would tell stories of children born since
that night with the dark eyes of strangers.

Jane Hoogestraat

Bridges

Driving across the city this morning
over bridges fragile in the rain,
I thought of iron balconies surrounding
the places we used to live, how we used
to lean over them, talking the night away,
watching the light glisten on the magnolia
in the courtyard below, watching the smoke
from our cigarettes rising toward the stars,
noticing the tangible that delivered us
from too much wordless thought.

And just past a gap in the guard rail,
twisted aluminum where the night before
a driver had missed a curve, I thought
of the night on the balcony when you said
you wanted a mind so open it would never
close on anything again. We were watching
a storm, holding to the balcony railing —
the metal vibrating like the pulse of a nerve
as the trees above us bent away, the leaves
blended together, the wind receded from us,
tearing boats loose from moorings downstream,
we learned later. When even the touch of iron
disappeared beneath our fingers, you said
this is what it's like: to know you are
standing in the center of the storm.

And when I passed the trees in bloom,
driving almost blind through the rain,
I thought of the last night we leaned
against the railing, in late August
when the crepe myrtle blossoms were falling
to cover the asphalt in bright patches
that would fade before morning
like chalk drawings. You asked that night about
the point of poetry, and what to do
with pain. We talked until morning about how
the light makes patterns in the rain,

the paper on a cigarette burns in rings,
about how the mind looks for order,
for the railing that will hold.

Lynda K. Hull

Tide of Voices

At the hour the streetlights come on, the buildings
turn abstract. The Hudson, for a moment, formal.
We drink Chablis on the terrace and you speak
in the evening voice, weighted deep in the throat.

They plan to harvest oysters, you tell me,
from the harbor by Jersey City, how the waters
will be clean again in twenty years. I imagine nets
burdened with rough shells, the meat dun and sexual.

Below, the river and the high rock —
where boys each year jump — from bravado
or desperation. The day flares, turns into itself.
And innocently, sideways, the way we always fall

into grace or knowledge, we watched the police
drag the river for a suicide, the third this year.
The terrible hook, the boy's frail whiteness.
His face was blank and new like your face

in the morning before the day has worked
its pattern of lines and tensions. A hook
like an iron question and this coming
out of the waters, a flawed pearl —

a memory that wasn't ours to claim.
Perhaps, in a bedroom by lamplight,
a woman waits for this boy. She may riffle drawers
gathering photographs, string, keys to abandoned rooms.

Even now she may be leaving the room,
closing the door for some silence. I need
to move next to you. Water sluiced
from the boy's hair. I need to watch you

light your cigarette, and the flickering geometry
of your face in matchlight, as if underwater
and drifting away. I take your cigarette
and drag from it, touch your hand.

Remember that winter of your long fever,
the winter we understood how fragile
any being together was. The wall sweated
behind the headboard and you said you felt

the rim of consciousness where dreams crouch
and every room of the past. It must begin in luxury —
do you think — a break and fall into the glamour
attending each kind of surrender. Water must flood

the mind, as in certain diseases, the walls
between the cells of memory dissolve, blur
into a single stream of voices and faces.
I don't know any more about this river or if

it can be cleaned of its tender and broken histories —
a tide of voices. And this is how the dead
rise to us, transformed: wet and singing,
the tide of voices will pearl in our hands.

Joseph Hutchison

Vander Meer Holding On

Slouched behind the steering wheel of his new
used Ford, Vander Meer sights down the gap
between his ex-house and the neighbors'.

A view of the swingset he assembled,
skinning his knuckles all the raw morning
and howling, "Why the hell do we *never*
have the right tools?" Now his daughter's
swinging there like a stone in a sling.
Off and on, a glimpse of his wife —
shoving . . . making the child's hair
float behind her like jet-streamed clouds.

It all reminds him of his own swinging youth:
the way ground seesawed as he pumped, head
thrown so far back his vision hung trees
by their heels from a heaven of grass!
And the buoyant tug of links in his hands,
tug of the pulse in his eyes . . . so strong
he believed he could always let his body
flirt with such sweet falling . . . .

But his daughter, sailing higher, shrieks
with joy . . . and he grips the wheel —
white-knuckled Vander Meer! Shutting his eyes,
hearing his wife laugh and call, "Hold on!
Honey, hold on tight!" Her every push
pushing him farther out . . . .

Kit Irwin

The Pinboys

There was a rumbling always in the basement
of the Community Center.
She'd been told it was bowling,
once had been allowed to follow her brother down
to the lanes, the bright yellow wood
gleaming under the earth.

For weeks after
all she could think of were the pinboys
lying above that murderous intent,
that dark power
heading for them. They'd lean back on their narrow ledges
as if danger were beneath
them. They were quiet as puppets
gazing into time.

Then as if their strings had been pulled taut,
they'd spring to their feet.
At once the ten pins would be up and wobbling

and then perfectly still
and the boys draped on their ledges again
as if they'd been carefully laid down there
so their strings wouldn't tangle.

After school she'd watch them,
young enough
so she could stare at boys without being teased,
sent away. At home it helped
to think of such bright parallel lines under the earth,
and such rumbling
and the pinboys
dreaming on top of the thunder.

Sibyl James

(01)

This is not Vienna, not the old country.
No ribboned czar spins czaress slowly.
This is two a.m., summer windows up,
next door, one couple waltzing.

The song gets lost in ballrooms,
all those strangers. Here,
it floats its round shape in the silence,
expands like brandy on the warm night's tongue.
Nothing like it for the heart.

They could dance without their clothes
and still she'd lift some satin.
They're old, he wears suspenders.
He might have walked across the room,
arms out, taking stacked plates from her hands.
He might dance, still holding his cigar.

I know they smile.
Waltz face to face, turning
on their eyes. They know by heart
the steps between the pushed-back table
and the door, open for the stars.

The lights burn down like candles.
I fall asleep,
half-turned inside my own arm.
Somehow it isn't sad.

(translitic based on the *Love Sonnets* of Louise Labé)

Marilyn Kallet

The Ladies

        August, Montgomery, Alabama

98° and the dogs
are digging holes
to cool their
bottoms in
  mining
    digging
you write of
your search for
    your father's past
in the coal mines
of Harlan
& what we do
to each other
in the 100° heat
digging,
wanting to go
    deeper,
even with the
shades closed
to hide your
married body
my unmarried skin
digging each other
the neighbors
so mean so
    stupid
they don't take
their dogs in
the ladies wonder
what the beasts are doing
beat them for holes
in the yard
for their urge to find shade
& dig

Chuck Kinder

Disneyland

The pool was in a garden of palms and flowering plants in the center of the motel's courtyard. It was kidney-shaped with a small cabana, tiled like the pool red and white, at its larger end. At the pool's smaller end stood a small marble statue, a pink cupid with a thin stream of water arching from its pursed lips into the pool. Blue and green spotlights were arranged in the palms with their beams playing on the pool. Here and there in the thick flowering bushes under the palms stood brightly painted plaster-of-Paris peacocks.

It was a lovely, late-May evening, and Ralph Crawford, thirty-seven, an American author, sat fully-clothed at a poolside table on the eve of his second bankruptcy hearing in seven years. He was holding a glass of whiskey and ice. On the table was one of those motel-room cardboard buckets filled with mostly melted ice, a half-full fifth of Four Roses, and a small transistor radio which Ralph had tuned to a Dodger game. His wife, Alice Ann, floated on her back in the large end of the pool.

Ralph told himself again and again things could be worse, for he and Alice Ann had been smarter about the situation this time around the bend. For one thing, they had *homesteaded* their house, which was simply legalese, meaning they wouldn't find themselves on the street. I am a *homesteader,* Ralph kept repeating to himself, awed by this irony. They had initiated the bankruptcy proceedings here in Santa Barbara, three hundred miles south of their home in Menlo Park, a smart move to avoid local embarrassment and creditors. By hook and crook Alice Ann had hung onto her red, Cadillac convertible, signing its title over to her mother for safe-keeping. The convertible was parked in its appointed place in front of the motel. They had driven down this day in the thing. The drive had been leisurely. They had stopped at a seaside park just south of Big Sur for a picnic Alice Ann had packed of her famous fried chicken, some German potatoe-salad, assorted cheeses, a good jug chablis. At one point Ralph had said to Alice Ann: Alice Ann, this is all crazy.

Right now, what worried Ralph the most was Alice Ann's calmness of late. There had been no recent snarls, no shouting, screaming, laying of blame, not one drop of recently shed blood. Ralph took a long drink. He watched his wife floating peacefully in a pool shaped like some giant organ. From the surrounding darkness under the palms fantails of terrible eyes fastened onto Ralph's every move. Alice Ann was saving it up. Ralph was no fool. It was not fair. Any moment, plaster birds of prey would pounce shrieking across the crazy light for Ralph. Ralph exhaled, closed his eyes and rubbed them until they hurt.

We have our health, Alice Ann said.

Ralph jerked and opened his eyes.

Our health? Ralph said.

Alice Ann kicked and backstroked toward the pool's smaller end. Slivers of blue and green light twitched over the water's surface like severed nerves. Ralph drank down his whiskey. He put fresh ice in his glass and covered it once more with whiskey. He leaned toward the radio as though he hoped to catch the game's score.

We have our health at least, Alice Ann said.

Alice Ann draped her arms over the poolside near her glass. She rested her long chin on the backs of her hands and looked up at Ralph's face. Her eyes looked black. Ralph could see the backs of her long legs floating out behind her in the pale red water. Behind her knees had been a favorite place for Ralph and Alice Ann.

And our children have their health, Alice Ann said. — That's the main thing. Mom used to say that when you have your health you have everything.

Health, Ralph said, — What are you talking about, Alice Ann? What in God's name does your mother know about health? That woman has been having the same pitiful heart-attack for thirty years. And what about her brain tumors, Alice Ann? A dozen of those babies? Fifteen? Don't ask me how many.

You're the one with all the little symptoms, Ralph, Alice Ann said. — All those little fainty vapors. The seven warning signs like clockwork.

A minute ago you said I had my health, Ralph said. — Which is it?

It's your diet, Ralph, Alice Ann said. — You have a rotten diet. Your stomach is a graveyard, Ralph. It is a cemetery for the dead flesh of fellow creatures.

I know the state of my health all right, Ralph said. — I have no illusions. I know I'm a shell of the man I once was. I'm not even the man I was six months ago and I know it. Or yesterday, for that matter. I don't kid myself. But it doesn't have a thing to do with red meat, I'll tell you that.

Come on, honey, Alice Ann said. — Perk up. You are in the prime of your life.

That is probably the cruelest thing you could say to me, Ralph said. He drank down his whiskey and poured another. He lit a cigarette and watched its smoke rise in the pool lights.

This time tomorrow it will be all over, Alice Ann said. She pulled herself out of the water and sat at poolside, her back to Ralph. She hugged her legs to her chest and rested her chin on her knees. Her long blond hair was darkened with water and hung down her back in a rope. Ralph followed the soft slope of spine down her brown back to the dimples above her hips. Those dimples had been a favorite place.

Why don't you come over and sit beside me, Alice Ann said.

I'm listening to a game, Ralph said. — I'm smoking.

Let me have a puff, Alice Ann said and wiggled a hand behind her.

You're all wet, Ralph said. — I'll light you one of your own.

No. Forget it. Later maybe. Are you getting hungry yet?

I don't know, Ralph said. — I hadn't thought about it. I guess my graveyard is still pretty full of that fellow creature you fried up.

Chicken is not red meat, Alice Ann said. — Chicken is fowl, and fowl like fish is better for your blood than red meat.

You mean, in the great scheme of things chickens are less our fellow creatures than our bovine brothers?

Red meat is just not good for your blood, that's all, Alice Ann said. — I just wanted to fix you something you liked, Ralph. That's all. I knew you wouldn't be satisfied with a nice salad. All I needed today was to have you carrying on about bean sprouts, choking and gagging the way you do. I wanted us to have a nice picnic together like old times. I didn't want us to drive down here today grim as death.

It was great chicken, Ralph said. — I mean it. It was a nice picnic too. I don't remember a cross word. Do you? I don't anyway.

Remember how we used to set out deliberately to make memories, Alice Ann said. — We'd set out for a picnic, or just for a drive, a movie, or anything, remember, and we'd vow to each other that we would each do one thing at least to make the time unusual, memorable. Special. And we would try to surprise each other. Outdo each other even. So the time wouldn't just slip by and be forgotten and lost. Then we would lie in bed later and try to remember every little detail. To get the memory just right.

I can remember times things got totally out of hand, Ralph said. — We'd outdo each other all right. You following my left hook with a round-house right.

I don't mean when things got crazy. I mean when we'd do silly, sweet things. Goofy things. Like that time in the dead of night we made the snowman on that horrible neighbor's car hood and you gave it a carrot dick. Now we seem to live as though we want to forget as much as possible. Even the crazy times were better than having nothing to remember.

There's nothing about this situation I want to remember, Ralph said. — Nothing. Especially tomorrow in that courtroom. I want to blot out everything about it. If that means blotting out that nice picnic today in the process then so be it.

In the old days even the bad times were good for a few laughs, Alice Ann said. — We got in our share of scrapes, sure, but we always shot our troubles the bird.

Those days are over and gone, Ralph said.

Remember that time we went skinny-dipping in that motel pool? Drunk as sailors. Three o'clock in the a.m.

That was your idea, Ralph said. — You put me up to it.

Well, whose idea was it to make love in the water? Remember? Alice Ann said. — We were all naked and slippery. You kept diving after me underwater. Muff dives, you called them. 'It's dark and lonely work,' you kept saying, 'but someone has to do it,' and down you'd dive.

We woke up the manager, that's something I remember, Ralph said. — We're lucky he didn't call the cops.

The poor man was struck dumb by my bare-assed beauty, Alice Ann said. — Don't you recall his falling jaw when I alighted dripping.

I remember that, Ralph said. — Sure. I remember you parading around nude in front of that perfect stranger. I remember that. I bet he does too, wherever he is, to this day. I realized then there was nothing you weren't capable of.

Ralph, tell me how it's going to be after tomorrow, Alice Ann said. She finished her drink and handed Ralph her glass. — Light me a cigarette now, too, please.

What it's going to be like, Ralph said. — What kind of question is that? What can I say? How can I answer a question like that?

It will be another fresh start, Alice Ann said. — That's the only way we can look at it. What frightens me the most is someday running out of fresh starts. Let's really do things differently this time, Ralph. Let's pretend we really are new, different people.

What about the past? Ralph said. — All those memories we mapped out.

We'll only save the best parts. We'll make up new pasts. What's important is what we do now, from here on out. We'll live in the present and future. We'll set goals. Common goals.

What kind of goals? Ralph said. — I'll admit it, Alice Ann. Talk like that gets me edgy. You talk about goals and things like preachers and fund-raising and football pop into my mind. It's crazy, I know it. But there it is.

I mean little things, Alice Ann said. — Just doing little things in our life differently. At first. To get started. Things like watching our health more. Getting some exercise. Really. Things like that. We could start taking walks. Long brisk strolls after dinner together. Maybe start hiking in the woods on weekends. Who knows. Maybe later really getting back to nature. Backpacking into the high country eventually.

You must be going crazy, Alice Ann, Ralph said.

We could both quit smoking, Alice Ann said. — Now that's something we really could do. We'll set a date and then just do it together cold turkey. We'll encourage each other, Ralph. Give each other moral support. We'll be the two mouseketeers of moral support, Ralph.

What about those two kids at home? Ralph said.

We'll cut back on the booze some, Alice Ann said. — Think of the money we could save. We'll open a savings account. We'll take the kids on family vacations. Before it's too late, Ralph.

Maybe we could take the kids backpacking into the high country with us, Ralph said.

I mean all this, Alice Ann said. — I do. We'll take family vacations. We'll go to places like, I don't know, the Grand Canyon maybe. Carlsbad Caverns. Places like that. We'll get tourist stickers and put them on our bumpers. *See The Grand Canyon* will be on our bumper and people will know we're a family who has seen the Grand Canyon together. Disneyland. We'll take the kids to Disneyland.

Alice Ann, the boy is fifteen years old, Ralph said. — And he's a hood. Your daughter is sixteen, Alice Ann. And she's a hood too. The only way we could get those kids to Disneyland is on acid.

I want to take my children to Disneyland, Alice Ann said. — I've never even been to Disneyland myself. I've lived in this state all these years and not once have I been to Disneyland, Ralph. I want to take our kids to Disneyland, Ralph, and I want us to get a bumper-sticker to prove it. We have to make a commitment to each other right now, a vow, Ralph, to take our children to Disneyland as soon as we get on our feet.

Don't tell me you're drunk, Ralph said. — Alice Ann, it's not even seven yet.

Before it's too late, Ralph. And we lose them for good. Are you willing to make this vow with me, Ralph? Here and now. I mean it, Ralph. Right this minute.

Yes, Jesus Christ, yes, Ralph said. — Right. Wow. Disneyland. You got it. It's done. The check's in the mail.

Take me seriously, Ralph, Alice Ann said.

I am, Ralph said. — I do. I do.

My parents took me on one vacation when I was a child, Alice Ann said. — And it was pitiful. Three months later they separated.

Did you save any bumper-stickers? Ralph said.

It was their last chance. It was their last honeymoon. Only there I was, the fruit of their first. I remember being so upset because Father got ajoining rooms, and I had to sleep alone in one, instead of sleeping with Mom in her bed as I was used to doing. I cried and cried. They wouldn't even leave the door open. At first they wouldn't.

This is a story I've never heard before, Ralph said. — I thought I knew all your stories. Why haven't you told me this one before? Did something terrible happen?

No, Alice Ann said. — Nothing happened at all really. Not that a child could see. Like in one of your stories, Ralph, everything was undercurrent. We went to Florida. It was horribly hot and muggy. We spent several unscheduled days in St. Augustine going around to all the historical sites. The oldest house in America, the oldest school, the oldest fort. I remember being so frightened at these Indian burial grounds Father had to carry me. Rows of open graves full of skeletons. It seemed as though they were in some huge garage and you walked among them on these elevated wooden walkways. Your steps would echo. For years afterward when I would see a sign above some garage saying Body Shop those burial grounds would flash before me. Seeing all those sites was for my sake I suppose. I'm sure my parents told themselves that. Educational. We were supposed to spend several days in Miami, where my parents had actually spent their first honeymoon. But we never got that far. The extra days in St. Augustine, and then I was badly sunburned. So at some point Father just turned around and we headed home. At some point I was sleeping in the same bed with Mom. This sounds like a story you would write, Ralph. Doesn't it? Like that critic said, right, full of homely, unexceptional, colorless people going about the business of their colorless lives, but full also of, what did he say, warnings, malignancies. Ralph, do me one favor. Forget this story I told you.

Too bad they hadn't built Disneyworld down in Orlando yet, Ralph said. — Or is Disneyworld in Jacksonville?

Did you hear me, Ralph? Alice Ann said.

Consider it forgotten, Ralph said.

But this was not true. It was too late for this. And then Alice Ann went on.

I remember we stopped in a place called Silver Springs. Or maybe it was called Crystal Springs. Something like that. The water was just crystal clear. You could see to the bottom anywhere, and this was deep water. They had what I think were called Jungle Cruises, which you took in glass-bottom boats. As we cruised along the captain, or guide, whatever he was called, pointed out things of interest underwater. What looked to me like the encrusted trunk of a fallen tree the guide told us was a mast from one of Ponce de Leon's sunken ships. Another encrusted trunk he called the fossilized backbone of a dinosaur. My parents smiled at each other. The guide tossed pieces of stale bread on the water and fish came up to feed. All the fish had personal names. There was Captain Catfish, Hungry Hilda, Bait-Breath Bob. The guide pointed out fish couples to us, some married, some just courting he said, some he pointed out had brokenhearts. He related several fishy love stories to us. My parents, sitting on either side of me, smiled above my head. I thought they looked so happy.

Then the guide told us a human love story and I thought my heart would break. At where he said was the deepest spot at the springs, the guide pointed out a huge open hole, an underwater cave, where the spring water bubbled out of I guess. He said that years and years earlier a handsome young man, who had been horribly wounded in war, wounded in such a way he could never marry his sweetheart and have babies (my parents looked at each other; I felt my Father stir; my Mom looked out over the water toward the shore), this handsome, wounded, young man took a jungle cruise one afternoon just like any other tourist, and when the boat passed directly over the mouth of that underwater cave this handsome young man dove off and while all the real tourists watched through the glass-bottom in horror he swam all the way down and disappeared into that hole never to be seen again. The story wasn't over. One year later to the day his beautiful sweetheart did the same thing. She dove, clothes and all, off a glass-bottom boat to join her love forever in that hole.

Alice Ann stood up at poolside and dove into the water. She swam underwater slowly to the pool's shallow end where she surfaced in the spray from the cupid fountain. She stood up and turned slowly, letting the spray fall over her body. She tilted her head back and let the spray splash over her face. She opened her mouth and let it fill with spray. Ralph followed the arch of water from the cupid's mouth to his wife's mouth. Alice Ann had her hands cupped under her breasts. Water ran in thin streams from the corners of her mouth. Ralph turned off the radio. He heard sudden laughter from somewhere behind him and he jerked around in his chair.

What's the matter? Alice Ann said.

Nothing, Ralph said.

Ralph stood up and peered about. He could feel his heart racing. He sat down.

Is someone coming? Alice Ann said.

I don't know. I heard something. I don't see anyone. Haven't you had enough of that water? You'll look like a prune.

Alice Ann breaststroked back to poolside near Ralph. Between the slight separation in her front teeth Alice Ann spit a long thin arc of water toward Ralph.

Hey, there, Ralph said, and scooted his chair back. — You got my shoes all wet.

Oh, bullshit, Ralph, Alice Ann said. — Come on in. The water's right.

I have a headache coming on, Ralph said. — A migrane.

Oh, Ralph, Alice Ann said. — Go put your suit on. Come on and play. I won't tell anyone.

I've got this headache, Ralph said. Ralph turned the radio on and bent toward it.

I still say it's your diet, honey, believe me, Alice Ann said. She jangled her glass at Ralph and he bent to reach it. He filled it with ice and whiskey and handed it back to her. Alice Ann took a long drink then crunched an icecube between her teeth.

I wish you'd go on that karma-cleaning diet I learned at the Zen center, Alice Ann said. — You'd be a new man in no time.

I don't want to be a new man, Ralph said. — I just want to be the old me. The way I used to be. Back then.

Back when, honey?

I don't know. Back sometime. Back before everything. Back before all this, Ralph said and slowly waved his glass about him.

I think the worst is over, honey, Alice Ann said. — We've suffered, sure. But we're going to start getting some good out of this incarnation, Ralph. Both of us. I know it. And we're going to be made stronger for all our suffering in the long run. If not in this life then in the next. We have to work on our karma, that's all.

Alice Ann, would you just answer me something? Ralph said. — And don't fly off the handle. Please. This is just a simple, honest question. What's with you and those zen-birds anyway? Where do they get off, Alice Ann? Just tell me that.

You never fail to amaze me, Ralph.

I just don't understand those birds, Ralph said. — I'll admit it. All right, so it's just me being ignorant. Maybe that's it. I don't know. But I honestly think they're all a bunch of nuts.

You are ignorant, Ralph, Alice Ann said. — You're right about that anyway.

All right. All right. I've admitted it. I've said it. So set me straight. Explain things to me. I'm willing to learn. Really. Explain India to me. You take India. Over in India people are starving, right? Everyone knows that. It's a fact of life. Starving people in India. But do you think those starving people would have sense enough to barbeque up some of those cows they have roaming around all over the place in India? Cows everywhere. Roaming the streets. All over the sidewalks. Cow-shit everywhere. Piss. It's awful. And do they barbeque up any of that grade-A beef? Not on your life, Alice Ann. And do you know why, Alice Ann? I'll tell you why. Because they believe one of those bovines might be their dead daddy returned to life on the hoof.

I've tried everything to get you to expand your horizons, Ralph. There is a spiritual dimension to this world. You just won't let yourself open up to new possibilities. You live in a closed system, Ralph.

My Dad has been dead for years, Ralph said. — I bet I've put away ten thousand hamburgs since my Dad passed and I'll tell you something, Alice Ann, I'm not one bit worried. You'll never in a million years convince me I ever took a single bite out of Dad.

The final thing about you, Ralph, is, you don't want to probe new possibilities. You don't have the imagination for it. And your stories suffer for it too.

Leave my stories out of this, Ralph said. — My stories don't have a thing to do with this business.

Your stories *are* out of it, Ralph, Alice Ann said. — And this is the reason why. You don't have the . . . no, you won't let your imagination probe deeply enough. You won't let your imagination seek the deeper mysteries in this world of veils. That's why your stories are about colorless people going about the business of their colorless lives. There is no spiritual dimension to your stories, Ralph.

That's crazy, Alice Ann, Ralph said. — Just non-sense.

It's true. It is. Malignancies, Ralph. Malignancies make up your stories. And this is one reason I pity you.

You pity me? Ralph said. — That's a laugh. What about those zen looney birds over there in India who walk around with nails in their dicks? Don't deny it, Alice Ann. It's a true fact. That's just what some of your zen pals do, Alice Ann. I've seen pictures. In *National Geographic.* They pound nails through their dicks then roam around the countryside carrying these begging bowls. You call that spiritual. Are those the kind of nuts you think I should write about? It's pathetic. That's no way to worship God.

I'll bet it keeps them out of trouble anyway, Alice Ann said.

What's that supposed to mean? Ralph said.

Do I have to draw you a picture, Ralph?

Come on, out with it. Let's get our cards on the table.

Well, honey, if you had had a nail in your weeney you certainly would not have done much womanizing. Am I right?

There! Ralph said. — There it is! I knew it. I knew all day you were just waiting to drag up dirt. That picnic didn't fool me a minute, Alice Ann. All that fried chicken. That tasty potatoe-salad. I knew all along you were just waiting to catch me off-guard and nail me.

That's not true, Ralph, Alice Ann said. — I mean it.

That's a likely story. We weren't going to bring up that old business I thought. We agreed I thought. That business was dead and buried I thought.

You're right, Ralph. Alice Ann said. — Would you believe me if I told you I was sorry?

What? Ralph said. — What?

Would you believe me if I told you I was sorry?

I don't understand this, Ralph said.

Would you believe me if I told you I have never been unfaithful to you?

What? Ralph said. — What is this, some kind of trick question?

No, Alice Ann said. She drained her drink and placed her glass at poolside. She pushed off backwards and floated to the center of the pool where she treaded water.

You've got me all worked up now, Ralph said. He turned up the radio and then poured more whiskey into his glass.

What's the score? Alice Ann said. She breaststroked back to poolside.

I don't have the first idea, Ralph said.

Freshen my drink too, Alice Ann said. She handed her glass to Ralph and when he returned it she drank deeply. — I may as well tell you something, Ralph.

Tell me something? Ralph said. — What? Tell me what?

You're not going to be very happy about this, Ralph.

Jesus, don't tell me then. Yes, tell me. Go ahead. Jesus, Alice Ann.

You'd find out sooner or later anyway, Ralph.

Oh Christ, Alice Ann. Just tell me. Just do it.

Ralph, I wrote your ladyfriend a letter.

What was that? Ralph said. He turned off the radio. — What did you do?

You heard me, Ralph.

Jesus Christ, Alice Ann. Jesus, what possessed you. That business is dead and buried.

It is now, Alice Ann said. She took another long drink from her glass.

What in the world did you say? Alice Ann, I don't understand. What did you write?

The truth, Ralph, Alice Ann said. — The truth about us.

Alice Ann swam backwards across the pool then returned breaststroking. Ralph turned on the radio. He turned up its volume.

When she reached poolside Alice Ann said: — Why don't you go get into your swimsuit, honey? You need the exercise.

I didn't bring my swimsuit, that's one reason.

We always have our birthday suits, Alice Ann said. She undid her halter top and tossed it toward Ralph.

Are you going crazy, Alice Ann? Ralph jumped up. He waved his hands at her. — Stop this, Alice Ann.

Alice Ann bent beneath the water and tugged off her bikini bottoms. She swung them around over her head and threw them toward the nearest peacock among the flowering bushes. Ralph ran to them. He ran holding the bikini bottoms before him to the pool's edge. — Here, here, Alice Ann, Ralph said and shook them before her face. — Do you want to go to jail? Is that it?

We're a married couple, Ralph. We've seen each other naked, Alice Ann said. She pushed off backwards again from the poolside and floated to the center. Her nipples looked black. Ralph watched the smooth muscles of her stomach and thighs flex. During Ralph's last desperate stay at Duffy's, a drying-out facility for alcoholics north of San Francisco, Alice Ann had, with no explanation, begun shaving her pubic hair.

There's someone coming, Ralph said. He glanced about behind him. — Really, Alice Ann. It's probably the manager, Alice Ann. Jesus Christ, Alice Ann.

Alice Ann arched backwards into a dive and disappeared beneath the water. Ralph threw the bikini bottoms into the water after her. He kicked the halter-top in. He turned away then turned back and kicked her glass into the pool. Ralph stumbled back to his chair and sat down. He pressed his fingertips against his temple and shut his eyes. Somehow he would call his friend. Tonight. Set her straight. Give the lie to Alice Ann's letter. The crowds' roar rose from the transistor radio. The Dodgers must have scored, Ralph thought. He wished he knew the game's score. He hoped the Dodgers were ahead. The Dodgers had been his Dad's team. Ralph could just see his Dad sitting at the kitchen table, eating his supper, having a beer, a highball maybe, the radio on, the crowds' roar as someone, Peewee Reese say, came up to bat, his Dad laughing with his mouth full, pointing to the radio, giving Ralph the A-OK high sign, summer evening air coming in the open kitchen door, outside the sounds of treefrogs, distant traffic, the smell of coming rain, of mown grass, the sudden crack of Peewee Reese's bat sending some ball sailing into the stands.

Ralph stood up suddenly and hurried to the pool's edge. He stared into the pale red water. He knelt down at poolside. Ralph braced himself and bent as far out over the water as he dared.

The narrow hallway he was standing naked in was only vaguely familiar to Ralph Crawford, but somehow he wasn't afraid. Ralph walked past numbered doors toward a glass door at the hall's nearest end. Fascinated, he watched his naked reflection gorge in the glass. When Ralph slid the glass door open he looked out over a parking area one floor below and beyond it to a small garden of strangely blue palms. He smelled sea air, and knew somehow it was the Pacific. He heard a faint tinkle of wind-chimes, the hum of neon, a distant car's tires, television from some room behind him. Taking his penis in his hand, Ralph stepped beyond the doorway onto a narrow balcony. What was Alice Ann's convertible doing parked below? Through the palm trees Ralph saw a pool. Where was Alice Ann? Ralph thought. When had Alice Ann licked that champagne from his stomach? She had sucked champagne from his navel. Ralph aimed his penis toward where he imagined the Pacific Ocean was, thinking, Why can't I piss? He looked at his penis. It was stiff in his hand. Ralph aimed his stiff penis toward the Cadillac convertible and gritted his teeth.

Alice Ann was deep asleep when loud voices from the hallway half woke her. After a moment she remembered where she was, but she still lay with her eyes shut. She felt small and safe in this enormous bed, which continued to vibrate from that fistful of quarters they had stuffed into the slot on its headboard earlier in the evening for hours of healthful, fingertip toning-touch.

Alice Ann and Ralph had paid an arm and a leg for this suite and why not? What did it matter she had asked Ralph. Even bankrupts deserve a bone. She had borrowed the money from a colleague at the community college where she taught, so the debt was hers and hers alone. For the price of this suite a complimentary continental breakfast was included, so tomorrow morning Alice Ann planned to put that one o'clock courtroom business out of her mind and just savor it, while Ralph sucked his screwdrivers.

Alice Ann stretched and felt for Ralph. The sheets on his side were still damp with champagne. Alice Ann opened her eyes. Across the darkened room the huge color television screen was a silent red, white, and blue rippling American flag. The bathroom was dark. Alice Ann got up and put on her robe. Alice Ann heard her name called from the hallway.

Unhand my husband! Alice Ann told the burly, uniformed man who had Ralph in a headlock in the hall.

Alice Ann! Ralph called. Ralph was naked. His voice was muffled in a coatsleeve. — This is crazy, Alice Ann!

Remove your hands from my husband this instant, Alice Ann said.

Listen, lady, the guard said.

That man is my husband, Alice Ann said.

Lady, the guard said.

He's got me in a hold, Ralph said. — Help me, Alice Ann.

You are assaulting an ill man, Alice Ann said.

Lady, this man is naked in public, the guard said. He tightened his grip on Ralph's head.

Kick him, Alice Ann, Ralph said. — Give him one.

My husband is ill, Alice Ann said. — He walks in his sleep. He needs help not this physical abuse. He is under a doctor's care. My husband needs medical attention.

Lady, this is a drunk man, the guard said.

A woman opened the door of the room across from Ralph and Alice Ann's. She stood there motionless, watching this scene, her hand on the doorknob.

Would you call the desk for me, please? the guard asked the woman. — Get the manager. Get anyone around down there.

Another door opened down the hall and a grey-haired man stuck his head out.

Are you people getting your eyes full? Alice Ann said. — A sick man is being assaulted before your eyes and you people just gawk. This poor man needs someone's help.

Call the desk, someone, the guard said. — Have them send someone up quick. Please!

This has gone far enough, Ralph said. — Alice Ann!

This man is an important American author! Alice Ann said. — How can something like this happen in America? Where is this, Germany? Are we in Germany? Help, someone, before it's too late! Don't let it happen again in this century. We must stop it before it's too late. Stand up and be counted! Don't let them silence my husband. You could be the next one to go. Remember that.

Someone call the desk! the guard said.

Alice Ann! Ralph called.

Don't you people dare look upon my husband in this state! Alice Ann said. — Shut your doors. All of you. You shut your door! Alice Ann said and stepped toward the woman. The woman backed into the room and shut the door. Alice Ann looked at the man up the hall. He shut his door.

Call the desk, someone, the guard called out.

That does it, Alice Ann said. — Who do you think you are? Who are you anyway? That man is an important American author.

Kick him! Ralph said. — Do it, Alice Ann.

Come on, lady, the guard said.

The guard ducked away from Alice Ann's roundhouse right, but it caught him behind his right ear and knocked his cap flipping to the floor. Ralph broke the guard's hold and lunged for the door. Ralph slammed the door behind him. The guard bent to pick up his cap. Alice Ann aimed a kick at his face which he blocked with an elbow. The guard ran several yards down the hall before turning and shaking a finger at Alice Ann.

Lady, you are under arrest! the guard yelled.

I will sue you for every nickel you have, Alice Ann said. — I have friends in high places. Senator Tunney is a personal friend. Ted Kennedy is a personal friend. I know Frank Sinatra.

The woman from across the hall cracked the door.

Lady, I don't want any more trouble, the guard said. — I told you you are under arrest by the powers invested in me by the state of California. Lady, put your hands up against that wall. Right now. Spread your legs.

You heard that, Alice Ann said to the woman behind the door. — You are my witness. Rape! Help, rape!

Are you crazy or something? the guard said. — Lady, are you crazy?

Rape! Alice Ann screamed.

The guard turned and hurried down the hall toward the stairwell exit.

God bless you, Alice said to the woman behind the door. — God knows what that man would have done to me if you hadn't been my witness.

The woman closed the door. Alice Ann knocked on the door to Ralph's and her room.

Open up, Ralph.

When there was no answer Alice Ann pounded on the door.

Let me in, goddamn it, Ralph!

Who is it? Ralph said from behind the door.

Who do you think it is, goddamn it! Open this door, Ralph!

Is there anyone with you?

Open the goddamn door, Ralph!

This is the worst thing that ever happened to me in my life, Ralph said. He shut the door behind Alice Ann and locked it. He was dressed.

This is just too much for one man to handle, Ralph said. He walked over and sat on the bed. He put his face in his hands. — I was innocent. I was just hunting for the bathroom. It was an honest mistake, Alice Ann. This is the straw that broke this camel's back.

Get your things together, honey, Alice Ann said. She began packing her overnight case on the dresser with her makeup.

Being naked out there in that hallway was my worst dream come true, Ralph said. He lay back on the bed. He pulled the covers up over his head.

Come on, honey, Alice Ann said. — Where did you put your shaving kit?

Let them come and get me, Ralph said. He rolled into a ball under the covers. — Let them just take me away now.

This is like old times, Alice Ann said and laughed. She put her robe and nightgown in the suitcase. She dressed quickly in her jeans and blouse. — Where's your underwear, Ralph?

In my pocket, Ralph said. — Did you get him a good one?

Not really, Alice Ann said. — Come on, honey, get out from under those covers. You should have seen it. He ran down the hall then turned around and announced I was under arrest.

You mean, you're under arrest? Ralph said.

Can't you tell, Alice Ann said. She held the opened champagne bottle before the television's light and shook it. She split its final inches between two plastic cups and carried them to the bed.

Am I under arrest too? Ralph said.

Here, baby, Alice Ann said and sat down on the bed by Ralph. — Look what Momma has for us.

Ralph looked out from under the covers. Alice Ann handed him a cup.

Let's have a toast, Alice Ann said.

To what? Ralph said. — To what?

To whatever, Alice Ann said. — To our fresh start. I don't know. You make the toast, honey.

To Disneyland, Ralph said.

To Disneyland? Alice Ann said. — Disneyland, Ralph?

To our trip to Disneyland when we get on our feet, Ralph said.

What about the kids? Alice Ann said.

What about the kids? Ralph said. — We'll get them stoned out of their minds. They'll love Disneyland. We'll cover every inch of that Cadillac with stickers.

Ralph, what I said about your stories, I didn't mean it, Alice Ann said. — I love your stories. Your stories *are* spiritual, Ralph.

Really? Ralph said. — Do you really think that?

Your stories are spiritual, Ralph, Alice Ann said. — And you are spiritual. You are a spiritual man, Ralph. More than you know.

Honest to God, Alice Ann?

You are, Ralph. Believe me.

Sometimes I worry I'm just turning into an old drunk, Ralph said.

We just need to get on our feet, Alice Ann said.

There was a loud knock on the door.

To Disneyland, Alice Ann said and raised her cup.

They're here, Ralph said.

Come on, honey, Alice Ann said. — To Disneyland.

Right, Ralph said. — You bet. Why not? To Disneyland.

Alice Ann and Ralph touched cups and then drank the flat champagne down.

HOWARD JOHNSON'S MOTOR LODGE
OPPOSITE DISNEYLAND

Phyllis Koestenbaum

Criminal Sonnets

III.
Leaving one man, my friend fantasies
Immaculata's city for a sex-
ier one and a job in paradise,
Macy's. Human intercourse is heaven-
ly hell. She aims human, I aim for work
that is pleasure. Fuck Freud and his love
and work. You can count on the fingers of
one hand who loves and works. Are you in their
bed. They might not be fucking, like Gandhi
or Woolf. Why couldn't she be satisfied
in books. This imperfect body climaxes
as it can. Would I reach nirvana, gay.
Moot question: my psychic mother wouldn't let
me sleep at Arlyne's, and I acquiesced.

Kendra Kopelke

Jonnie Richardson

> At the age of 16, Jonnie Richardson climbed
> into a big double bed in his parents' isolated
> mountain shack to rest. Fifty years later,
> he's still resting, the victim of an illness
> that he says left him permanently exhausted.

1.
I was born here
on Ashe mountain in this bed
the middle child of Sara and Jon
and my life went along
blurred and unnoticed
among milk cows and litters of cats,
clothes whipping on the line,
startled rabbit skins
stretched on the porch.
Between seasons my mother
would pound out the dents
in the blackened pots
while father's silhouette
dreamed long into the fields;
I was no different then.
On Sunday we would wash
lining up to have our hair
parted and combed straight.
And each day,
as the sun rolled over the ridge,
we would pray
that the rains not forget our farm,
the blue Chevy resist the rust,
the roof stay tight
against our walls. We would pray
for Michael, the brother
we buried in his night clothes
at two, that his fever
had lifted him. Then
before father whispered
the final *amen* across the table
he would thank the Lord

for this old mountain, which
momma used to say
gave us a better view
of Michael and quiet.

2.
> *speech is a little thing;*
> *in these raw and clouded moons,*
> *space is little too.*

I forget sometimes
that speech is a virtue —
a way of protection,
of making sure I am more alive
than the apparition
of my own hollow face
waiting at the window.
On the radio I hear
the young winged voices
flapping against thin air
and I imagine
their caged hearts pumping
behind the microphone
as the sentences sputter
into the crowded room.
I forget how once
I too, wanted more
and would swing my arms
in wide circles on the lawn,
where rattled chickens
scattered like leaves
and always my mother
emerged on the back step
wearing a look
so distorted in daylight
I tried not to sense
its warning. Still
it wound a knot around my heart
that twisted for weeks. Later

the storms came through
and uprooted half a century
of trees against this house.
We lost a spring's migration
of birds and spent mornings
picking splinters of glass
from branches and twigs.
In autumn, as clouds
grew accustomed to a bleaker
sky, there arose
from high branch a song,
a voice that knew what space
it came to fill —
I listened for its answer
felt the mountain hold me in.

3.
Afternoons, you come up the path
carrying tea and cereal wrapped
in newspaper. You unlatch the door,
call out, shaping my name
like a question. Fifty years
Bessie, and your voice has carved
a statue in this empty hall.
Yet lately your visits grow silent
as if you've become more acquainted
with an older wilderness
and its ghosts: our people
are dwindling to stone so near
to us I can smell the air
thickening to dust. Even you
do not seem my sister,
who would climb the roof
to hammer a shingle during
a strong rain. Though
the clocked days still rise
to the same distance in the sky,
you crouch low
to stoke the stove, stare

into the fire, watching
patterns break free
from the flames. Or the thin
pencil line of smoke
drawing light from the room.
Outside, sparrows disappear
into the evergreen
knocking snow into the wind
until the scene is nothing
but a shock of white
caught on the glass
one of us turning away.

4.
I remember the heart
she drew around my initials.
When she kissed me behind the ear
I saw the sun break apart. After that
I took my time along the road
kicking stones into stones,
watching the light blossom at my feet.
When her father became ill
the family hauled a lifetime
of furniture out to the yard,
auctioned it off in a day.
"I'll write," she called
as she disappeared into the back seat,
but her voice was already cold.
Sometimes
I see in the floor boards
a woman's shape. I imagine
a soft shadow stitched to my heart,
the sound of clothes
dropping into the water,
the water encircling itself.
Sometimes my hands
become another's; they grope,
hesitate, as if questioning —
a man, a woman . . .

neither body fits mine.
What lives inside
finds its shape pressed
between folds of blackness
like the hand
the lover puts across his mouth
quieting the scream.

5.
The *click*
when I pull back the trigger
should be enough protection.
Up here, in night's common quiet
any sound enters the body
through the pulse, animals
pull away from their sleep.
I keep my shotgun close,
and when the moon's crystal edge
pierces the window,
I stay awake, waiting.
I like to think about the night
I'll grip the gun in my hands
and fire bullet after bullet
into this house, shattering
walls, photographs, tv, radio,
toaster, tea kettle, lamp.
Outside, leaves would tremble
while stars fell forward
towards the earth.
I would tell reporters
it was a moment
of confusion —
footsteps heard on the path,
a swollen heartbeat,
while daylight opened
each wound. I would lie flat
then, as before
with both eyes open
to this room where even

a friend's trailing hand
burns for days beneath the skin.

> In innumerable overcrowded "homes" in Stepney there is no room for the growing lad; he is forced into the streets with all their perils.
>
> **What will become of him**
>
> unless helpful hands come to his rescue? We hold out such hands. Numbers of youths have been, and are being, moulded into good citizens by the efforts of our workers, a large proportion of whom are honorary.
>
> Contributions will be gratefully acknowledged by the Rev. Percy Ineson, *Superintendent,*
>
> DRIFTING
>
> **The East End MISSION**
>
> Central Hall, Commercial Road, Stepney, London, E.1

Judith Kroll

After the Snowfall

*Months of silence, then a parting of mist.
I heard you say:*

It was all your misunderstanding.
My stopped touches
were merely the chill of the wind.

My secretly loving another
had nothing to do with your being lost in the forest,
frozen by my absences.

Those cold letters that choked your breath
were a coffin of snow, growing all night
as you lay there helplessly,
scarred by shadows.

You did not feel
a subsiding of love, but the passionate storm
fitfully dying.

I lied about nothing.
Can't everything be true?
It is not that I do not want you,

but just
that I do not want you.

Judith Kroll

Winter Birth

Why should I wake at four in the morning
into my mind, already up and singing
*I am thirty-seven, I have a new baby,
how can I live with a man I no longer trust?*

My breasts aching, flushed with milk —
but the baby sleeps.

When he sucks, he looks up at me
wide-eyed, adoring,

the eyes of a deer in the first garden
before he learns
man can't be trusted.

I want to walk where my head is light,
on a path lit only by stars
in the still and compassionate mountains.

I want to say to the god inside

*Only pick me up and hold me,
I too will stop crying.*

Judith Kroll

Same Time, Next Life

Are you lonely today in your magical house,
silent among
those mirrored tapestries and painted dolls,
the wands of fiery gladioli?

Everyone loves an enchanted forest.
Remember the one that enclosed us, wherever we were,
in the dazed aura of our widest selves?

Then you sank into being human.
It is all right. I respect letting go,
even if it is me you let go of.

But do not call it by another name,
leave me the touchstone of truth.

Are reasons birds, to be caged or trained,
flung into the sun before they are ready?

You have turned away, and I still cannot
let go of you.
That is my sentence, patiently waiting
for the transformation that may never come —

a beggar sits in the dusty road,
playing with coins and flowers.

Maxine Kumin

In the Absence of Bliss

> Museum of the Diaspora, Tel Aviv

The roasting alive of rabbis
in the ardor of the Crusades
went unremarked in *Europe from
the Holy Roman Empire to 1918,*
open without prerequisite
when I was an undergraduate.

While reciting the Sh'ma in full
expectation that their souls
would waft up to the bosom
of the Almighty, the rabbis burned
pious past the humming extremes
of pain. And their loved ones with them.
Whole communities tortured and set aflame
in Christ's name
while chanting Hear O Israel.

Why?
Why couldn't the rabbis recant,
kiss the Cross, pretend?
Is God so simple that He can't
sort out real from sham?
Did He want
these fanatic autos-da-fé, admire
the eyeballs popping,
the corpses shrinking in the fire?

We live in an orderly
universe of discoverable laws,
writes an intelligent alumna
in Harvard Magazine.
Bliss is belief,
agnostics always say
a little condescendingly
as befits mandarins who function
on a higher moral plane.

Consider our contemporary
Muslim kamikazes
hurling their explosives-
packed trucks through barriers.
Isn't it all the same?
They too die cherishing the fond
certitude of a better life beyond.

We walk away from twenty-two
graphic centuries of kill-the-jew
and hail, of all things, a Mercedes
taxi. The driver is Yemeni,
loves rock music and hangs
each son's picture — three so far —
on tassels from his rearview mirror.

I do not tell him that in Yemen
Jewish men, like women, were forbidden
to ride their donkeys astride,
having just seen this humiliation
illustrated on the Museum screen.

When his parents came
to the Promised Land, they entered
the belly of the enormous growling
silver bird, not knowing whether
they would live or die.
No matter. As it was written
the Messiah had drawn nigh.

I do not ask, who tied
the leaping ram inside the thicket?
Who polished, then blighted the apple?
Who loosed pigs in the Temple,
set tribe against tribe
and nailed man in His pocket?

But ask myself, what would
I die for and reciting what?

Not for Jahweh, Allah, Christ,
those patriarchal fists
in the face. But would
I die to save a child?
Rescue my lover? Would
I run into the fiery barn
to release animals
singed and panicked from their stalls?

Bliss is belief, but where's
the higher moral plane I roost on?
This narrow plank given to splinters.
No easy answers. Only questions.

Maxine Kumin

Visiting Professor

At MIT on the oval
my students stretch out like corpses
this day of budded maples.
Like the dead of Beirut in the sun.

Here everything is hopeful
because unconsidered. Fierce in
their indolence my students
turn themselves over sunning.

This evening under fluorescent lights
in a cooling classroom we will discuss
poems of the apocalypse
which serenely never happens

in their dreams. In mine, that one
Poseidon submarine carrying
like the fish, its eggs enough
to flood the pond, warheads enough

to level every medium
every large city in
the Soviet Union, that one
Poseidon sub sticks up its snub nose.

Diogenes at ninety held his breath
until he suffocated, so goes the myth
that says how much we want to be in charge.
My students will colonize

outer space. They will
domesticate the solar cell.
Syzygy and the molecular
cloning of genes will not overpower

their odes to the 21st century
their love poems and elegies.
Meanwhile their illegal puppies
wrestle among them on the oval

in springtime, in Cambridge again
in a world where all, all is possible.
The chrome of new dandelions
assaults the sun.

SNOW CHAINS FOR SHOES

WALK SAFE   DON'T SLIP

Be prepared ! Avoid nasty accidents. The same as snow chains make tyres slip-proof GRIPPEX will make your shoes or boots slip-proof on wet ground, mud, snow and sleety ice.

HOPES 3.95   PER PAIR
+ 35p pp
Dept. EE, 27-29 Blenheim Gdns, Ldn SW2

James Howard Kunstler

The Rise, Fall, and Redemption of Mooski Toffski Offski

"I am Mooski Toffski Offski, Sultan of Bungwah, Caliph of Poona, Archduke of Soodna, Tsarovitch of the Imperial Russian realm, so what else is new?"

The author of this speech, delivered to a full-length mirror in the bedroom of a Manhattan apartment, was an eleven-year-old boy named Jeff Greenaway. Since he had finished his homework — a "report" on the state of Iowa, its history, products, official song, et cetera; plus two pages of fractions in the odious math workbook — and since there were fifteen minutes remaining before *The Untouchables* television show would come on the air, Jeff worked on his latest comedy routine. He was an accomplished mimic and the accent sounded a lot like Nikita Khrushchev, who had recently visited New York in order to bang his shoe at the U.N.

Jeff rehearsed telling several jokes, first in his normal voice, then in his Mooski dialect, and the second time around they sounded so hilarious he could barely finish them. He tried to imagine the circumstance where he might do his routine for Wendy Waldbaum, whom he adored, and sweep her off her feet on gales of laughter. The ultimate triumph, of course, would be to somehow get on *The Ed Sullivan Show* and take her by complete and overwhelming surprise. But Jeff realized that he was unlikely to get on the show, at least for a few years, and by then he and Wendy would be in different schools. Then again there were the "talent shows" held in the school auditorium where the children sought refuge at recess on rainy days. Impromptu affairs at first, they had become boringly predictable as the school year wore on. Barry Goldblatt would amaze the audience at the piano with "The Theme from the Million Dollar Movie," after which Bobby Bedrosian would play "Me and My Shadow" on his cornet. Richard Schnabel, the class dork, would do his birdcalls. After that it would all go downhill. Jeff had mixed feelings about debuting in such company. New acts always had to wait until after the established ones took their turns. By the time he got up there, the crowd would be ready for blood. What if they didn't get the jokes? What if the jokes weren't any good? Wendy Waldbaum wouldn't be caught dead talking to him. He'd have to move to a new city, change his name . . . !

Jeff approached the mirror and examined himself. Gazing with dismay at the image, he decided that short arms and legs might be fine for comedy, but they were no help at all in the romance department. He thought of his rival for the affection of Wendy Waldbaum, Lee Talbot, and how Talbot towered at least a foot over him. *How's the weather up there, Lee?* he would ask on line, as Mrs. Snipes's class moved in formation down the hall toward the gym. Lee would pretend to laugh, but it was obvious he simply didn't get it. Jeff loved the fact that Talbot didn't get it far more than he liked the wisecrack itself. Then, during the game of "bombardment" that comprised the daily gym period, Jeff would fire volley after volley of big rubber balls at Talbot, seeking not merely to eliminate him from the game, but to ring his bell, to cause brain damage, if possible. Once, he nailed him right between the eyes and Talbot sank to his knees on the varnished hardwood floor like a gut-shot Indian. Mrs. Snipes put a moratorium on "head-hunting" after that, but the rule was unenforcable. " . . . I couldn't help it, Mrs. Snipes, honest . . . ." What Wendy Waldbaum saw in the big jerk, Jeff couldn't begin to imagine, but they'd been spotted together buying tickets at the 86th Street RKO theater one recent Saturday by Jay Skolnick, who was not known to lie about such things.

Jeff stepped closer to the mirror and smiled as if at a photographer. His teeth were very large, and he noticed a similarity between his smile and the expression on the muzzle of the alligator that adorned the polo shirts his mother bought for him.

"Frank Nitti traveled all the way from Chicago to New York for the sole purpose of exterminating Lee Talbot," Jeff declaimed in his best Walter Winchell voice. Then, he turned on the TV at the foot of his bed and watched that week's episode of *The Untouchables* in which Special Agent Elliot Ness sent yet another batch of

Italian-American miscreants to that great speakeasy in the sky.

Noon recess at Public School Number 6 on Manhattan's upper east side was surprisingly informal. Patronage of the school cafeteria was strictly voluntary, and most of the older children, the 5th and 6th graders, scorned it for the liberty of the playground and the streets. Lunch could be gotten, for instance, at the Copper Lantern Coffee Shoppe across Madison Avenue, where a hamburger, french fries and a cherry coke cost $1.03 plus tip. An equally nourishing, if not exactly wholesome, lunch could be had for half that price from the Sabrett hot dog man who parked his pushcart on 81st Street every day. A squat, furtive, melancholy figure dressed in a grimy quilted jacket and a laborer's hat with three earflaps which he wore in all weathers and all seasons, and with stumpy, permanently blackened fingers (the stains etched in tiny cracks of his skin like scrimshaw), the hot dog man spoke a language which not even Jeff Greenaway, with his love of mimicry, could identify. But there was not much to go on, for the hot dog man never said more than the two words *mustard* and *saurkraut*, which he pronounced "moostahrokrot" and posed in the interrogatory.

Now, on this particular noon, a blustery March day when newspapers blew down the avenues like tumbleweeds, Jeff went off by himself at lunch hour in foul and turbulent spirits. That morning, he had overheard Lee Talbot describe his 12th birthday festivities, upcoming this Saturday. First, Talbot's father, a bigshot Broadway attorney, would be taking Lee and a horde of his so-called friends to the matinee of *The Sound of Music.* From there they would proceed to the F.A.O. Schwarz toy store on 59th Street where Lee would be given 12 minutes to grab everything his heart desired. Finally, the group would debouch up Fifth Avenue to the Talbot duplex for a birthday party with cake, ice cream, soda and favors.

As far as Jeff was concerned, it was obvious that the whole purpose of this party was to impress Wendy Waldbaum. In the first place, Talbot didn't have any friends, just acquaintences who liked to play with his slot cars and mooch candy off him. It was Talbot, in fact, who had given Jeff his first insights onto the true nature of the political mentality. (Talbot was "President" of class 6-B, meaning he got to sit up at the teacher's desk and lord it over everybody while Mrs. Snipes visited the "powder room.") In any case, the prospect of this party — to which he had been pointedly *not* invited — filled Jeff with loathing and nausea.

All morning long he had done nothing but stare diagonally across the room at Wendy, so demure in her green jumper with the red tights. From the angle where he sat, Jeff could see inside the bib front of her jumper where a little mound of budding breast swelled beneath her white cotton turtleneck. The sight of it made him half-mad with a desperate yearning he could not quite account for. He had started out the year with no more interest in girls than in math. For the last several months, however, since Wendy had moved her desk to its present site, Jeff had slowly begun to acquire an interest in Wendy Waldbaum that seemed, at times, utterly consuming.

He would haunt the corner across the street from her building at 85th and Park and try to guess which of the 400-odd windows on each side belonged to her apartment. One Saturday, he waited six hours — hiding behind the trash bins in the alley of a catholic school across Park Avenue — for Wendy to emerge from the canopied entrance, just to confirm that she had an existence beyond P.S. 6. But she never did appear, and Jeff subsequently learned that she had been skiing in Vermont with her parents that whole weekend.

Then, one abnormally mild afternoon in February when everyone was lining up in the playground to return to class from recess, Jeff found himself paired with the black-haired, brown-eyed, inexpressibly beautiful Wendy and, on an impulse that he would rue for weeks, reached for her hand, leaned close to her ear (her hair smelled like the florist's shop on 83rd Street), and whispered, "I love you."

She recoiled from him, not reproachfully, but with a look of pained bewilderment on her face, those dark eyes searching every inch of him as though she were trying to understand how he fit together, and then she said, quietly, in a voice that was not unkind, "But I don't love you." The three flights of stairs from the playground to the classroom were the longest climb of his life. But what really confused him was that she continued to hold his hand the whole way up, as though consoling him for his terrible humiliation. His love for her, therefore, not only went on undimmed but reached a new and blinding degree of intensity.

And so, having overheard the demoralizing details of Lee Talbot's upcoming birthday bash, and having spent the morning in a torment of gazing and longing, Jeff bought two hot dogs with "moostahrokrot" from the Sabrett man and then headed toward the Metropolitan Museum of Art a block away, to look at the old swords and armor and to try out his Mooski routine on one of the guards.

In the days before art began competing with showbiz, department stores and bigtime sports for the tourist dollar, the Metropolitan Museum of Art would be well nigh deserted late on a dreary Friday afternoon in March, especially the great, gloomy, Gothic hall where the white and black knights perpetually faced off, lances bristling, on rearing plaster-of-Paris chargers. It was here, among the echoes of chivalry, that Jeff found his captive audience, a nervous young Negro security guard, so thin that his uniform looked as stiff and bulky as a suit of armor, and with a downy mustache which, contrary to its intended effect, actually made him look younger than his 21 years.

"Hello, guardski. I am Mooski Toffski Offski, official Russian tourist, from Babooski, Sovietski. Could you tellski meski which way to the mumski?"

"Say what?" the guard said.

"Mumski, deadski."

When the guard still failed to understand, Jeff lay down at his feet on the marble floor, crossed his hands over his chest and sucked in his cheeks to convey the idea of ghoulish emaciation.

"You can't do that here," the guard said. "Come on, get up."

So, Jeff got up and began circling the guard in a lurching, limping gait, dragging one leg stiffly and holding both arms out as he had seen various types of the undead do in a host of movies.

"Tana leaves!" Jeff croaked hoarsly. "I must have my tana leaves . . . !"

"If you don't go away, I'm gonna have to call my supervisor."

Jeff added a disgusting snorfling noise to the act, a sound halfway between a rooting pig and a man dying of tuberculosis.

"Get out my face, boy!" the guard finally exploded in exasperation.

Jeff loped across the great hall crying "sanctuary!" and disappeared through an arched portal into the world of the high Renaissance. He counted the tryout a resounding success, and thus cheered up, made his way through the art of the ages back toward the main entrance. Just short of the lobby, he paused to visit the reconstructed tomb of the Pharaoh. The exhibit was set up so that one entered a narrow stone passageway enscribed with hieroglyphics, taken from a real mummy's tomb, and thus experience what it must have been like for the art plunderers who emptied the great troves of Egypt. Jeff liked it especially for the accoustics. It enhanced the effect of any of the accents he was proficient in —

Mooski, Dracula, Quasimodo, Walter Winchell, Amen-ho-tep. He stepped under the lintel guarded by a bas-relief of the jackel-headed god Anubis, and had only taken a few steps when he detected the echo of somebody weeping within.

It frightened him for a moment, until he remembered that he was not in a real mummy's tomb, but a museum in the middle of the biggest city in the world, and then, curiosity bolstered, he advanced down the passageway and turned a corner. There, in her camel hair coat, face to the hieroglyph-covered wall, was Wendy Waldbaum. Having gazed at her from so many rearview angles that he knew the back of her head as well as her face, Jeff recognized her at once. Uncertain what to do, afraid to reach out and touch her, yet unwilling to skulk quietly away, he decided the most polite thing would be to clear his throat.

"Ahem...."

Wendy glanced furtively over her shoulder at him, her face swollen with misery.

"What's wrong?" Jeff asked.

But seeing him only added indignity to her anguish. She tore herself away from the wall, wedged past him in the narrow corridor (he could smell her tears), and ran out of the tomb. Jeff did not follow. His own emotions were in a tumult, and he sensed somehow that to inflict himself on her would only make matters worse. When he emerged from the tomb, she was not in the lobby; when he left the museum, she was nowhere to be seen on Fifth Avenue or 82nd Street; and when he returned to Mrs. Snipes's class at one o'clock, she was absent from her seat and did not reappear.

During the course of that afternoon — an hour of geography in which Lee Talbot held forth smarmily on the wonders and virtues of the state of Texas, and a final hour of the detested fractions — Jeff slowly came to the conclusion that whatever had driven Wendy Waldbaum to the mummy's tomb in tears and desolation was directly attributable to that lumbering, toothy, would-be Texan whose initials were L.T. They burned themselves into Jeff's brain like a smoldering brand. When the bell rang at five minutes to three, and the boys and girls put on their coats and lined up, Jeff had half a mind to push Talbot down the stairwell. But he refrained, and also checked an impulse to shove Talbot in front of a Madison Avenue bus, once they got out on the sidewalk. After all, Jeff tried to reason logically, he ought to make sure that the big jerk really was to blame before doing anything that might land him in the electric chair.

After school, he returned to the museum, thinking that perhaps Wendy might be hiding in another part of it. But though he searched the place high and low — from the 17th Century bedchambers in the most obscure corner of the American wing, to a sepulchral gallery of Etruscan sarcophogi in the ground floor, rear — he encountered no sign of her. Still trying to puzzle the matter out, he returned briefly to the hall of antique weaponry and savored a vision of the havoc that a thirty-pound iron mace could wreak on the person of Lee Talbot. He imagined Talbot hacked with a halberd, cleaved in twain with a battle-axe, blind-sided with a broadsword, and shot with so many crossbow bolts that he looked like a porcupine.

On his way out, Jeff crossed paths with the thin, Negro security guard again.

"No trouble, you," the guard warned him, sternly pointing an index finger.

Jeff just smiled.

He got home to the apartment on 79th Street between Park and Madison at four-thirty. His parents were going to the theater that night.

"Not *The Sound of Music*, I hope," Jeff remarked to his mother as he ransacked the kitchen cabinets for a snack.

"No, *The Threepenny Opera*," she informed him. "Say, what's wrong with *The Sound of Music*, incidentally?"

"Mom, it's the stupidest play on Broadway. Only a complete moron would go see it."

"The Strombers adored it."

"They must have brain damage, then."

"Jeffery!"

"Promise me you'll never go see it."

"Don't you think six oreos are enough, young man?" She took the package away from him and put it back in the cabinet. "Alma's coming over to cook your dinner and to . . . to . . ."

"Go ahead, say it."

" . . . to be with you."

"To babysit, you mean. Yaagghh! I'm eleven years old, for crying out loud. I'm going to be twelve in September!"

"We can't leave you here alone, darling."

"Why not? Whaddaya think I'm going to do? Burn the building down —?"

"I don't have time for this, I don't have time," she chanted in a not-entirely-playful sing-song. "Look, we'd just worry about you, okay. Starting in September, no more babysitters. I promise."

"Promise you won't go see *The Sound of Music.*"

"I swear by all that's holy, I will not see that abominable play, ever. Happy?"

"I've got a lot on my mind, Mom," Jeff muttered and shuffled out of the kitchen.

There were three phones in the apartment. The one Jeff customarily availed himself of was in the den that doubled as a guest room. Here, his father kept all his tennis trophies and the reference books they needed to complete the crossword puzzle in the Sunday *Times.* The room was paneled in dark wood and its single window thickly draped. Jeff liked it for many of the same reasons that he liked the mummy's tomb in the museum — it was easy to forget you were in the middle of the biggest city in the world.

Though he had already done this once or twice before, Jeff looked up the name Waldbaum in the Manhattan telephone directory. 83 of them were entered, but only one of them, a Harvey Waldbaum, was listed at 1014 Park Avenue, the very building Jeff had staked out from behind the catholic school's ash cans, and so Jeff had every reason to believe that the seven-digit number printed beside Harvey Waldbaum's name could feasibly connect him, via the magic of electricity, to the object of his heart's desire. He held the telephone handset until it was clammy with sweat and the dial tone turned into an angry klaxon, like an air-raid siren. He slammed the receiver down, breathing shallowly, his mouth as dry as a mummy's. He repeated this bungling operation almost a dozen times, having gotten as far as the sixth digit once before chickening out.

At six o'clock, his mother barged into the den, looking quite lovely in a dark skirt, shimmering blue silk blouse and pearls, with a fur coat over her arm.

"I'm meeting Daddy for drinks at the Edwardian Room, pussycat," she said and stopped to kiss him on the forehead. "Say, are you all right?"

"Sure, I'm all right."

"Alma's here."

"Hot diggity dog."

"Who are you trying to call?"

"I'm not *trying* to call anyone," he said irritably. "If I wanted to call someone, I'd call."

"I suppose so," his mother agreed with a sigh. "Well, 'bye, darling."

She floated out of the room on a stately cloud of *Joy de Patou.* As soon as the door closed behind her, Jeff snatched the phone back out of its cradle and dialed all seven digits. The first ring at the other end had as much terrifying potency as the whine of the dentist's drill before he inserts the tip in an inflamed tooth. The second ring seemed to physically scramble Jeff's brain and he doubted he would even be able to speak when someone answered, let alone remember his name. By the third ring he had entered a psychological wasteland as vast and empty as the Sahara desert, where there is no hope for the stranded wayfarer, nor any hope of hope. But, on the fourth ring, a strange rapture of almost religious dimension began to well inside him. And on the fifth ring, practically delirious with relief, Jeff toppled back into the yielding cushions of the convertible sofa. Nobody was home. Most particularly, Wendy Waldbaum was not home. After that, he let it ring and ring and ring, gleefully allowing the phone to violate the silence of the empty Waldbaum apartment.

Alma the babysitter prepared Jeff's hamburger to his exact specifications ("burnt to a crisp on a buttered English muffin with velveeta melted on both halves") and gave him permission to take the sandwich into his room, as he requested. He turned on the TV. A program featuring candid interviews with movie stars, taped at their own Hollywood homes, was in progress. An oleaginous actor of the Latin persuasion, known for his portrayal of cads in second-rate feature films, was explaining his philosophy of matrimony at poolside. Jeff hurled objurgations at him in his Mooski accent. Meanwhile, a movie about romantic villainy starring Wendy Waldbaum and Lee Talbot began to flicker on one of the silver screens deep inside Jeff's head. He pictured Talbot taking Wendy out on the town: hamburgers and onion rings at Prexy's, where the food was delivered on electric trains; then the two of them at a Broadway show (the vile and execrable *Sound of Music* — he had no idea what it was about, so he imagined a stage full of clashing tympani, xylophones, bassoons, blaring horns, assorted screeching strings, like a symphony orchestra in the throes of a revolution); then Talbot escorting Wendy into F.A.O. Schwarz and flinging money at the obsequious clerks; finally, Talbot luring Wendy to the Metropolitan Museum of Art, seizing her by the shoulders and kissing her right on the mouth!

Jeff shook his head to disperse the horrifying fantasy. The actor on TV had been replaced by a woman dressed as a plumber selling drain cleaner. That had to be it, Jeff thought: Talbot had taken her to the museum that lunch hour and done something disgusting to her in the mummy's tomb!

After that, and for the next three hours, Jeff labored in a veritable blur of activity. First, he cut his leather briefcase up into strips, pointed at one end, and stapled these strips around the waistband of a pair of his summer camp shorts so that it ended up resembling something akin to a Roman foot-soldier's battle tunic. Next, he carefully clipped the collar off one of his blue oxford button-down shirts, cut off the sleeves just above the cuffs, and scissored the remaining sleeves into long fringes. Finally, the *piece de resistance,* he chopped the brim off one of his father's hats, fashioned two great horns out of shirt cardboards, and fastened them to the crown with tufts of colored yard hanging off the tips. By the time *The Twilight Zone* came on the air (a grim little tale featuring Mickey Rooney as a washed-up, alcoholic ex-jockey living in a miserable furnished room and waiting for the Angel of Death to knock on his door — it finally appears in the guise of a nine-year-old girl), Jeff stood before the full-length mirror in full regalia. The effect was impressive. At eleven o'clock, promptly, Alma came to his room and told him to get ready for bed, and for the first time in several years, to her vast astonishment, Jeff did not utter a peep of protest.

On Saturday morning, his father invited him to come along on a ride to Mamaroneck to inspect a sailboat he was thinking of buying, and to his father's surprise Jeff begged off, citing a "report" on dinosaurs he had to get done for school by Monday. "I could get left back," Jeff explained gravely, and his father agreed that he had better see to it, then.

At one o'clock, his mother went off to do the galleries on Madison Avenue and meet one of her fellow-mothers for lunch at a French place. As soon as he heard the elevator door close, Jeff changed into his costume. He could tell by looking out the window at the pedestrians bundled up on 79th Street that it was another blustery day out, so he put on his ski pajamas under the fringed shirt and battle tunic. He decided it looked even better that way. Finally, he helped himself to one of his mother's raincoats, a plain tan poplin model that came down to his ankles, thus concealing his warrior's outfit. He stuck his horned helmet in a Bloomingdale's bag and left the apartment.

At 78th Street, he ducked into the candy and newspaper store and purchased a pair of those plastic eyeglasses that come complete with bushy eyebrows and a fake nose. He put these in the shopping bag with his helmet. To avoid any chance encounter with his mother, he swung over to Fifth Avenue and began the trek downtown, walking on the Central Park side of the street. He reached his destination by two o'clock. From his seat on a stone bench in front of the Pulitzer fountain on 59th Street, Jeff could surreptitiously observe all those who entered the F.A.O. Schwarz toy store diagonally across the street. The Grand Army Plaza swarmed with college men checking their watches as they waited for their dates. The horse-drawn cabs were lined up in seedy splendor along 59th Street, and though Jeff wanted desperately to go over and pet the horses, he made himself stay on the bench and watch the toy store entrance. Time crept by with agonizing slowness. One hour. Two. Several people sat down on the other end of Jeff's bench, lingered awhile to watch the passing spectacle, then left. One of these was an elderly gentleman, fastidiously attired in a worn brown overcoat and shiny brown brogans.

"Say," Jeff asked him, "do you happen to know what time the matinees of the Broadway shows get out on Saturday?"

The old man shrugged his shoulders.

"Have you seen *The Sound of Music* by any chance?" Jeff inquired further.

The old man shook his head.

"Don't go, even if someone gives you free tickets. It stinks."

"You are a critic?" the old man spoke for the first time, his voice thick with the dialect of Eastern Europe. Hearing it had an electrifying effect on Jeff.

"You are Sovietski?" he asked excitedly.

The old man recoiled, wincing.

"Sovietski!" Jeff insisted. "Sovietski Ruski, like meski: Mooski Toffski Offski!"

The old man got up off the bench, spat on the ground, and walked stiffly away. Jeff would have felt chagrined by the encounter, but he had hardly fastened his gaze back on the entrance of F.A.O. Schwarz when whom should he spy before its bountiful windows but Lee Talbot, all dressed up in a tie and Chesterfield coat, hair plastered slickly down, along with a handful of schoolmates, all of them led by Talbot's towering, cigar-chomping father. Jeff got up anc crept over behind a chestnut peddler's smoking pushcart. He was already shivering with anticipation.

The Talbot party remained in F.A.O. Schwarz for more than a half hour, then emerged absolutely loaded down with boxes and bags. They mustered briefly at the corner, then started north up Fifth Avenue, Talbot's companions burdened like native bearers on an African safari. Jeff followed them stealthily up the Central Park side. In a little while, they turned into a canopied entrance between 64th and 65th. Jeff waited fifteen minutes, then crossed Fifth Avenue and approached the doorman, an imposing figure in his gilt-frogged green uniform.

"Is this where Lee Talbot's birthday party is?" Jeff asked in his most retarded-sounding voice.

"7-E," the doorman said gruffly and let Jeff in. The elevator was down a long, carpeted corridor lined with gilded, marblized mirrors, far fancier than his own building. Jeff turned up his collar. The elevator operator was an ancient, white-haired Irishman whose head was permanently cocked to one side by arthritis. He was not much taller than Jeff.

"Seven," Jeff told him in a firm, rather froggy fake voice.

"Goin' ter see the birthday boy, are ye? Got yer present?"

Jeff hoisted up the bag to show.

"He come in through here a little while ago like the Aga Khan," the elevator man muttered acidly. "Well, here we are, sonny."

Jeff stepped out into the seventh floor hallway, his heart racing. The door to 7-E was directly across from the elevator, and the elevator man waited for him to ring the doorbell. Sounds of merriment could be heard within. Jeff thought he would have a heart attack waiting for the elevator man to get lost. He turned and smiled.

"Yer a shy little lad, aren't ye?"

Jeff nodded his head. Just then, the elevator buzzer sounded and the old man was constrained to depart, leaving Jeff alone in the hall. When he was gone, Jeff raced frantically around the hall trying to find the fire stairs, then ducked inside. Panting with fear, he removed his raincoat and dumped it on the landing. He put on the helmet and magic eyeglasses, took a deep breath, and went forth to the door of the Talbot apartment, ringing the bell for two full seconds. Footsteps on a hardwood floor could be heard within. The door swung open, held by a glamorous blonde in a puffy skirt. Far beyond her, amid heaps of paper and cardboard boxes, and a table laden with cake and sodas, was Lee Talbot in a blue metallic pointed party hat that made him look like the world's richest pinhead. He was surrounded by his fawning cronies.

"Why, look Lee, another one of your friends is here," the woman announced brightly, then said to Jeff, "What a cunning costume."

Jeff stalked past her, ignoring the compliment, until he was ten feet away from the great horseshoe of sofas where Talbot and his friends were assembling his booty of new playthings. Talbot's mouth tried to form a smile, but it was a cracked, uncertain thing.

"Who is it?" he asked timidly.

"It is Mooski Toffski Offski," Jeff replied, his voice growing louder and more shrill with every syllable, "Sultan of Bungwah, Caliph of Poona, Archduke of Soodna and Tsarovitch of the Imperial Russian realm. I have come to take my vengeance!"

"It's Greenaway!" Bobby Bedrosian cried.

In a matter of perhaps fifteen seconds, an interval that would live in his memory and imagination as an eternity, Jeff bounded around the room amid cries and shrieks and alarms and the original cast recording of *The Sound of Music* — which just happened to be playing on the hi-fi — grabbing Talbot's birthday presents, his chemistry set, his gleaming new brass alcohol-fired miniature steam engine, his microscope kit, his electric train, his upgraded slot-car set, his telescope, his electric football game, his Frank Nitti machine gun, his drum set, his plastic models of the U.S.S. Enterprise and the Cutty Sark, et cetera, et cetera, et cetera, and to the horror of all present, most particularly Lee Talbot, began hurling these things against the rose-colored walls of the apartment, concluding with the upending of an eleven-pound marzipan-bedizened birthday cake right on top of the stupified Talbot's pointy-hatted head.

Of course, he tried to get away via the fire stairs, but he was nabbed by Talbot's father before he could make it back out the front door.

The ensuing 36 hours were glum and embarrassed ones for the Greenaway family, his parents left to try to explain their offspring's deplorable conduct — and to settle for damages before the courts were notified. All tolled, it ended up costing Jeff's father in excess of $300, the same day he had shelled out $1,000 on the down payment for a 25-foot motor-sailer. Jeff remained sequestered in his bedroom, visited, at first, only by silent adults bearing food trays. But he remained strangely placid throughout the ordeal. Deep inside, his heart throbbed with glory. He accepted the possibility that his parents might disown him and he even made plans for running away to Iowa, a state whose products, history and waterways were familiar to him. He figured that he could learn all the words to the state song on his way out there, and that it would help him get into the better sort of orphan asylum.

Then, early Sunday evening, his father came to see him, sitting on the edge of the boy's bed while Jeff hugged his knees in his padded swivel desk chair.

"Why did you do it, son?"

"Love," Jeff said.

"What did he say?" Jeff's mother asked her husband when he returned wearily to their bedroom.

"He says, 'love.' "

"Love? What could he possibly mean by that?"

"I don't know," Jeff's father sighed. "Well, he's eleven. That's almost a person."

Somewhat later, Jeff's father went back and told his son what had been decided:

"We're sending you to a special private school next year," he said quietly, "where you have to wear a uniform and they make you work very, very hard."

The cloud over Jeff took an exceedingly long time to lift. Suspicion and recrimination lingered for weeks, not only within his family but among his schoolmates. The story of his crazed exploit was the talk of the upper grades at P.S. 6; and even among the children, whose sense of acceptable comportment is highly elastic, he was treated a little standoffishly, as though he were a walking bomb that might go off at the slightest provocation.

Then one day in early May, it began raining buckets five minutes after the boys and girls were let out for the noon recess. The auditorium, therefore, was opened up and very shortly filled to capacity. Mr. Peevis, a fourth-grade teacher on recess duty, soon organized a rainy-day talent show, and Barry Goldblatt led it off at the piano with a rendition of "My Favorite Things," a song from (unbeknownst to Jeff) *The Sound of Music.* He was followed by Bobby Bedrosian ("Life Is Just a Bowl of Cherries") on the cornet, and Richard Schnabel, who had added a whole program of wild animal cries to his formidable repertoire of birdcalls. A newcomer, Raymond Hosner, tried to sing "I'm a Yankee Doodle Dandy" but forgot the words; Esther Grubka related the heartwarming saga of her family's recent audience with the Pope; and Joseph Fucci, prime candidate for the soon-to-be-vacated role of official 6th-grade dork, performed a dance that had to be stopped by Mr. Peevis on account of incipient lewdness. It was at this juncture, with seven minutes left to the bell, that Jeff took his turn.

He peered at the audience from the cleft behind the heavy velour curtain, then stepped out to the forestage. A thrill of recognition crackled across the audience, not necessarily of the approving kind.

"I am Mooski Toffski Offski . . ." he declared loudly. A great roar of laughter swept up at him like a warm, friendly breeze and drowned him out. The younger children especially squirmed in their seats with delight. While they laughed, Jeff duckwalked up and down the apron of the stage, as he had seen Groucho Marx do in several movies. This too provoked gales of laughter. He noticed Lee Talbot get up and leave. When the noise subsided, he told a joke about the kamikaze pilot who signs up for tango lessons. The audience ate it up, even though they laughed in the wrong places. He followed this with a dramatic vignette out of *The Untouchables,* Jeff acting out the voices of all the principal characters himself: Elliot Ness, Big Al Capone, Frank ("The Enforcer") Nitti, a flapper. This earned laughs throughout and a smattering of applause. He wrapped up the routine with a joke about Adolf Hitler meeting Superman in heaven. The cheers and clapping that followed would have guaranteed him an encore, but the bell rang and the children were instructed to line up by class.

Jeff climbed down from the stage and fought his way up the aisle to his classmates. En route, many of the other children slapped his back or touched him, saying things like, "Nice goin', Mooski." He was still in a daze when he felt someone take his hand and looked to his left to discover Wendy Waldbaum beside him.

"You were great," she said.

Mr. Peevis yelled at everyone to start marching out of the auditorium. Wendy held his hand all the way up the stairs. His heart fluttered inside his chest like a bird in a cage. On the third floor landing, Wendy leaned over and whispered in his ear, "Meet me at the museum after school."

"Where?"

"You know where."

He remained in a transport the rest of the afternoon, oblivious to the recital of state capitals, the voyages of Ferdinand Magellan and the boggle of fractions. For two hours, the highly musical name *Wendy Waldbaum* reverberated through his skull like the notes of a heavenly choir. At five minutes to three the bell rang and Mrs. Snipes's class filed downstairs to the exit.

It had stopped raining. Jeff waited on the corner of 82nd Street thinking that he and Wendy might walk the block up to the museum together, that perhaps she would like to hold his hand again. But she paid no attention to him and skipped uptown on Madison with a crowd of her female classmates. Jeff considered the possibility that she had been playing a practical joke on him earlier, but his life had grown so consistently absurd in recent months that he felt immune to further disgrace. So, he walked up to the museum alone and went directly to its heart, the mummy's tomb.

Twelve minutes later, when he had given up all hope and was about to leave, she came to him. Her eyes, her mouth, the little brown mole on her cheek, seemed to him utterly original elements of beauty, previously unknown on the planet Earth.

"I heard about what you did at Lee Talbot's party," she began directly.

"Oh . . .?" Jeff replied, gazing into the stone floor and mulling over the costly escapade. A moment later he looked up at Wendy and, a smile spreading across his face, said, "It was great. It was worth it. You should have been there."

"You know why I was crying that day in here?"

"Because of him: Lee."

"No. My parents are getting divorced. I found out the night before."

"Oh . . . ? Oh, God. Divorced —"

"It's okay. Well, it's *not* okay. But *I'm* okay now. Only, we're moving, my mom and me, to a whole new state."

"Not Iowa by any chance?"

"Connecticut."

"Oh. I've been there."

"It's real New Englandy."

For quite a while neither of them said anything.

"My parents are sending me to this special punishment school next year," Jeff finally broke the silence.

All of a sudden, he felt her incredibly warm body press against him. His spine touched the wall as her lips touched his, soft and slippery, her hair like flowers. Jeff's heart seemed to fly up to his throat, then out of his very body.

"Hey," he said breathlessly when she pulled away, "do you want to run away with me and move to Iowa?"

"What's in Iowa?"

"Oh, it's great there, Wendy," Jeff told her, taking her hand and leading her out of the mummy's tomb. "They've got corn, soybeans, oats. The state flower is the wild rose. I'm learning the state song now. Herbert Hoover was born there."

Dorianne Laux

Skipping Stones

I was thirteen the summer the family went to visit
Grandma Laux in Oregon. We passed her place three times
before we finally saw her, running
down the middle of the street in her house slippers screaming
"This is it, park the damn thing."
She was still alone at sixty-five and the neighbors
thought she was crazy; sitting at the attic window, her angora cat slopped
over the sill, typing up her autobiography.

I learned to skip stones at Miller's Pond. Grandma's nephew showed
me how to sift the low slope of bedrock and choose
only the flatest smoothest stones. His loose arm
shot over the shallow part of the pond a million times
that summer. At dusk I would watch his silhouette ripple,
his curved wrist scythe
the air between the water and the scooped out moon.

On the last day of our vacation I waited while he hit
every drug store on the outskirts of town. He finally
showed up, with a thin smile and a rubber. His face was flushed
with the heat and I was nervous, but when he opened
the door to his basement bedroom it was cool and smelled
like wood shavings and Testor paints. He kept his pants on
just in case, and when I lifted my best dress carefully,
not to wrinkle it, he giggled and I closed my eyes.

I will always wonder how we didn't hear
the car, or the footsteps on the ancient stairs.
I do know that the look on my father's face
and the beating that came after killed
any ideas I had about romance.

Eighteen years and as many lovers later, we stand on the edge
of Coniston Water skipping stones. Every day this vacation
I have been moody and distant; every night we've come
into a new town too late and had to struggle
with our bags up three flights of stairs to the small
attic flats where you fall on the bed exhausted and I set up

my portable typewriter, rinse out my angora sweater
and hang it over the window sill to dry.

When the only sound is the skipping of stones, I tell you
I'm beginning to like it:
these small one windowed rooms with a view. You had given up
on romance until now, when you point to the ringed water and tell me
this is what your heart does every time I touch you.

It would be simple, in the moonlight, to say nothing
and reach for your hand. Instead I ask you to show me again,
how to arc a stone into the middle of the lake so that it sounds
like stabbing a watermelon.

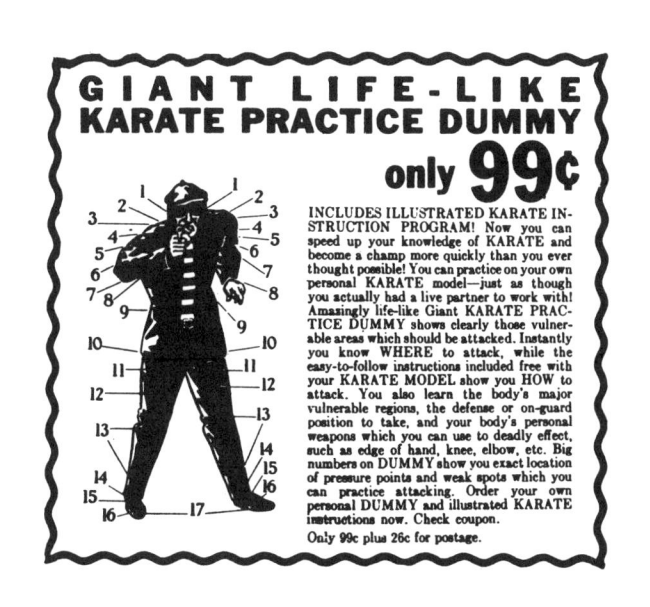

GIANT LIFE-LIKE
KARATE PRACTICE DUMMY
only 99¢

INCLUDES ILLUSTRATED KARATE INSTRUCTION PROGRAM! Now you can speed up your knowledge of KARATE and become a champ more quickly than you ever thought possible! You can practice on your own personal KARATE model—just as though you actually had a live partner to work with! Amazingly life-like Giant KARATE PRACTICE DUMMY shows clearly those vulnerable areas which should be attacked. Instantly you know WHERE to attack, while the easy-to-follow instructions included free with your KARATE MODEL show you HOW to attack. You also learn the body's major vulnerable regions, the defense or on-guard position to take, and your body's personal weapons which you can use to deadly effect, such as edge of hand, knee, elbow, etc. Big numbers on DUMMY show you exact location of pressure points and weak spots which you can practice attacking. Order your own personal DUMMY and illustrated KARATE instructions now. Check coupon.

Only 99¢ plus 26¢ for postage.

Sydney Lea

Reckoning

Minus twenty-five outside. Second
month, third day. Inside my child it's one
hundred and three. For five straight nights this
torrid thing (or things) has wandered in
my girl at will, and I therefore will
magic on the hand that wanders on
her forehead, my own. Perspiration
in its coursing seems so odd in this
unmoving weather. I remember
hearing of a child who crashed through ice
while skating our Unami River,
the father or mother only one
field away, which was one too many
to call back the body: remote, gray
newspaper story. And yet it chilled.
One field too many. The body is
so full of many things, I'm frozen
here before it, praying for a lull:
crudely, like a man, so like a man
to exercise his fascination
with figures, to take measures, helpless
though he be: helpless — so myth has it —
as a woman. That old myth: *And which
of you by being anxious can add
one cubit to his span of life?* O,
it's not my life, but hers. I'd gladly
die. I start the thankless blasphemous
act of self-distraction: counting hairs
upon her head. I fail at forty,
I for whom the grayest terror is
profusion. If I still can number
it, it's not beyond me. I begin
again, despite the Christian doctor's
copious assurance, spendor of
ice crystals on her window at dawn
like so many amulets against
catastrophe, making of her room
a rainbow; or, outside, like soldiers,
jays who squabble over scattered seed

in sequenced shrieks. Morning takes over,
stars retreating, and the sky diffused
in the undifferentiated
blue-near-gray of twenty years ago.
We gathered in the parking lot ten
floors from great uncle in a tower
— head bald as a snowman's dented with
his knowledge, age, and hot with fever —
quaking in the hospital, while I
counted storeys, counted a hundred
autos bright with snowflakes, tried to count
the beds within the building: number
of rooms by number of floors . . . The wards
confused me, prolix, gray with patients.
Everything appeared to multiply
past my computation — exotic
tears that all my elders were crying,
remarks that, flown, kept falling:
"Uncle does nothing," said my mother,
"but tell his own telephone number,
over and over." Somebody said,
"Yesterday he made as if to knit,
calling out the stitches and the purls!"
O, he was sinking . . . Heads bowed, motors
caught, the family disappearing now
into the incalculable throng
on the freeway. And my father, soon
to disappear himself, womanly
laying a hand upon my mother's
head, and mine. My sisters were rebuked
for "trooper's language," in their mouths so
bizarre. We were home. Tiny figures
in an ordinary tragedy.
"Still, count your blessings," each one of us
was told. And I counted all night long.
The rows of fissures in the plaster;
headlamps coursing in upon the walls
in squares; the radiator's protests,
regular, inside. These summoned me

back from all that terrified outside,
without degree or limit — tower-
tall, field-wide, and more, immeasurably —
but were no blessing, for I wandered
in that undecipherable maze,
the *idea* of the body, wherein
my cells were like my uncle's making
headway undetected; like the boy's
who drowned in that far childhood river.
Or was it a girl? I couldn't then
remember, much less now remember,
life at eighteen was already sunk
in myths and questions without number.
Why, I wondered, was I born? And why,
once born, did I turn out a man? I
put hands upon myself, but gently.
Every seed, so I had heard it said,
like every bird is tallied: nothing
falls but is accounted for somewhere.
I mark my daughter's fiery breathings.
What keeps me wakened here will keep me
present at the bed of my own seed . . . .
I feel my breasts like a mother's start
to fall, I reckon all the bristles
graying on my face. I count the charms
that I've invented in my vigil:
utterance unnumbered, ignorance
manifold as beatings of our hearts,
once to summon one loved soul from harm.

D. Leitman

An Affair, I Guess

I am working on the theory (unproved) that I love you. You make me laugh because you keep dropping your keys. Your hair grows commas along the back of your neck. And there's a question mark too. Soon my diligence will lead to a new problem, the corollary theory that you love me. When I don't see you, I forget many things.

There you are, licking my breast. How small the world is growing, to cunt-size. Come, unfold your prick. You're pushing my thighs apart. I could do that myself, but it's so much nicer when you do it. Take charge. Charge.

Not yet. First you will turn me over. This is the way doggies and horsies do it, boys and girls. And houseflies and camels and gnus. Dinosaurs did it this way when they were doing it. You nip at the back of my neck, you enter me, you withdraw. I'm trembling and sighing. Now you're turning me over again. Maybe I'm being barbecued, I'm burning for sure. You grapple with my clitoris, make my cunt contract. Your tongue declares itself and, as it does, you swing your body round and offer your prick my mouth. On this exotic matter I chew without teeth, I am so happy I could die, let me die now. You take the prize away, put mouth on mouth to pour my cunt juice into me again, wrong end on purpose. Please, I've lost my body, I'm all cunt, come inside.

You stab at me, slick road, you've missed the opening, I grab your prick and show it where to go. You slide in me up to your nonexistent hips, I exhale loudly. But no, you pull away, uncork me. I'm hissing like an old radiator. One of your hands holds my wrists together on pillows above my head. Unassisted, your prick sniffs out my cunt. You'll have it your way, on your own, and so you do. This entry makes me gasp. My dance card's full. You're moving in and out, I'm wrists and cunt you've pinned. Your fingers buff my clitoris, I ring and wring your prick with muscles I've acquired for that purpose. You're riding now, I'm being ridden, my toes are pointing east and west, spread-eagle ballerina. You're in no hurry, you detour here and there, I think I'm going crazy. We ride for miles, desert and oasis, an arching bridge, the West Side highway. I'm dreaming that I'm talking. I see your eyes see mine. We climb a hill, we're over treetops, there's a star or circling satellite. There's no more place to go. One of us is moaning, I can't tell which.

We're lying side by side. You want to know if I believe in God.

You're telling me your wife's name, which isn't Carmen or Mary Sue. I'll have to memorize it. You want to see a picture of my husband; I show you what I've got, my driver's license and a Band-Aid. You suck my teeth. You say you have to be going. You do, by the way, believe in God, even if I don't.

How We Met

I was looking for someone to pay attention and you did. I reminded you of a girl from your childhood, late adolescence, or so you said. You held me closer to the light, inspected me. Your gaze was wonderful, the rest of you was odd. I didn't know you were torturing me, bestowing your attention in order to withhold it later. You recommended coffee. Sex waited everywhere, even in your patience, but I didn't see it. I asked, How can I ever thank you? You said, looking up seriously from a depressed chair, You can go to bed with me. I laughed and stammered something, tried to make a joke of it. Your eyes, which can sometimes seem small as the eyes of a bear, bared nothing.

Weeks later I came back to see you. I think I know what I'm doing now, I said. You mentioned you had to find someone to reverse your shirt collars. He's strange, I thought. You said, My wife is charming but passionless, she just lies there. Exit cue for me, and I went out waving.

More time. I worked with the unreasoning endurance of an animal, which is why they're called dumb. My husband was kind, cruel, all-encompassing. He struggled with his life, I shook my head. He bent my arm, I cried. He went to work. In the new silence of the apartment, I saw that all I had was my own destruction.

Frightened, I called you up. Frightened, I came to see you. I thought I wanted order, honor, help. You offered me a fuck.

Now you're curled up naked on the white bed, talking, lighting a cigarette. I miss every third word because you whisper. Sometimes when I whisper to you, I can tell by your answer that you haven't understood me, either.

Why You're Sad

Because you're spent, you're overspent, life is seeping out of you, not from the prick, that miracle, but from your pores, your eyes, the dead cells of your fingernails. You have had and still have too many women. You long for sleep. Ghosts lie down with us in bed. Transparent naked women, some of them the same woman at different times, at different ages, observe our passion. There are too many women and you are keeping them all. The collection owns the collector. They weigh you down, they drag you down, they kill you with your children. The women are your ballast; without them, you fear, you'd drift away from earth. Wanting to stay, wanting to keep alive, you add me now, a plummet to an anchor. You're sad because you're getting the uncomfortable feeling that I love you.

Your Wife

She has dinner set out, porcelain and blood, and greets you in the kitchen with a chaste kiss. Your children have already met you at the door, crying. The youngest holds your hand as you kiss your wife. What's wrong, you ask, what's all this crying? They will tell you stories, they will let you be the judge. Your wife bending to open a low cabinet displays a great ass in jeans. You'd like to reach for it, but the children are explaining Occam's razor. What tragedies they deliver you try to measure. Your wife stands up, the ass that was so pretty tucks away. You send the children off to wash their hands — With lots of soap, you call — then stealthily, a cartoon wolf, you stalk her jeans. You hug her from behind, place unwashed hands on breasts, your stirring prick against the backside groove. She says, The children. You say, They're washing. She says, That doesn't take forever. You let her go. Half in apology, she kisses your mouth. Can she smell me there? Not over the tobacco and the Scotch. Why don't you take a quick shower, she suggests, and I'll keep dinner warm. Keep me warm, you say. You don't want to shower, you want to fuck her with your body still wearing our fuck. You want to link the women through yourself.

This idea compels you to pursue her. She runs, hands full of salad, to the dinner table, where the children play with salt. Don't do that, you say; and the children, thinking you mean them, stop playing.

You eat, you drink, you hold your children as if your love could keep them young. You kiss their foreheads when you say good night, a reed of parent over their breathing beds. You shower — I go down the drain — then stroll naked to the living room, where your wife untangles yarn for needlepoint. Or paints. Or sculpts. Or weaves hair baskets from your brush's gleanings. You ask her, Do you love me? Yes, she says, I do. Take off your clothes, you say. Not here, she says. Then where? you want to know. Let me bathe, she says. Don't bathe, you say. You're angry, she says.

Naked, you sit at your desk and stare at paper. She drapes your bathrobe over you. She kisses you the way you kiss the children.

She thinks in colors: the sofa will be blue, she'll have persimmon streaks across a pillow, the walls are beige, the walls of colors make her home. Your sex needs decorating.

I imagine this woman smaller than life. She is older than I am. So are you, so is my husband. Everybody is older than I am, though this won't always be true. Against that day I stroke clear cream into my pained expression.

My Husband

Has seen me crouching, ratlike, in our room. Has told me, Don't panic; sensing I'm about to run, and run blindly. I don't trust him anymore, he talks so well, he does so little. Refinement's costly. I need a winter coat. With you things are easier, I have never trusted you, not from the beginning.

My husband lives to waver, watches from the sidelines while others scramble, thinks being on the side is being up above and looking down. It's not. His eyes are beautiful and unmatched, his soul is flawless as a baby's. He blames me for his terrors. I'm drowning, I don't want him on top of me, it hurts too much. One breath, another.

He understands the concepts of rent and health insurance. He understands the word *please*. He thinks I'm hanging him, I think he's strangling me. The truth is not electric. Manners are better than nothing at all.

Fears
Your wife will take sex lessons. My husband will read what I'm writing. You'll die. You won't want to see me. I'll discover you aren't the one thing that's keeping me sane, you're the one thing that's driving me crazy.

Facts
I never wanted to have a baby. Bring life into despair? I knew my husband wouldn't be the father of my child. I swallowed pills, dammed up the cervix. I spat out sperm.

The first time you entered me, I wanted to have a baby with you. My husband needs a different woman, I need a different man.

Solutions
Your wife will conveniently develop terminal movie-star disease and die peacefully in two days. She'll feel no pain, only a flicker of surprise before the lights go out. My husband will die instantaneously in a plane crash, boom against a mountain, so I won't have to hurt him with my departure. He'll be pleasantly stoned at the time. You'll need someone to care for your children. Interview me. I'll learn to cook if you insist. We'll all live happily somehow.

And After That
You'll have other women. I'll meet you for illicit fucks even though we live together. You'll never know what I'm thinking. I'll never believe what you're saying. We'll be alive, we'll be alive.

But If Not
Then let's continue as we have until we stop. Put your prick in my mouth. I have to find an apartment because I'm leaving my husband. You have one finger in my cunt, one up my ass. I'm scored, I'm skewered, I'm screwed.

Lisa Lewis

History of a Partial Cure

There was one year, or maybe
It came to me suddenly,
When a past was all
I wanted, the mindlessness
Of childhood no longer
Enough to love. I am tough
Through my own hard work
At forgetting. Trouble
Is the core, made clear
By the contrast
Of my walk under the railroad
Bridge, now, at twenty-six,
Nothing more a threat nearby
Than construction sites
And their arrogant rivers
Of mud, with the dog day
Ten years ago when I hitchhiked
And knew better. Two men
Picked me up, I lied
About my age, and we three
Sat under a railroad bridge
And smoked. I wore
A puff-sleeved blouse, with tiny
Eyelets, no bra. One man
Said, "Why are some
Of those holes white inside
And some of them brown?"
I don't know why I liked that.
It's not as if I didn't know
I had nipples, not as if
I didn't know he could see.
Those men didn't touch me,
Though it's not as if
I could have stopped them,
Or would have. I can't help
What flattered me then,
But admitting this now
Is one way to make sure
I won't be dumb again.

*Go through it again.
It can't have changed much.
Trouble doesn't change.*
But it has, is changing
Now. Either I am wrong
Again or the past was not,
And everything, ridiculous
As it seems, is like
The toilet with the stopper stuck.
I could repair it that easily.

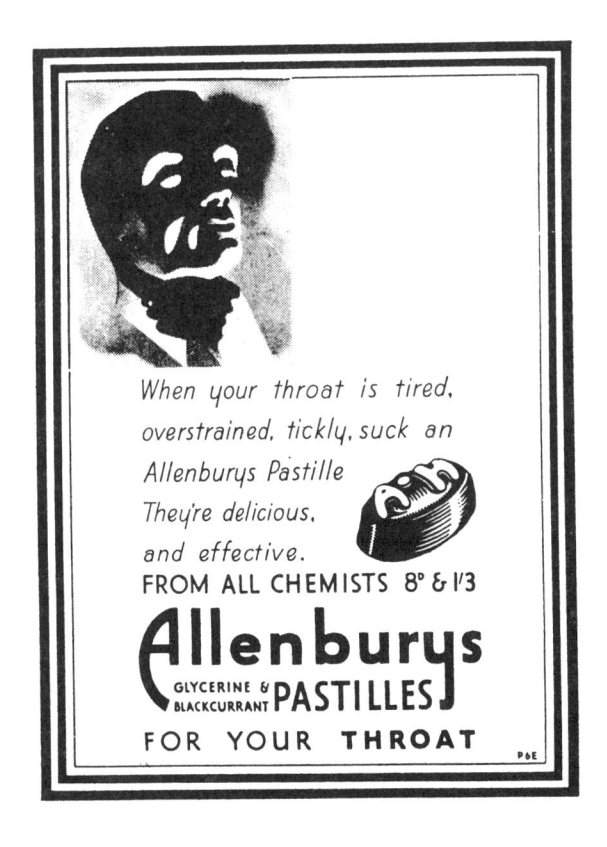

David Long

Great Blue

Paul's grandfather cut the engine and the boat drifted into a dark cove on the far side of the lake. It was a sweet late time. Paul was happy his grandfather had picked him to fish with tonight, and not let any of the other cousins come along. They were older than Paul, most of them, and they'd gone out with their grandfather dozens of times. They already knew how it was that the bats careening back and forth above the boat kept from colliding with your head. They knew about the glaciers that gouged out these lakes, they'd heard how Father Marquette traversed these woods around Lake Superior three-hundred-odd years ago . . . . Not that his grandfather seemed to feel obliged to pack every spare moment with grandfatherly wisdom. No, he could be a stony quiet, the cousins all knew, not to be budged with their best antics.

None of the other cousins lived more than a day's drive from camp, but Paul had come from out West on the airplane, alone. He'd only come once before, a rushed pilgrimage he and his mother had made at the tail end of last summer, a few clear days just cool enough for a jacket around suppertime. But it was hardly long enough. Everyone seemed lost in the work of closing things up for the year by then, and his mother was still coaching him on names by the time they left. Still, camp haunted him all winter . . . the lake, and the cabins spread along the edge of the pine woods, and all the people kin to him in one fashion or another, most of all, the grandfather he'd been named for. So this year his mother'd arranged for him to stay as long as he wanted, living with Aunt

Hallie, her next-youngest sister, and Uncle Ray, and their two girls. "Miss us, will you?" his mother had teased him in the car . . . now, out on the water, he did a little, but it was a feeling he could live with.

"You put me in mind of your mother," his grandfather said after a while. "You know, Paulie, I think of her best up here, when she was your age or thereabouts. One summer she wore long pants and a long flannel shirt with the cuffs snapped and a little blue cap, all day long, hot or no. Not a one of us could talk her out of it. She was so serious. And how we tried to get her into a swim suit . . . but no dice. I said, *Shirley, you afraid of poison ivy? Or yellowjackets? Something of that nature?* But no, it wasn't that."

Paul smiled and waited for his grandfather to finish, but he didn't.

"She swims a lot now," Paul offered finally.

His grandfather nodded. "Well, that summer," he said, "I don't know, I think she just wanted to be *prepared* . . . set for things. You're a little that way, too, are you?"

Paul stared down at the fishing tackle. He guessed maybe he was. He liked to know what he had to do . . . the flying by himself, for instance. They'd boarded him and a woman in a wheelchair first, and let him take a window seat, and he tried to act like it was nothing to fly. He watched the prairie for a while, but then the clouds thickened and he read the rest of the way. He'd saved his best book for the trip, *The Voyage of the "Dawn Treader,"* hid it in the back of his pajama drawer so he wouldn't know the whole thing by heart. He read it slowly, read a few pages over and over before going on. He pictured the "Dawn Treader" as it navigated a sunny stretch of ocean . . . and struck with no warning a patch of darkness, pictured the crew pulling that raggedy man from the water, who screamed for them to turn and fly back where they'd come from. *This is the island where dreams come true,* he told them. *Not daydreams: dreams.* Paul looked out at the tops of the clouds and considered what that would be like and it gave him a shiver. But he kept reading, and in the end, the story was beautiful and he managed to not be afraid.

He lifted their home-made anchor over the side of the boat and ran the rope through his fingers until the weight settled on the silty bottom. There were no cabins on this side of the lake. The firs reached the water's edge and the forest was heavily shadowed. The reeds at the shore rocked with the boat's last ripple.

Paul held his pole ready but waited for his grandfather to

make the first cast.

"I imagine this is the spot," his grandfather said. He sat in the stern, straight-backed, his eyes almost as drained of strong color as the sky, around each a bed of sharp creases. He wore a canvas cap with a long stained bill. Under it he was bald as a hen's egg. His arm drew back, his lure skipped once and sank near the reeds. The boy cast then and began reeling in, trying to copy his grandfather's patient whirl of the wrist. He hoped they'd get something, hoped it would be his grandfather who got it . . . but he wouldn't mind too much if they didn't. The mosquitoes hadn't found them yet. He heard the buzz of another boat far across the lake, but it was peaceful there in the cove as the light began to die.

Suddenly, just to one side of where he'd been staring, came an explosion of water and reeds and wingbeats, so startling him that his pole rang against the aluminum gunwale. A great bird rose and skirted the water, its wings dipping in long fluid strokes. The boy was transfixed.

"The great blue," his grandfather said. "Our heron. You've never seen it before?"

"I . . . no, I've heard them talking about it," Paul said. "I guess I never saw it close-up."

The bird leveled off just above the treetops. The boy watched it trace the outline of the lake . . . as if marking off its territory before dark, the sharp beak jutting out, the legs trailing down. He felt the goosebumps shoot down his legs and tried to smooth them away through his jeans. Minutes passed before he thought about fishing again. When he looked over at his grandfather, he saw that he'd been watching the heron too, and he was weeping.

There were always secrets at camp. Some were even his: once last summer, walking along the bluff above the big lake, he'd spotted Aunt Leah's oldest girl . . . Lara, with the shiny black hair . . . down on the rocks with a boy, seen her suddenly jump up in front of him and pull off her T-shirt and let him look at her, which Paul understood she'd never do back at camp, but he kept it to himself. Other secrets he glimpsed because the adults still felt free to talk in his presence — over a drink on the screened porch of his grandfather's cabin, called The Folly, or at the stove of Aunt Hallie's or Aunt Leah's: who'd broken her word, who Grampa Paul was going to have to lend money to, whose grown child was having mental problems. It didn't much bother him that he didn't get all they were saying . . . he was happy just to be there, happy to fit in as well as he did. And the cousins were friendly most of the time, only at rare times drawing back from him, as if to say there were still things he hadn't a right to yet. Some secrets he yearned to understand.

He slept on a pallet in the cabin's loft. Aunt Hallie and Uncle Ray had the bedroom, and the girls, Billie and Gwen, shared the hide-a-bed below him in the front room. Curled in his bag, he'd hear the soft-spoken tallying of the cribbage hands at the kitchen table, then the sounds of the game ending, and the last relations slipping off to their cabins. Someone would reach up and shut off the gas lanterns and they'd gutter for a moment then go quiet. In the dark, he'd hear the two girls whispering, sometimes breaking into talk or laughter loud enough to draw a muffled yell from Uncle Ray. Or he'd hear their bare feet slapping as one, then the other, got up to use the pot. Tonight their voices were different, though . . . hushed, pointed. He lay still, afraid to move his head against the railing.

" . . . only because he's dying," the boy heard.

"It's pretty weird," Billie said.

"Uncle Duff said they'd have to build the cabin over. It's all rotten underneath, it's so *old.*" She rolled over and the rest was swallowed by her pillow.

After a long silence, the older girl said, "I think it's *awful.*"

Outside, pine boughs grated on the gable screen. He didn't have any trouble sleeping at home. He'd read and next thing it would be morning and his book would be over on the bedstand with the page marked. But the dark was different at camp. It brought raccoons with red-glowing eyes and claws that scuttled across the porch boards. And wind flew down off Mt. Charles at night, whipping the lake up, leaving the shore strewn with foam. Men didn't use the pot, so if he couldn't stand it anymore, he'd talk himself down the stairs and back toward the outhouse. He'd never make it the whole way. He'd stop beyond the woodpile and go there, then, find himself looking up through the blowing limbs of the pines at the stars, so needle-bright and endless that he imagined himself falling out into them . . . until he'd look away and hurry back to the porch steps, hating himself for not being brave.

But now these worries vanished. He waited in the loft and thought: *Who's dying?* For a minute or two, his mind beat with wondering, then, just as suddenly, he was gone.

When he woke, the air in the loft was rich with cooking smells. At home, the mornings were frantic . . . his parents throwing themselves together for work, prodding him to get his belt on, get his teeth brushed, get his lunchbox. At camp, they let him be, so he didn't get up yet, resting happily and listening to the breakfast talk. He couldn't hear his Uncle Ray and guessed he'd gone into town early. Now and then, he caught Aunt Hallie through the clatter of the girls' voices. He liked how she sounded, a little slower and deeper than his mother. He rolled over and peered down at her through the railing. In her blue bathrobe, arms folded low at her waist, gazing beyond her daughters to the morning light in the front window, she looked almost exactly like his mother, he thought.

Just then, his grandfather came up the steps, stopped for a breath, and squinted through the screen door. Aunt Hallie and the girls looked up at once and their talk skipped a beat. As he made his way into the room, they seemed to part for him. Cousin Gwen got up, stuffing the last wedge of toast into her mouth, and gave him her chair at the dinette.

"How'd you sleep, Dad?" Aunt Hallie asked him.

He waved the question aside. Paul couldn't see his face, only the back of his head where wisps of hair stuck out from the cap and brushed the collar of his wool shirt . . . light as a dandelion gone to seed.

"Well, I see we have another good day," he said, not to any of them in particular.

"Yes, haven't we been lucky this year?" Aunt Hallie said.

Paul caught the change in her voice — his mother did that, too. He could always tell how well she knew someone by how cheerful her voice got. She saved the darker velvety sound for her family. Funny that Aunt Hallie was talking to her own father in such a voice, Paul thought. Maybe it was because he didn't hear well.

Then the room froze, as Paul remembered the words he'd overheard in the night . . . and knew what they meant. Daytime made it worse. Everything was plain to him and he couldn't say these were only terrible thoughts flung at him by the darkness. People died when they got old, he understood that. And after that, they went to heaven, his friend Lynette said. *All your family'll be waiting for you,* she told him over Monopoly one afternoon. She made it sound like a holiday dinner, everyone arranged around a huge table with tall candles and the best dishes and no empty chairs except the one he'd fill. Lynette acted like she was excited by the idea, but Paul wasn't sure, not at all.

"You wouldn't be so dumb about it if you went to Sunday school like you were supposed to," Lynette said, and he'd said they didn't do that in his family.

But a few days later, he'd gone and talked to his mother, out at the picnic table under the willow, and she'd looked right into his face and told him: *No one knows.* And when she said it this way, she made it sound mysterious and not to be feared. "Don't you think there's more going on than we can see?" she said, "Besides, Paulie, look how young you are, I don't want to think of you worrying yourself about all that." He remembered how she sat with him, not getting impatient, and how the gold light struck her face and how her hair streamed down like the willow branches.

Well, his grandfather was old, but not old like the old people he saw going to eat at the cafe near his house, or like Lynette's greatgrandmother who lived with them next door part of the year, who was born in the 1800's. Paul felt his face burning. *His parents really didn't know,* he thought. *And his grandfather didn't either.* He felt himself plummeting and grabbed the bars of the railing and squeezed them hard. He locked his eyes on his grandfather's figure below and imagined that he turned his face and smiled up at him, raising one of his soft hands in a greeting. *Come along, Paulie, you're one of us.*

But no, the room was alive and loud again. His grandfather was stirring his coffee listlessly, and Aunt Hallie was saying, "Our girls are walking down to the barrens this morning . . . Paulie, too, I guess."

"No!" Paul said aloud, though he'd only meant it as a thought.

Everyone turned and looked up at him. Aunt Hallie's mouth drooped open. "Paulie," she said. "Well, good morning." Her composure gathered again. "You don't have to go if you don't want to," she said. "But why don't you."

Paul hadn't meant he wouldn't go walking with them, but now that he thought about it, he knew he didn't want to. He didn't want to do anything.

"There's nothing to be afraid of," Billie said.

"You can look for arrowheads," Gwen said.

Paul could hardly talk. He'd gone numb. He dug under the sleeping bag for his clothes and slipped back out of sight to put them on. In a moment, the talk below resumed, as though he'd never broken it.

Aunt Hallie lifted the big tea kettle two-handed and poured steaming water over the breakfast dishes. Everyone had gone. Paul sat by the Franklin stove, paging through old *Field and Streams*, waiting for a break in her work. But she moved from job to job so smoothly that Paul finally went and stood by her as she drove the fine sand from the rag rug to the linoleum and out the door.

"It's a wonder we have a beach anymore," she said, an old camp joke.

"What's wrong with Grampa Paul?" Paul asked.

He had no idea what she'd say. Some things, his mother reminded him all the time, weren't any of his business.

"Here, Paulie," Aunt Hallie said. "Give this a shake for me."

Paul took the mat she handed him and followed her to the porch. He held it over the edge and shook and the dirty sand showered the ivy below. As he finished, he saw she was watching him, so he gave it another little shake.

"That's good," she said, but didn't take it back from him. Her eyes had shifted to the lake. Through the pine branches, Paul saw the hazy sheen of the water and down by the lake's outlet the glint of a boat at anchor.

"Somebody said something, sounds like," Aunt Hallie said, back with him again. "Haven't they?" She walked to the edge of the porch and patted a plank beside her for him to sit, and he did.

"Honey," Aunt Hallie said. "Your grandfather has a cancer. Do you know about that?"

Paul nodded, but he hoped she wouldn't ask him to say what he knew.

"Your mother didn't tell you anything?"

"No."

"Just as well," Aunt Hallie said. "The truth is, we don't expect he'll be here when you come again next summer. We'll miss him terribly, won't we?"

Paul felt that numbing in his chest again, but then Aunt Hallie put her hand to his forehead and smoothed back his hair . . . just what his mother would've done. He didn't know what to say. He tried to smile the way his father sometimes smiled when he didn't feel like it.

"Be nice to him, Paulie," she said.

"Oh, I will . . ." Paul said.

Everyone knew his grandfather's routine at camp — even now it wasn't much changed. He woke early most days and took the boat out, alone. The chug of a far-off motor was the first sound people would notice as they lay in bed. If he took any fish — northerns or walleyes (rock bass he said ruined the lake and these he stuck through the gills with his pen knife and threw back to die) — he cleaned them on a board grown between two maples by the water, a few of the younger cousins crowding around. He took his time, now and then picking off one of the questions pitched at him, letting most of what they said fly past. But often he took no fish. After beaching the boat, he'd make the rounds of his children's cabins, then shut himself in the workroom, where he oiled and sharpened the tools, or fixed things that broke around camp, or if nothing was broken, where he just sat and read whatever newspaper he found in one of the outhouses, back to front, until he retired to The Folly and treated himself to deviled ham on Ry-Crisp and some black tea, then shooed out any remaining cousins, drew the bamboo shades and slept.

After his aunt went back to her work, Paul drifted down the path toward Grampa Paul's. The day was getting hot. The lake was flat and nothing seemed to move. Someone called to him from inside Aunt Leah's, one of the girl cousins, but he skipped down the hill past the tangle of rosehips, as if he hadn't heard. A lantern was burning in the workroom. Paul veered off the trail and came around the shaded side and sat on the chopping block and waited for his grandfather to come outside. But he didn't, and after a while Paul climbed up on the pile of birch rounds below the high screened window and tried to listen . . . but all he could hear was some jays up in the hardwoods, so he let himself down and stood by the door for another few minutes . . . then edged away.

It was too late to catch Gwen and Billie, even if he wanted to. He crossed the strip of road behind the cabins and started running down the wide footpath through Uncle Mac's swath of thinned-out woods, called The Pinery, which lead a quarter-mile to Lake Superior . . . and by the time the trail opened out above the rusty sandstone bluffs, he was crying and coughing and trying to get his breath. He went to his knees and covered his face from the glare of the bay, and before long the spasm began to ease. Leaning back into the roots of a cedar, he heard Aunt Hallie's voice again, and somehow the sound of it outweighed what she'd told him. He took a few deep breaths and gradually his hands unclenched. He sat up and stared out at the big lake. Miles out, an ore boat crept along the horizon, above it a wash of bright clouds, too far away to look like anything.

Before supper, everyone gathered on the porch of The Folly for happy hour — Uncle Ray and Aunt Hallie, Uncle Duff, Uncle Mac and all the others. His grandfather sat in a high-backed wicker chair and slats of light crossed his shirt and rippled down onto his hands folded in his lap. Paul walked through to the table and grabbed a handful of cashews and looked for a place to sit, but all the chairs and even the bench under the window were taken, so he backed against the wall and tried to be invisible.

"How's the boy?" Uncle Ray asked. Paul smiled blankly. It was all the answer his uncle seemed to want.

The talk was about electricity. One of the original land owners across the lake had brought in power and had a TV in his cabin. The road was still dug up in spots and even Uncle Ray complained.

Uncle Duff drank down the last of his beer and snapped the aluminum sharply between his fingers.

"What're you all afraid of?" he said. "What's going to happen is going to happen."

"It's better than listening to that god-awful generator of his," Aunt Leah said.

"I'll tell you, they don't even make gas iceboxes anymore," Uncle Duff added.

Uncle Mac gave them both a stare. He was oldest of the five, the most like Paul's grandfather, everyone said. "We all *agreed* about this, as I remember it," he said stiffly.

Uncle Duff was known as the family hothead, and Paul could see for himself he was itching to let loose with something more. But another look flew between the brothers, accompanied by the slightest nod toward their father. It was the same kind of thing that'd happened in the cabin that morning. They *did* have an agreement . . . but it was about more than electricity. They were all going to get along for a while, and they were all going to be nice to him.

The porch fell to silence.

Paul looked at his grandfather. He wondered how the sickness could be inside him and not show. Maybe everyone else knew what to look for, he thought. They acted as if they could see it, as if they felt it in the room with them, breathing and growing. Aunt Hallie came out from the kitchen and brought his glass back, filled mostly with ice, and fit it into his hand. "There now," she said. Paul saw his eyes flick from it up to her, lingering just a second, then out to the rest of them fanned before him . . . all his family . . . and then saw the slow, tired-looking shake of his head.

After supper, Paul slipped away from his aunt and uncle and the cousins, and sat on the dock by The Folly. The evening birds came out, the swallows like bits of quick shadow, then the loons and grebes. Far off, Paul heard a woman's voice calling, but it only made the lake seem quieter and farther away from the rest of the world . . . then his grandfather was standing beside him. Without a word, they made the boat ready. They loaded the cushions, the poles, the tacklebox. Paul dropped into the bow and hugged a life preserver around his middle. His grandfather rowed out much farther than he had the night before, as if reluctant to break the stillness, and both looked back, still not saying anything, at the slice of cleared land where the cabins were, a few lights just coming to their windows. Finally he primed the engine and started it. Paul turned and faced into the wind and watched the black choppy water separate before the bow, letting the rush of air scour his thoughts.

Near the far shore, his grandfather eased the engine back to a slow chug, then let it die, though they were still a ways out in deep water. Out of the corner of the sky, Paul saw the great heron again, just as it thrust down its long wings and braced itself to land.

"There!" Paul said, but his grandfather had already seen it.

Paul looked down at the fishing things and could barely think what they were for. He wanted to keep talking now, before his voice froze, though he couldn't think of what to say.

"I'll miss you terribly," he blurted . . . then gulped and felt his face flush. That was what Aunt Hallie had said, not his words at all. His grandfather was still watching the heron, the oar grips squeaking on his callouses.

"After you go home?"

"Yes," Paul said. "And after that, I mean . . . ."

"Don't you think you'll be seeing me again?"

"No," Paul said. "Not really."

His grandfather thumbed up the bill of his cap and studied him, as if he hadn't really taken full reckon of him until this instant. "I guess maybe you won't at that," he said. "Hardly seems fair does it? Just when I get to know you."

Paul struggled to look straight up at his grandfather's face, but when he did he saw that his grandfather's eyes were looking off now, following the treeline around the lake, slowly, the way the heron had done.

"We always called this God's Country," he said in a minute. "There's no place like it, I guess, not a place so beautiful, so full of all of us . . . but Paulie, God's Country?"

His gaze came suddenly back and fixed hugely on Paul. "Paulie, can I tell you something? I don't know if God has a country."

"I don't either," Paul murmured.

"Nor anyone," his grandfather said. He let go of the oars and let them drift back along the hull. "Nor any living thing, Paulie."

The heron lifted its beak toward the sky, and a harsh rattle escaped from it and echoed across the open water. The blue air deepened quickly, speckled by the dark shapes of insects, then by the first stars. A fish jumped near the boat, but neither Paul nor his grandfather made a move toward the tackle. They'd come out too late and soon they'd have to turn around and go back, but for a few minutes more, they sat in the boat together, watching the heron as it disappeared into the darkness of the reeds.

NO MORE ROUND SHOULDERS.

KNICKERBOCKER SHOULDER - BRACE
And Suspender Combined.
Sold by Druggists and General Stores, or sent, postpaid, on receipt of $1 per pair, plain, or $1.50 silk-faced. Send chest-measure around the body.　Address
KNICKERBOCKER BRACE CO.,
N. A. JOHNSON, Prop'r.　　　　　EASTON, PA.

Gary Margolis

Her Apprehension

This morning, as I look out, I see
a doe feeding on the June grasses
in the back meadow. I call you
to join me, knowing
by the time you reach here,
she could disappear. Yet something
holds her until you come,
and we stand fixed in her apprehension.
It's not often, at this bright time
of day, a deer wanders out
of the woods. At dusk, the last
feathered light helps each emerge
and keep its distance.
Once, driving home late, I hit
a doe, crushing her rear legs.
She must have felt she was alone
or the fast light safe enough
to cross through. When I tried
to move closer, to kill her quickly,
she dragged herself across the road
and down into the darkness of a lake,
barking with all the bloody air
in her nose. She must have died
on her own, no matter how often
I dream up another night to drive home.
Today there is just air and field
between me and this new doe, and now
you near, still as meadow light, watching
her browse. The doe's guard bird is
the breeze, which brings us to her
faster than a headlight, so she can
prick up and bound away.

Paul Mariani

Minneapolis: At the Summer Solstice

What martyr's cry quickens our civil blood,
Wolfe Tone's, Parnell's? Whose sacrifice
on a noche triste centuries alive
enables an ultimate homogeneity?

John Berryman

About this northmidwest polis abrupt
the plane had dropped me in I thought & yet again
I thought. Five days, five full days *and* nights
I tried spying out its soul or, if not *that*
imperious Emersonian immensity, then at least

some centering primal nucleus of riverbed or track.
Minneapolis: a mishmash appelation half Greek/half Sioux,
flat anomoly of broad boulevards & concrete looming granaries
& spiffy, dutiful, high-polish-boots police.
And yet: like oatmeal after Venice's canals,

the ducal stone of Florence, rococco Rome, without even
slum Dublin's gorgeous Georgian doors. No, *this*
was not so very unlike New World Syracuse and Rome
or, even closer home: a 91-beribboned Springfield,
home of basketball and the repeating rifle.

Except for old New York and maybe Bourbon Street
Orleans & the quaint grey quais of palmetto-laced
old Charleston, the post-blue highway cities
of America, let's face it, are like this.
It took chutzpah to build Paterson from those old

rejected stones, the which Doc Williams pretty much
avoided, I see better now, for the far more interesting
issue of himself. There are no holy cities in America,
at least none *this* side of the border, north
or south. No Quebec shrine, no maternal Guadaloupe,

no Czestochowa, Zurick, Canterbury, Rome,
and surely no Kyoto. No angel's wing to brush sacred
mosques or crypt or wall: that painted golden light

which has stood these four thousand years for Jerusalem.
Ah, if the tonsured fathers of the companie of Francis

could see L.A. or San Francisco now, how they'd
slap their fevered brows. And yet here I was: one more
exhausting pilgrimage to go, twenty pounds the lighter,
the trick of leaning into the fiery furnace
until my eyelids curled & singed as once

with Ananius, Azarius & the others. Minneapolis:
this singer's final nesting place, the exhausted
martyr's star upon those expansive coalpiers that skirt
the adolescent Mississippi, star glinting in the rubble
from that morning when he tilted out & leapt.

Ah, who could write like him, count poem for blessed
poem? the whirlwind polyvalved bellow of that deeply
wounded man who builded him an altar to outlast plastic
food & foodstands & exfoliating lots, the city over which
he'd brooded, this swarming vital northern desolation.

Lynn Martin

It Is Sunny

(after Carlos Drummond de Andrade)

Because love is always sad, at nighttime
and especially during the day, and because
these four walls in the long hours become
too bright a mirror, I think of the busy

apples. Today I turn on the sprinkler.
Tomorrow it will be raining. There was

that kiss the other week, and today
there is only the memory of the kiss,
and it is weeping in some blank corner
of the living room. And nobody knows

what will happen on Saturday, the day
of breakfast and chores, when there is
no time to kill yourself. Maybe there

will be another night, when you will meet
that hard part of yourself and not be afraid.
There won't be a racket, but simply prayers.

Meanwhile, the dying poppies are getting water
and so are the tall grasses. Yesterday, a woman
drove her car into a telephone booth. I walk
outside and it is sunny and I am unhappy.

Lynn Martin

Shaving

I have no questions your body is not answering
by the way your hair, in its puzzled arc, lifts
to curve and just touch your ear, by how your hands
take hold of the tea cup and bring it to your lips

as if they were a child's lips or mine, the gesture
opening and opening into the lost places in between,
to where people will be able to tell one another
what happened, where love cancels what is lonely,

and where what is asked to be seen is fully seen.
There is much I do not know, but I do know that
at this moment, while sitting in your kitchen,
the way you look out of your window is all about

loss. We were talking about shaving, how you won't
let anyone watch you, how I used to watch my father.

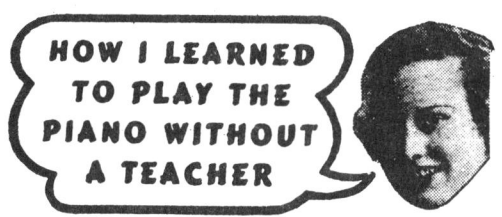

Mekeel McBride

The Kiss

In an empty room two people kiss
and it becomes a university.
As Dean the Kiss wallpapers
each classroom with redwood forests,
star charts from the childhood
of Nostradamus. Clear tranquility of rain
invited in to give guest lectures.
And angels, their wings swelling
like orchids, peach orchards
teach wool-gathering, loitering.

Valentines arrive from the ghosts
of forgotten children, invisible
twins long neglected. And textbook
representatives leave free seed catalogs,
samples of rare August-blooming lilies.
Papers appear about the Kiss, first
praise, then the careful critical
approach. Finally, claims of larceny,
infidelity, perjury. **Meetings occur**
in rooms with impeccable roofs,
the interiors as dark as the heart
of a politician. Secret votes taken.

Found lacking. Eased out. The Kiss,
that shy zodiac spinning
in glitter-filled laughter
through inestimable dark doesn't
have the sense to worry. Instead,
studies in solitude the common sense
scripture of seagull wings
sweeping winter's iciest sky.
Investigates meadow mice, poultice roots,
and the sacred potato, all inheritors
of the misunderstood underground.

Invents the healing property of one
snowflake caught and cherished
in the black hair of the crippled girl.

Oh, and it built a house, the Kiss did,
a very small house in the shining disk
of a thrown penny descending
into the bottomless well of a possible
wish. And it lives there, reading
the love letters Marco Polo wrote
to continents he never discovered.
In the end, insisting on nothing but
this — in an empty room, that two people kiss.

Mekeel McBride

The Plainest Signs

One hundred miles of interstate, north,
the route Godzilla would take
after ravaging Boston, past life-sized
plastic cows, topless joints,
the orange dinosaur guarding
a miniature golf course. And then
no services for a long, long time.

This is where I pass my ex-husband
doing forty in the slow lane. Ex?
Mark on the map that means, most likely,
the treasure never will be found.
I step on the gas, suddenly wanting nothing
more than to keep the past
behind me but still visible.

It's like the way I watch
horror movies on TV, from the next room
letting myself know just enough
to come in when the trouble's taken care of.
But special effects have become too good
and the script promises
the worst is over when it's just about

to get a whole lot worse.
I hit eighty, eighty-five, already rehearsing:
Officer, it was a way to make the past
last a little longer in proper perspective.
Dream on sister, he'd say, you were speeding
pure and simple. But it never comes
to anything that simple. Not even
in the old movies. Taken out of his element

what could Kong do but climb
out of reach and try to stay that way?
And wasn't it inevitable that the heavens
would open up and put an end
to an honest attempt at fairly intelligent

escape? The inevitable never is a comfort.
My husband, my ex-husband catches up,

gets ahead of me, falls back, gains
like a lazy pendulum on an old clock, the time
perilously close to correct. Nothing
as simple as an officer of the law
to put a stop to this. I stop, finally,
just before a toll booth for the next
state, beside a sign that says

Hospital Next Right, another, No Stopping.
The plainest signs, the most misleading.
And sitting there, stopped all right,
I remember the first movie I ever saw.
An entire civilization burrows in the center
of the earth. Ritual requires that they
place virgins in a chamber of simple

daylight, filtered down mile after mile
where the thin-skinned, obedient women
will burn. Until the hero from *on* the earth
blunders his way down, finds the woman
who is sacrificed to our world's
ordinary light but survives, thriving
on his stories of bright and endless air.

As they begin their difficult ascent
through dusk and rock, an earthquake occurs
closing her world
of quarter-light behind her;
the one who cajoled her out of it, dead.
Plainest signs, the most misleading.
The only way that she can go, ahead.

Mekeel McBride

The Thief of Light

He stole light and in his case, it was true — he
couldn't help it. Snatched coins perched on church
candles; lifted the golden highlight from his wife's
eye. Secretly, the way any infidelity begins. He
perfected his art on the lit tips of cigarettes, warning
signals at railroad crossings. Still, the world only
seemed to grow brighter. And his own heart, smaller,
darker, shameful as a raisin. He culled electricity
right out of the bed-lamp bulb, chanted his black
lament on rosaries of coal. The King of the Thieves
of Light! He will not be trifled with! Grows so thin
that a moonless night is enough to excite his hunger.
And no one is trying to stop him. But even the old
blind woman on the corner, the one who sits with her
patient face turned toward this late winter sun can
tell you. The world, in a way that is, as yet
unexplained, seems only to grow brighter.

Gardner McFall

After a Fairy Tale by Oscar Wilde

Loving the idea of love, a nightingale
pressed her chest to the thorn of a rosebush
so a rose might bloom red as her blood.
The harder she pressed, the sweeter she sang
until in the purest ecstasy of song,
her heart and the thorn of the rosebush met.
A man picked the rose for a woman he loved,
but the woman disdained it. The man discarded
the rose near the wheels of a cart. He went
back to his books. He forgot about love
with a valid excuse. Love, let us be neither
the man nor woman, but the nightingale:
the sharper the pain, the greater the song,
the deeper the red: the miraculous blossom.

Martin McGovern

Near San Gregorio

Fog curls between the redwoods
and the ocean. It was this gray light
that kept me at the window,
held me close there, looking out
at my brother in the yard.
He threw a leather ball
while the setter, named for water
in some old language, leaped
high as the wet, pink blossoms
of crabapple and caught the ball,
brought it back. Again and again.
Redwood, driftwood, ocean just beyond
the bank of fog moving slowly,
night tide creeping into this cove,
returning to the dark.
My brother asked if he had lost
his mind. I said whatever words
I thought would keep him,
one day, from jumping.
When I go home now I drive
across the bridge he chose.
There is a love that separates,
just as high tide pulls close the foam
and sends it farther out again,
or as the echo lingers
a moment when a chant is over.
Regret's a kind of bringing back.

*

The lighthouse juts into fog,
seeming simply, in the afternoon,
something harmless and familiar:
winter rides in the blue Ford
or days in grandfather's store,
damp wood walls of the tobacco room,
old men coming for coffee and pills.
My brother and I'd spin fountain stools
until we caught some daylight on shelves

the winter sun never touched.
We said we were the lighthouse men
bringing the ships safely in
or warding them off the rocks.

*

Each morning the tide goes out,
pocking the beach with pools,
leaving inevitable tangles of wood.
Summers, we put up shacks barely smaller
than the scrap and driftwood houses
between a levy and the Mississippi.
Families who live there live on nobody's land.
They tell no one of their past:
an old farm, a child somewhere,
five long years of debts. A man
by the river once started to wave to me
but stopped himself as if I'd returned,
some lost brother, from the dead.
If my brother would come back,
I'd rise to greet him, and there'd be more
than the loneliness of moss water
lapping at a bank, its low chant
of regret. Perhaps we would both rise up
and touch and forget nothing
but the grave between us. Until below us
at a distance, the tide coming again,
beach fires go out in the last
corners of a cove.

Thomas McGuane

Beyond the Infield

The moon lofted off the horizon to drift low over the prairie, white and imperious as a commodore. While the two walked, their shadows darted over the ground and through the sage. The boy went along, concentrating on the footing which was secure and reliable except where the washes had undercut ledges that sloughed quickly beneath them. His father strode ahead in silence, his boots making a steady beat unmodified by the boy's breathlessness. The boy still wore his baseball jersey and had a green sweater tied around his waist. The wind came out of the draws and breathed through them toward the lights of town.

"You out of breath?"

"No, sir."

"Keep moving."

His father made forward in vengeance, then asked. "Do you feel like you've been stolen? Like I took you away?"

"No, sir."

His father had returned after hiding from his mother, hiding in, of all places, Arequipa, Peru, where he had cooked on sheep dung and drunk too much and mailed deranged letters to his son until his son flunked his courses and got kicked off the baseball team. Then on a morning when the boy spent still another Saturday at home, away from his beloved third base, the father walked in and said, "What'll it be, Lucien, where do we go?"

Lucien, a small town boy buried in Ernest Thompson Seton, said, "Up in the hills." He was baffled by his father's dramatics but more than anything, happy to see him again.

Now they were lost. They had been lost for two days. Not seriously lost because they could see the lights of Deadrock; but they had lost their own camp on the rocky escarpment of the Crazy Mountains. And though they could have walked to the highway in a few hours, they still hadn't had food in days. Their feet were blistered; and twice the father had curled up on the ground, before walking the great circle again with fury and self pity. When he heard the boy's hard breathing, he said, "You're a baseball player and I'm fifty. Keep walking." Lucien was silent. He thought of his books and wondered if they were still on the study hall desk, in the nearly empty room with its clock, superintended by a history teacher one week, an English teacher another, some bored man with a paperback spending his time miserably. Lucien's sudden fall to nearly flunking seemed strangely permanent. One upperclassman called him a forceps baby. The light of detention fell through institutional windows upon Lucien and the books that had suddenly gone dead on him. He was homesick and there was no home, nothing to fill a caissonned heart, until the blazing satisfaction of his father's arrival, descended from the inexplicable Arequipa, Peru, where Lucien pictured Indians and colonials circling his father through the divorce. It was the year of vicuña scandals in Eisenhower's administration. The profanity of his father's departure seemed to the boy to infect national politics. Furthermore, his mother didn't want to give the family another try. "It's quits," she said of the marriage.

Lucien began to think: if we cannot find the camp, we'll have to go to Peru. Moreover, his last history lesson, possibly still open on the study hall desk, concerned the Teapot Dome scandal. Lucien knew that Teapot Dome was out here somewhere, maybe between here and camp; and around it were the ghosts of crooks in vests and homburgs, crooks with money. He had already learned that in America the very good and the very bad had money to burn.

"If you want to give up," said his father, "we can start toward the highway." His face was charged with suffering and there was a slight whistle in his breath. Lucien looked him over. "I don't want to quit," said Lucien. "I want to find our camp."

"We did this sort of thing at fifteen thousand feet," said his father shakily. "In the Andes." Lucien knew his father's companion in Peru, a Billings car dealer named Art Clancy, also on the run from divorce. Art weighed two hundred thirty pounds. Lucien had a harder time picturing him at fifteen thousand feet than he had picturing his father. Art was a famous lady killer, even at his weight; he had a secret apartment and a Corvette. There was some connection between these things and the separation of Lucien's parents. One hungover morning, according to Lucien's mother, Art Clancy and his father had joined the winter segment of a thing called "The World Adventure Series". It was a tour that went to Peru where the Indians wore stocking caps with ear flaps and where Lucien's father, deprived of his secretary, wrote Lucien the only handwritten letters he had ever seen of his. The writing was strong and linear and spoke romantic escape: sometimes Lucien's father was alone the romantic escapist; sometimes Lucien and his father were depicted in the letters as escaping; sometimes there was anger and glory, sometimes just anger. In all cases, it was the world that was against them, a world which no longer cared for the individual with his dread of homogeneity. Sometimes, not one word of the letters could be read. It was like the night Lucien's mother made a tape recording of his father, and he had gone after her. Because of that Lucien's father went out the door with the police and the next thing was the World Adventure Series to Peru with Art Clancy. She called Lucien's father a "coward," a strong word.

Lucien began to know where they were. He could have said so right away. Instead, he took a very slight lead until they were around the bottom of the low cliff. His father didn't know they were on the trail again. Above them, the rock was black and spilled stars in a bright trail to the lighted clouds. It was the perfect trail to get jumped on from above, by a cougar or a gook: Lucien had no idea who lived around here. But he did know it was more than a backdrop for his father and himself, more than an illustrated letter. For some reason, he didn't tell his father they were on the trail once more. He could hear the whistle in his father's breath as though some small rigid thing were stuck in his throat, some forceful thing.

A cloud of crows lifted from a depression between small hills, revealing the most remarkable hot spring imagineable, a deeply colored blue hole with pale steam blowing from its surface to tangle its streamers in the trunks of sage. For a brief time, the two forgot their troubles as they floated in thermal blue. They saw the world through a gentle fog and they talked in the simplest statements.

Lucien's father spotted some ranch buildings in the distance. "This must be private," he said; and they left.

Then you could see their camp, a grim, improperly erected

pup tent with canned food in a pile by its entrance. They had been gone nearly two days and when his father saw the tent, he groaned and trotted toward it. He threw himself on the ground beside the cans; his curved and exhausted back heaved for a long time. Lucien wondered whether this was a heart attack. "Are you okay?" he asked but got no answer. He hated himself for not knowing appropriate first aid. His father slung himself up.

He said, "We better eat. We better eat now."

Lucien began to build a fire. There was plenty of dry wood. There were matches and a patented product that he squirted into the wood. In a moment, they had fire and heat.

"Our time in the desert is at an end," said Lucien's father. Lucien had not thought of it as desert. He thought the two days following the sun round a long corner had been beautiful. He wasn't sure in what way his father had been present, but his father had been present in the minimum way a boy will accept.

The tent was an old one, bought by mail when Lucien was in the first grade, for a trip to the Boundary Waters of Minnesota, a trip they were unable to make because of the Recession, or something about middle management. The tent had been treated to waterproof it, a tar smell. The moon outside revealed the weave of the cloth. Lucien watched his father's wonderfully peaceful sleep. He couldn't make out if he was in worse trouble at school and would never be returned to the baseball team; or that his father's terrific intervention cancelled that world and its rules. In fact, he couldn't exactly make out if his father was glad to be back. It was as if the same master stood over them with a stick and not only drove them but drove them in circles, around the mountains, around their camp, around their tin cans.

His father had brought a fancy Zenith radio for the trip, so that they would not be surprised by weather. Lucien got nine countries on it. He turned it as low as he could and dialed away at his sleeplessness. He got Mexico, an exciting thing in 1955. The speaker from Mexico spoke very rapidly, reminding Lucien that he was flunking Spanish. If he picked up "muy" once, he picked it up a hundred times. Then he ran the six foot antenna out the tent flap and dialed some more: he got an English-language Baptist station right in the middle of Port Au Prince, Haiti, right where they have voodoo, talking about Our Lord Jesus Christ; not at all the way a radio Baptist would carry on Stateside. You could tell the people of Haiti had put a civil tongue in his head. Then he got rough Northern languages he could not understand. Maybe they were Russians.

He tuned back to Haiti. Cold wind stirred the tent sides, a rocky wind that murmured through the imprecations of the stranded preacher in Haiti so anxious to make friends among the heathen he pronounced their country I.T. as the Hatians did; the wind murmured over the tired Peruvian traveler and a son still early in his journey.

The day broke blue and northern on the basin of gravel, a basin lined with thin glittering springs and the delicacies of vegetation that spilled their edges all the way to the brisk willows at the creek bottom. The creek turned South till it fell off the end. Someone's lost saddlehorse stood exactly where the creek fell into pure blue sky, alternately grazing and staring across the gravelly basin to their camp. Lucien's first thought was to catch him, ride him back to school and get to play third base again.

"I could never catch him," he thought. He remade the fire for breakfast, building it in a single blast with the patent fire starter, a flame as tall as Lucien that wavered ominously toward the tent, then shrank into the firewood peaceably. His father woke to the smell of hash and eggs, crawled forth with a bleak squint into broad daylight.

"You left the radio on, Lucien. The battery is dead."

His father doubled over to scrutinize a blister on his heel, displacing its liquid between opposing thumbs. "Godalmighty," he said.

They breakfasted and Lucien cleaned the aluminum plates in the spring. The cold water congealed the grease to the metal and he had to scour them with sand to make them clean. Lucien was conscious of his father staring at the peaks, plain rock jumping out of ground that looked as soft as a stream bank. "No wonder nobody lives here, no wonder they stay back in town," his father said. "There's no reason to be here. You come here to get something and then out you go. Look at that poor damn horse. Can you feature that?"

This gave Lucien no feeling whatsoever, not unless that in itself was a feeling. It was like hitting a baseball and having it just not come down. You could hardly call it a fielding error.

His father circled the tent slowly, digging a finger into his disordered hair, inventorying the camp, the camp which a few days ago had been erected as a gateway to an improved world.

"We're looking at under a hundred bucks," said his father, standing at their camp. "Let's walk away from it." Lucien listened, awaiting some further information; but that was all: leave it.

They had nothing to carry, nor the struggle of climbing;

Lucien's father led the way with a jaunty step. Part of the mission was completed. The Lights of Deadrock were reduced to the dimensional outlines of the little burg, that and the brief gusts of stink from the hot springs south of town. Lucien wondered why unpleasantness and healing were always connected.

"I'm afraid I feel a little guilty," said Lucien's father with a laugh. "A little guilty, a little hungry and a little thirsty."

"Guilty for what?"

"Taking you away from school."

Lucien walked on for a minute, scuffing along the dry, stony trail. "I wasn't doing well," he said. "You didn't do any harm."

"I'm sure I did a *lot* of harm," said his father. Lucien wondered why he always made his father feel so guilty. They had had so very few adventures together, but each one of them made his father burn with guilt. Maybe they shouldn't try to have adventures; the thought choked Lucien with sadness; but maybe it was true. Not if the adventures were just going to make his father burn with guilt. They had gone to Cabo San Lucas and his father burned like a martyr because it was the first trip they had made that reflected the deterioration of his parents' marriage. That trip at least had been on a school vacation, so the sense of irresponsibility had not been so hard on his father as this time. Lucien knew that this time his father felt more like a kidnapper than an adventurer.

For the last half mile, the trail was little more than a ledge in the granite. Beyond the ledge, soaring birds were seen from above, now and then diving feet first into the prairie. Their car could be discerned too: an almost vertical view, a rectangle of paint, like the toy car Lucien used to scuff one handed on the carpet at home. That was back when his mother and father had had famous parties where they displayed their outstanding dancing and where Lucien, already dying to please, had trained himself to be a perfect bartender, silent, and friendly, willing to overrule the jigger for family friends, later listening through the floor for the bellowed jokes and the trailing valkyrean laughs of the wives. It was when the census bureau harried Lucien's father for declaring himself an "entrepreneur"; Lucien still wasn't sure what that was, but all the adults banded together to throw parties to fight the census bureau, to pass the hat, to declare their faith in "entrepreneurs", a category which the census bureau would not accept. It was exciting. Lucien was the pubescent speedy bartender, who bracketed new people in town, the probational ones, with his strict jigger. Then suddenly things got so exciting that his father tore off to Peru with the man who sold him his last car: A car different from the plain business model the trail wound toward; the car Art Clancy sold his father was a Thunderbird, and now his mother had it. She had the house and she had the assets. Plus, she had done something Lucien couldn't quite fathom, she had let the memberships go. And now they were gone, his father had said dolorously: the memberships are gone.

They drove on toward Deadrock where they had rented the car. They weren't going to turn the rental in today; his father promised over and over that they wouldn't turn it in today, as though Lucien cared. "We've had this car for nearly half a week," his father crowed, "and it's got less than fifty miles on it!" As they drove, Lucien listened to stories of the living descendants of the Incas, how they hid gold in lakes, cut out hearts, sacrificed virgins. He heard of the astonishment of these small people, with their great Andean chests and earflaps, at the sight of Art Clancy's Corvette. Peru had been quite a deal. The Indians tried to put their hands all over the car. Art Clancy spoke to them in a kind of imitation Kruschev. "Hands off," he told the little Incas. "Gives a shot in the head." The year of Cabo San Lucas there had been a long aftermath of Mexican. "Eees good!" stood for approval. When Lucien hooked a trout in the ditch back of the house, his mother cried out, "Feesh! Ees good!"

Lucien suspected that his mother was as much on his father's mind, as she was on his own. It was his father's quietness as he made his way across the river bridge then the railroad tracks. Maybe Lucien's mother should have thrown his father out; but when she did, she threw everything out and maybe she shouldn't have done that. Who would ever know? Nobody. It infected everything from daybreak to baseball. It infected all things. It was a pestilence.

They drove into Deadrock. They were traveling light. The town crouched in front of the terrific mountains to the south, great wildly irregular peaks that seemed to say to the little town: don't try anything. No one strolled the streets, as Lucien and his father sat in the parked rental car. There were plenty of people visible but they just emerged from one store or bar and darted into another, short sudden arcs, escaping the same general gaze. This irresolute air suited Lucien and his father perfectly. The day felt too early and too late. Before the divorce, this was his father's home town too.

"We better get a room," his father said.

He restarted the car and began to hunt for a place. There were a couple of satisfactory hotels which they cruised past at very low speed. His father looked at them critically, then leaned out into the warm air to crane up at their higher stories either to evaluate their height and substance or to hope for an anomalous penthouse, more satisfactory than the lower rooms, rooms to which Lucien was sure his father referred when he uttered the single word, "Dandruff."

Then impatiently he gunned out onto Parkway and found Deadrock's only motel, a new place. In 1955 a motel was a pretty exciting thing, comfort and life alongside your car. Now Lucien saw that his father was okay once again, that there was volition and not a mind wandering through things spoilt. And the reproachful presence of your own child: Yes, Lucien felt that now.

Lucien's father went inside to get them a room. He came out with a ballpoint, wrote down the license number and went back inside. Then he came back and jumped in the car heartily. "15 B, I love it! 'B'! They only have one floor! You ought to see the owner. Get the feeling you don't take a room and the bank pounces on him." His father smiled wide with charity. Lucien glanced over and saw the motel lady, drawing back the venetian blinds, caught. He waved a little.

The room was another world: up to date, lightless. There were little things on the bedspread you could pick at. Lucien's father made his way sideways to each reproduction on the wall, thrummed his fingers on top of the TV, counted out ten dollars and weighted them with an ashtray. "I'm going out for a belt. I'm late and you get hungry, here's ten bucks." He was gone in a shudder of daylight.

Lucien read the welcome to Big Sky and thumbed the motel Bible. Kukla, Fran and Olly wouldn't be on television for a while. He pulled the curtain and saw their car was gone: he'd never heard it start up. He wondered if anyone would get some use out of their tent; maybe the owner of that horse — it would make a good combination for a man wanting to travel out in all those hills and mountains. He lay down for a moment trying to get control of himself. Very soon, he wasn't moving.

He woke up in the middle of the night. His father was standing bolt upright in his shorts, arm outstretched, finger pointing, a dynamo of rejection, a god casting someone out. "Go!" he roared.

Indeed, someone was being cast out; but she felt very strongly that she had not been given time to dress. She complained with acid bitterness as she crawled through her own clothing, holding individual articles up toward the bathroom light for rough identification.

"*Go!*" roared his father.

"I'm *gone,*" she wined. "But not like this."

She struggled a bit more, stood, and slanted through the small opening Lucien's father made for her into the night.

Lucien listened to his father walking around, stopping only for long sighs. Finally:

"Lucien?"

"I'm awake."

"I'm sorry . . . ?"

"I'm awake, sir."

"How long have you been awake?"

"Not long," Lucien said.

"Lucien when you were a small boy, I let you have lots of pets, hamsters, rabbits, and so on? Do you remember I allowed that?"

"Yes, sir, I do."

"That was so you could learn about animals, about how we are all animals."

"Yes, sir."

"And now I want to call momma."

He got the night operator or the morning operator, whichever, and revealed to Lucien's mother that they were no longer out in the mountains. "Momma," he said. "I'm with Lucien. We want to come home to you, Momma." Lucien could not devise an attitude toward this. His father suddenly fell to listening. He repeated "uh huh" a number of times in a deeper and flatter voice. He waved Lucien into the bathroom, then waved the door shut behind him. Lucien leaned on the faucet, turning it microscopically until a drop of water came out, shut it off, and did it again. Then he heard his father call for him.

When he went into the bedroom the reading lamp was on and his father sat right next to it, weeping, silently with heaving shoulders.

"What's the matter Pop, can't we go home?" Lucien was scared.

"It's not that —" He sobbed for a few more minutes and composed himself carefully. "Art Clancy was shot and killed by his girlfriend," he sobbed. "In Arequipa, Peru."

Lucien's father had coached him carefully as they walked across town from the motel. They stood in front of their house while his father ran a finger around the inside of his collar then gave Lucien a quick conspiratorial nod. He knocked. In a moment,

272

the door opened and there was his mother, all dressed up.

"When's lunch!" Lucien and his father cried together.

She looked from one to the other. "That hungry gang of mine," she said with a warm smile and turned into the house for her men to follow.

Chili was gone. He knew very well that his mother might have disposed of the small, blue, merry bird; or, at least, given the bird away, purely on the basis of its hispanic name. Lucien was sure she pictured Clancy of Peru in his shantung suits, his Corvette and his bad Spanish in a way that made a parakeet named Chili look bad. He already suspected that her greeting was camouflage so the crack of his mother's hand against his father's face came as not much of a surprise. His father just took it. There was little else he could do. Raising his hands in self defense would have made him a pantywaist in the eyes of his own son.

"I'll go," said Lucien's father.

"Where? Peru?" Her long patrician face always looked surprised when she was angry. What many took for astonishment was in fact a prelude to hysterical fury. "You and your Peru!"

Then Lucien's father did something very strange and yet wholly characteristic of him: he waved to an imaginary person in the window behind her; when she turned to look, he flattened her with a tremendous blow.

His father left the room, straight through the French doors into the side yard where the dog hid in its Tudor house, the chain making an abrupt circuit back into the little doorway as it always did in a family dispute. He sauntered over the highground beside the lilacs and took a final glance into the living room before retiring to the guest room over the garage.

Lucien's mother still lay on the floor, lightly fingering the discoloration around her left eye. "I'm a chump if I don't call a cop," she said, using a diction she seldom used unless she was trying to reveal the actual sordid texture she saw in her life. If this had all happened to an acquaintance, she would have said, "She's deluded if she doesn't call a policeman." She slung herself upright, got to her feet and headed for the stairs. "You had better find something to eat, Lucien. I'm in no shape to help you men. Not today. Perhaps, not ever." Lucien felt the excitement return at these last words. He still felt the raw electricity in the air. He made a sandwich.

When he had finished it, he went over to the guest room. His father was sitting on the edge of the bed like a man on his first night at boot camp. "I couldn't let her go on like that, kiddo," he said. "Not with you there." He looked up to see of Lucien was buying it. Lucien let no expression cross his face. "I don't even know whose side you're on." He flung himself on the bed with his hands behind his head, staring at the ceiling. "Out in those wide open spaces . . . now, that was another thing entirely. Out where they don't hamstring a man for standing a little tall."

Lucien took a pitcher of icewater up to his mother. She drank hungrily as though she had come in from a long journey only moments before. "I wonder who the real ring-leader on that Peru trip was. Now Clancy is dead. I guess I'll never know, will I? Clancy would have told me because Clancy knew better than to cross swords with me. Do you follow, Lucien? Of course you don't, you little angel with silver wings, you. —Brandy."

Lucien went downstairs and brought back the brandy and a snifter. His mother had a candle going in her room by now and swirled and heated her glass as she sipped. "No, Lucien, between your father and Art Clancy there wasn't a stick of decency." She held her glass so the candle danced on the other side of it. She squinted and continued. "Clancy? I hope he fries in hell." Lucien shuddered at this, to him, wholly realistic idea. "Your father is not man enough to deserve such spectacular punishment." She spit. "Did you have a lovely time out in the country?"

"Yes, Mom."

"What did you see?"

"Just this horse."

"Doesn't sound like much of a trip."

"It's hard to describe."

"Well," she said. "At least you're not old enough to have gotten into any trouble. Though that too, I suppose, is just around the corner." His mother's search for the combination that would tie them in an awful knot had begun to strike Lucien right in the stomach. His mother fished a mirror out of her purse and sized up the swelling on her face. Then she patted it with a powderpuff, as though she wished it could not be seen. She drew out a picture and held it close to her face. "Clancy," she said. "Who would have ever thought?"

There was something in the air that Lucien didn't like, didn't like at all. After this kind of talk, no one in the family would know to turn up the heat in the winter or close the windows when it rained or put antifreeze in the Thunderbird in November. No one would remember to send crazy Aunt Marie a thank you note when she forgot to send a Christmas present and Aunt Marie's Christmas would be ruined.

The long night got longer. First, Lucien's father stole down for a late snack and nearly collided with his mother. Lucien watched from the couch. The French bread under his arm, the six pack of imported beer, the cheese and the fruit, all fell to the floor. "It takes quite a bit to spoil your appetite, doesn't it, Gene?"

"Hunger and grief are absolutely compatible, you god damned whore," replied his father. "Lucien," he added, "get your mother a sweater. It's cold down here."

Lucien ran his hand up the long cool bannister and watched the candlelight from his mother's room flicker on the carpet. First he got the sweater, the cableknit cardigan she wore when sick, then he rifled the purse for Clancy's picture. He cut that up with his jackknife and flushed it down the toilet. He read a quick couple of pages from the Kinsey Report lying by the bed, and went downstairs where he found his parents hugging and cooing. Tex Benecke's band was playing "Marie Elena" on the record player, a sure sign of new weather. "I love you, you bugger," said his father, "you know I do." This last was slightly crooned to the big band sound in the air.

Lucien went out and sat in the rock garden and thought about the hills and the tent they had left and the old rock sheepherder's monument that looked out over the valley of Bangtail Creek. He thought of the rental car, the freedom vehicle that had almost succeeded, and his father banishing devils in the motel. The laughter and toasts that came from the house now seemed like a home-team faithfully cheered for a bad loss. His father's occasional riggish chuckle made Lucien uncomfortable.

The next thing he knew, Father Moore's big car came pouring up the driveway. The minister, not knowing he was observed by Lucien, climbed angrily out of the car, knocked and went in. Father Moore always bought season tickets with Lucien's father. In years past, they got into lots of trouble together. By the time Lucien went inside, Father Moore, in his sweatshirt and khakis, had a big drink of his own and was joining in on the spirit of things. Lucien's mother hung slightly forward from the waist in her cableknit cardigan and did not quite seem to know what was going on. The stars that had illuminated the rock garden were invisible through the brightly lit living room windows.

Lucien's parents stood shoulder to shoulder. His father was hugely animated and shouted everything he said. Lucien was given a small pillow for the ring. Father Moore — "Dicky" Moore — had his limp Bible splashed open on one hand while the other held his drink. He rattled through the marriage ceremony, stopping once for a refill; and at the end, when Lucien's mother was to say "I do," she instead screamed, "The man I love died in Peru!" and threw herself to the floor.

Lucien's father went out the door, never to return. Lucien sat once more in the starry lawn listening to Father "Dicky" Moore move through the vegetation, nervously murmuring his name.

When Lucien was an adult, when rain whirled up through the hayfield and scattered birds with its force, he heard his own name in the rock garden.

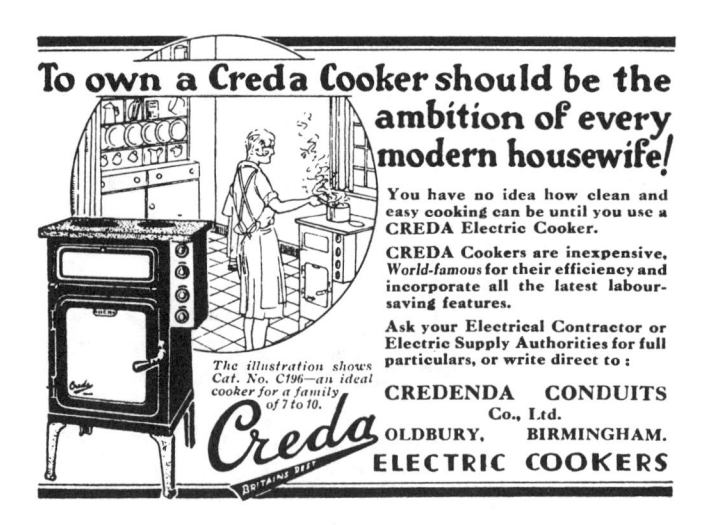

Sandy McKinney

The Body of Desire

Better to wear myself out with honest work
and end the day too tired to pace the floor
at midnight, picking specks of lint out of the rug.
Better than watching the smoke from today's
fortieth cigarette spiraling toward the lamp, than
testing the thorns on last winter's dried arrangement
against the hand that reaches for the face
I can't focus on, for how it differs from
the way I imagine it, even when I'm with you.

What will I name the day, the day you step
out of my dream and stand before me
in the flesh you were born in? How will I call
the emotion I haven't dreamed yet, the simple
unknown reality of the you you are?

The smoke from the forty-first cigarette is spiraling
upward toward the light. I want to know
the history of your blood. I want to be
your unborn twin, sharing the same placenta.
I want to be that waterstain on the ceiling,
the fly a spider's just eaten, food for something.
I want to go back to being the energy hovering
over the first tentative glob of almost
protoplasm, before it gobbled up life
and staked a claim on it. I want to be old
or stone or mist or God, be anything,
anything at all but halfway

Lynne McMahon

The Red Shoes
> *for Anna Akhmatova*

1.
The graininess of the place, first of all.
As in a photograph
The grainy light pulled up from the floor
Diminishing
Until the face is lost.
The floor has been paced out, the rug cut,
And the tamarind, which cannot live in another climate,
Pushes out white flowers
Which blur in the corner garden.
It is the place, first of all, and then the story.

2.
Fifty years and I am standing, as in a photograph,
On your street near the Neva.
The river is just as you said it would be,
That, and the blind red wall.
The freedom of the reader to march or stand back,
To nod thoughtfully over the black lake,
Was not your freedom.
Bitter tamarinds pushed you out into the street
And what fell into the water stayed fallen
Though you had called it back.

3.
What does a woman feel in her iron bed
Night upon night? Husband dead, child gone.
The river is just as you said it would be
And the women queue in the heavy air,
Red leaves in every season.
Each day as they watched you
I drew the covers up
Put down my book
Which said to me *This one is out of step.*
Which said *This one walks in the dark.*

4.
One shoe off and one shoe on
Where have all the husbands gone?

One eye open and one eye closed
The children go where the round sun goes

Into the dark into the dark.

5.
Talk to me. Across the Neva and the lake
And this narrow table.
Does it bother you that the trees are burning?
Bread and salt and the tablecloth in flames —
You said once that the lake had had enough of stars,
Enough of drowning. But you are so silent now
Crossing the window to watch the white flowers
Blur and scorch in the grainy light.
Do the pages mean so much then? Look at me
About to turn them.

6.
Two women sit at a table cutting bread and lemons.
One of them begins a story — an old one —
About a girl who wished only to dance. Only that.
She hadn't wanted the keys to the kingdom
Or the handsome soldier
Or the crystal cup.
And she hadn't known about the black lake
Or the burnings, of what becomes of love.
The women laugh at the story,
The little fool in her red shoes
The color of flames.
What a stupid child, one of them says,
And rises from the table.
She is crying, but the book is closed
And there is no one there to comfort her.

Jane Miller

Ozone Avenue

These days I love to dream,
then I go hear *Romeo Void*.

It's a gentle hell, beloved.
Teen-age boys with lead guitars

singing a number like
there is no like,

you're gone.
I suck the little megawatts of my memories

which are nothing
exactly like mirrors

in a bar in a different mentality,
L.A., Albuquerque, Berkeley,

queens drunk and choked to the teeth
for the imprimatur of the closing

bells. I imagine
I do you

riding toward my fascination
the speedway, and the next minute

the next minute
sniff jasmine no one sees.

I lose the image of myself the rest of the world has
to catch up with. How long are you going to be

the rest of the world? One long day
the lover you left me

for returns to sleep
with you, you can't do it, it's ancient,

like talking
about sex and not realizing the lead

singer has one leg squeezing the other around a mikestand.
Knowledge is useless,

Heaven in script on a turquoise sweatshirt,
with Private Clubs for Los Ojos.

Where is this room?
Just a sweater with nothing under it,

a blanket with the design of the future.
I can see how she is because we've only just met.

So used
to living intimately sometimes I wake

feelings in others I don't know.
Mornings the prostitutes

on Mission in halter tops and pumps
ignore me like I'm just another

voluntary miscarriage of an intellect.
Forever is getting faster,

air
traffic no one hears over a beach.

You make a small gesture on that beach, love,
flicking volcanic ash off a cigarette.

Judson Mitcham

Home

The TV's white noise
hisses me back, this first
awareness the worst one, lights on,
wine by the bed, stale cigarettes,
chicken box greasy on the Gideon.
An hour before dawn,
no lovers now rock me in irony,
and the low yellow moon
on the far wall's high school
watercolor is sad right art,
nowhere in the lake.

I remember my father's game.
Having come from the mill,
settled in his chair, he would say
"There is something odd in the room."
Unseen, either he had hidden
something in plain sight,
pencil in a flower pot,
or changed things slightly,
setting the clock back
or taking a knob off the radio.
He knew how simple it was
and watched us, giving no clue.

When the trucker overhead slams home,
his kicked-in turquoise door
not catching, the chain on mine
rattles. I recall
there was never a prize back then.
There was only the seeing.

Judson Mitcham

The Smell of Rain

A small boy catches this sweetness, and he knows,
standing at the edge of a field, watching the dust
swirl in the wind. A ball glove brothers oiled dark
hangs loose on his hand, and the friend he is waiting for
already has turned toward home.

                         An old farmer
walking slowly down the road catches it too,
then catches himself, the land gone years now, carved
into small lots, sold to anyone. In the air
there is something as sad as history touched by hope.

This morning it is there when I walk out
for the newspaper. I remember my mother
rushing to the clothesline, the sweet smelling sheets
lifting in the breeze, those first big drops coming down,
and I think of my children's lives.

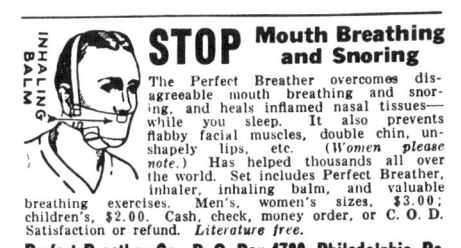

George Moore

Mexico Firsthand

We wake corrupted boyscouts,
near enough to the highway
that the semi's air horn sends us
into sudden terror. The desert
is no place to sleep alone,
even at twelve. Two are up early
making breakfast for forty,
an endless watery revenge
of scrambled eggs and white toast.
In the night my bag
has filled with sand,
and others are now finding scorpions
clinging to the smooth lips
of leather boots, poised
like dangerous blossoms ready to open.
A few stay out in the sun too long,
and at night we can hear them,
low moans housed in foreign flesh.
These are our first experiences,
nights along roadsides
in heavy industrial wastelands,
steel and steam and chainlink
singing us to sleep.
A few of the older boys
go into town and buy girls. And then,
because they feel we deserve it,
perhaps because we were not there
in the dingy rooms watching
as they fumbled with their clothes,
they bring us tequila
and we sit low, behind sarapes
draped between seats near the back
of the ailing bus, smoking
long black cigarettes
and talking about love. But
there is no magic in what we hear,
Mexico takes even the timid
and corrupts them. Later,
we will smuggle switchblades and

firecrackers back across the border,
and reaching Texas
we will become boyscouts again.

NEW!

FOR ALL CARS

STALLION HORN

Whinnies like a wild stallion

Wild-horse whinny lets them know you're coming! Novel new horn that works off battery, not manifold, attaches easily under hood to all cars, all models, makes any car sound like real live rip-snorting **stallion**. Precision-made by quality horn manufacturer. Complete with horn button control, wire, mounting hardware. 5" x 5½" x 6", handsome black enamel finish; 12-volt. When you blow your horn, be distinctive.

$9.95 each ppd.

Immediate shipment. Satisfaction guaranteed. Send check or money order.

HOBI INC DEPT E-86 FLUSHING, NEW YORK 11352

Fred Muratori

The Casket Maker's Proposal

Ten years out of high school — long enough to know
That summer's nothing special after all — I was hauling
Boxes out of state, a major sale for a little man like me.

She asked to come along, needed a rolled-down window
And that sense of stillness you get when you're moving fast.
I said sure because I never took her out enough.

We drank beer until our speech fell free as loose change
Jangling on the sidewalk, and then, deaf from road noise,
Caskets on the flatbed fit to rock right through the cab,

I popped it. Just asked it like it was *What time is it?*
And blind with love's sudden puff, she kissed me going 70.
All I could think about was owls when you find one

Out of happenstance, and you'd believe the whole white moon
Was taking off not three yards from your face.
She was thinking: Finally, finally. He's not much

But at least his work is steady as it comes. People die.
We passed a three-car pile up in the eastbound lane,
Big toys some giant kid tossed topsy-turvy.

Like anybody else we gawked. It was the first time
I'd ever seen a dead man out of formal clothes,
Splayed over a guardrail, his head suspended in the weeds.

I thought: Death is real, but so is everything this woman
Sitting next to me will do or say to make it less so.
I turned on the radio to find the song we'd need to remember.

Bea Carol Opengart

Erotica

Silk stockings and the belt that holds them,
garters edged with lace hand made by Belgian nuns,
their patience. The lives they left were less
and more than they gain. Their faith. The lace
they don't wear brings them closer to God,
who has no body. Undressing,

I cup my breasts in my hands and observe,
in the mirror, how stubbornly
the flesh resists restraint. If God had a body
it would be here, in my body, in everyone.

Legs, you have carried me this far,
I want to go on. Arms,
you have lifted, held and carried without breaking,
I want to go on singing. Mouth,
you have given such pleasure
that a man cried out beneath me and sleeping,
did not release my hands. Awake,
he couldn't keep them. Like fretful birds
they hovered, then accomplished
their sure hold on the air.

There was a boy who loved the sea and trusted it
too well. When his body washed ashore
they knew him by his teeth, the fillings
matched to a chart, all that was left. He might as well
have been driftwood, seaweed, beached jellyfish.
I think of death as an eclipse, the water
rocking him for days, gently. I press a finger

to my cheek to feel, when it's gone,
an imprint. As the mark fades, I diminish.
Love, what are you? These ghosts are what you are.

I'm with you in your nakedness.

Alicia Ostriker

The Game

Arrogance and loneliness. If a man
Knows only those three words, he runs away
Like a boy, when the larger children are fiercely playing

A violent game he does not understand.
Like a boy with a violin, or a boy
Whose eyelashes are suddenly wet with tears,

And who has heard a rough voice, not his own,
Call "give it back," emptying in a street
Among the grocery and music stores,

The cats, the pavement slates, and the fallen cans,
Glazed, pink, bricky, for it is four o'clock,
A rich smell pouring up from the river.

He digs, he pushes stones with his stubborn tool,
He sets his teeth together, and never,
Never again will they trick and fool him,

Those stinkers, those fuckers, and never
Will he butt his hungry head into the rubbery
Stomach of his grandmother, the wilted and baaing sheep,

That rocks and knits, half blind, exactly like
The illustration in *Alice,* and when you touch her
You feel clothing, corsets and blubber

All at once, embarrassingly.
You feel wet plants, bland food aromas. The boy
Closes his pocketknife and must go home.

They thought he was *her* boy. He is just waiting
For her dissolution into nightmare tatters,
Then swirling animalculae, then nothing,

Like when they blow up enemies in cartoons,
Or you solve a division problem
And it disappears. Like that. Now the boy, the future

Man is running.
He is happy, having begun to understand
The game, the ball, the sticks, the rule.

Soon you will see how the robes float from him,
Clean red and blue, and how the pebbled ball
Descends from heaven and plummets into his hands.

Robert Pack

Clayfeld Holds On

Shivered by his dream of her into
    a rancid sweat,
Clayfeld awakes in the weatherless dawn
    to find his right hand
has gone numb. As if examining
    a star-fish on the beach,
he steadies it then pokes it with
    a puzzled finger
for some residual response, assumes
    that he has slept on it,
that soon sensation will return, and so
    decides not to disturb
the mood of its glum privacy.
    The same repeating scene,
when first she told him she would leave,
    assembles in his mind:
the cove of swishing lily pads where they
    had landed their canoe,
spied on by golden eyes of bull frogs startled
    in their grunting
mimickings; the birch tree leaning
    from the slimy bank;
the water snake, uncoiling from its crevice
    in the slop of stones,
sunning along the border of the lake.
    Clayfeld remembers
exactly how the light reflected
    sleek upon the lily pads,
or shadowed inward on the moss
    upon the rocks, or mottled
on the birch tree's blighted leaves,
    but can't bring back
how he had felt — as if he had become
    only the story of his life.
He wonders — had he sensed within the gap
    of losing her
some unacknowledged rising of relief
    lifting his thoughts

outside himself into an air so easy
    in the lightness
of its flow, and so impersonal,
    that nothing moved in him
besides the patterns that his eyes perceived?
    An absent self — was that
the silence he had wished to vanish in
    beneath his fear
of losing even caring for her loss?
    He presses the moist chill
of his numb hand against the flush
    that swells his ear —
as if the curl and grip of fingers hardened
    his hand into a shell
in which he listens to the echoes call
    from the indifferent sea.
Clayfeld is drawn to let himself
    be washed back
with the tide of foaming sand,
    with horse-shoe crabs,
starfish and periwinkle, driftwood
    and anemone, but
something inside him won't let go:
    he can't give up
his memory of losing her; he holds
    to his possession of her
being gone. He feels her loosening hand
    as it released his own
when she stepped out of the canoe,
    pulling herself away
by clinging to the birch; he hears
    the jay's slurred squawk
as its warped shadow passes on the lake.
    Clayfeld wonders if
she has a child; and now he tries
    imagining her daughter,
grown and beautiful, beneath a tree,
    so he can watch her white hand

beckoning to someone who approaches from
    the glare of distant light
beyond the lake which Clayfeld has to shade
    his widened eyes to see.

Eric Pankey

Rhododendron

   Winter. Chickadees make their way
From the snow-tipped shrub to the feeder.
   I admire them: their resilience,
Their nervous flitter a measure
   Of the morning's minutes, familiar
Fright, full of greed and clear impatience —
   They take the given as if stolen.
One after another, but never
   More than one risking flight at a time.
The whole hedge quivers. The feeder sways.
   I remember that quick scene as mine.
A green life full of too many hearts.

Eric Pankey

Late August

While you are packing,
I go upstairs to write.
All the house's left-over heat
follows me up, it seems.
I sit by an open window
and sweat.
Nothing comes.
You have on the same album
you've played all summer.

Saxophones. A beat up record —
swing and jazz.
Gerry Mulligan, Stan Getz
and some other great I should know.
I try not to listen.
For a minute, I watch a mud-dauber
build its nest in a shutter slat.
A sliver of light
follows its body's thin curve,

a body balanced carefully
between flicks of wings
doing business with the air.
It starts to rain.
Lines of drops
gather on the shutter's edge,
each weighted with a fine mud.
The wasp continues
until I lose its shape

in the splatterings of dirt
on the driveway and the quick
irregular lines of water
blurring the window.
As always, I am watching.
As always, the record skips
on a low note, skips
three or four times
before you get to it.

I am pleased
for the first time
by the variation,
by the interruption,
and can't imagine the song
any other way.
I can hear the bath water
running as I watch
the screen smear with rain.

There is a breeze,
a thick slow wind still full of heat,
but it is motion, a relief.

Eric Pankey

The Guard: 1934

1.
Sometimes I wake up at night
and don't know where I am.
There's the train beneath me, a scent of dogwood . . . .
Waking is answer enough.
On the boxcar's side, a few damp leaves
are pasted, and the moonlight
shining through them and through the space
between slats is the thin brown-orange
of tea my mother used to make.
Every inch of the boxcar
is a changing shade of brown —
a color that won't stand still.
And always the smell of chickenshit.
Chickenshit. I hate that word.
That's what my brother called me
when I wouldn't join him
and the neighbor boys in the pranks they'd pull.
One time and for no good reason
they put a .22 up the ass
of a mean brindle sow.
My brother said her tits were uglier
than a fat woman's he had seen
at a freak show. But he lied.
He'd never been to one,
never even seen a woman's tits.
And how can something be ugly
when you see it your whole life?
There was no telling what killed the pig
— no wound. Just a crust of brown blood
along the line of the mouth,
blood matting the few jowl hairs.
Its thick flesh was a white, turning gray,
like talc dusted onto sweaty skin
when the only weather there is is humid.
It was noon by the time
the farmer found the sow.
I imagined by then
a fistful of flies covered

its eyes like so many seeds
in the middle of a sunflower.
It seemed like a waste. What's the point? —
I asked my brother. Don't you see, he laughed,
It don't mean a thing, not a thing.

2.
I get to where I can forget
the noise of the chickens, the train's clanking.
This is my fifth trip.
Sometimes when we pass a field
where someone is burning off hawkweed
or where, above the undergrowth
cluttering a creekbank,
peppermint grows,
I can almost ignore the stench.
But then a warm breeze passes through,
and you would think that would help . . . .
As we move on, the wind forces
shit-stink into my nose.
                                      At times,
the motion of the train
makes me sick to my stomach.
I slide the door open
but that only makes things worse —
the sun's glare racing on the water
which has gathered in the ditch,
the haze of heat lifting off that water,
the spiderwebs in the maples.
It all moves by too quickly,
all one blurred line like a wall.
The best bet is to focus
on something in the distance.
It doesn't matter what — a hawk,
a shack built up on a rise.
Once I watched a farmer
take a switch to his boy;
I mean, I thought it was his boy.
The scene, at such a distance,

was still, framed by solitary trees.
My stomach seemed to settle.
I don't know how many times
he hit the kid or why.
I just watched until the train darkened
into the length of a tunnel
and I felt better. I felt okay.

3.
I went into town for a half-hour —
Joplin, Missouri. The train stopped
to take on water. I needed a drink.
Although Joplin's just a bunch of Baptists,
you can buy a pint of bourbon
and even a woman if you want.
As I was leaving town, the rain started.
When you have a mile to go
you might as well walk —
no need to run like girls in the rain
from church to their daddy's new auto.
You can only get so wet.
I wasn't supposed to leave the train.

In the boxcar I call my office,
I was drying myself off with an old feedsack.
I heard board snapping and the chickens
stirring in crates at the car's end.
I had not lit the lantern yet —
I could see all right.
By then the shotgun was loaded
and the coolness of the butt
surprised me when I pulled it
into the shallow of my shoulder.
It felt good against my still damp skin.
I knew what I could do with it.

All I could see was an arm,
striped with railroad yard lights
that angled in through the slats.

It seemed whiter than it should be —
like that of a man who wore
long sleeves even late into July,
or a healed arm fresh out of a cast.
It was kind of frightening,
this arm without a body.
Its hand kept groping at chickens
until it caught one by the claw.
It was a left arm.
I had to imagine the man's face and body
pressed against the boxcar's side —
the man on his tiptoes as he reached in,
the boards rough against his cheek.
I aimed a little to the right.
I didn't care about the chickens anymore.

4.
After this evening's rain,
there's rust settled like brown soot
in the nicks and scratches.
But I take care of this gun —
don't get me wrong.

I can see just fine
through the splintered hole.

My brother told me something once
about the blood inside the body,
how it is blue. Something to do with air.
Nothing blue about this blood —
not even beneath the moon's light
which is almost blue in the puddles
along the tracks and on the tips of pines.

It's what you expect it to be.
Not pretty. Not bad enough to make you sick.

I killed a man with this shotgun.
It was easy. Easier than keeping rust

off the barrel's blue metal.
Almost too easy.
     As we move beyond a hedgerow,
it's as though a flash of sunlight
fills the car. It's just lightning against the dark.
Although there is coal smoke in the air
and a cool breath of snow, out of season,
as we pass the Joplin Ice Plant,
all I can smell is gunpowder.
I like that smell. The taste of the air.

LADIES' 'RATIONAL' DRESS.

For Cycling, Tennis, and Golf.

OUR SPECIALTY.

THE 'KNICKER-SKIRT'

From **5/11**, Post Free,

IS INVALUABLE TO ALL LADIES FOR

**FREEDOM,
HEALTH,
COMFORT.**

Patterns of Materials and Prices sent post free.

WM. SMALL & SON,
1 & 2,
CHAMBERS STREET,
EDINBURGH.

Wyatt Prunty

Rooms Without Walls

Late sunlight breaking through the room
And a boy's round face against the glass,
Breath clouding, eyes narrowed to the sun.
Outside, snow falls through the light;
The sky is granular and close,
All pattern of the wind's white slant,
That wind about the house, and branches'
Snow-muffled scrapes against the eaves.

Later, the power lines will fail,
And, twelve years old, I will stand outside
Counting the coal oil lamps that float
From room to room as though our house
Did not have walls inside but was
One space through which my family sent
Their liquid light without effort,
Like quiet conversation.

All this before the heart disease,
Cancers, and little suicides
Of cigarettes and whiskey turned
Events into a daguerrotype
Fading and slightly out of focus.
The snow, deeper than ever before,
Was in a frame I took outside
But never brought back in again.

Instead, with power lines knocked down
All over town, I stamped in the street,
My feet so cold they hurt, and gazed
Until I turned my family's warm house
Inside out, the snow's unfolding linen
And pillows deep as a child's gathering
Unconsciousness that sleeps through any sound
Made for the mind's stark furnishings.

Two blocks past where I stood, small shacks began,
Unpainted shotguns shouldered together
Into a row of narrow facings

I studied from the school bus window
Or counted as our car drove past —
Ten to a block, identical,
Each with its small front yard
Of bright red clay, as hard as pavement.

From that direction, over the stillness
The snow had brought, I heard the blows
And the high voice of a small girl
Who could not beg but only gasp
"Daddy, Daddy" between the cracking sounds
Made by whatever he'd picked up.
I stood more still than I have ever thought.
He beat her until there was silence.

And I think that action took forever.
More than the snow's cold multiplicity
Or all the lights that failed to work
In our small town, or hands that rested
In laps, in pockets, near telephones,
The hands of those who waited for
The power, thinking the novelty
Of such a deep snow, and that far south.

And later that night, beyond crying,
I began to shake for that small child,
For both of us; not in the arms and legs
But in the chest and gut. And I felt
As though I had a fishing line
In my head, drawn to the point of breaking.
And when I closed my eyes a light
Would flash, then run like iodine.

What I know now is that the frame
Made by the window where I stood
One afternoon was cold and arbitrary.
If anything, the snow's white sifting
Down my glass meant anonymity
Far past the best or worst we ever do,

Beyond all melting at our touch
Which like regret arrives past tense.

What I know is that our meanings work
Like games thought up by children in a street;
The space, number of players, goals
And objects moved are arbitrary.
And yet our games are serious,
As players go beyond themselves
Into a violence that winds,
And lets us say they were responsible.

The house I saw outside that night
Was covered by a heavy snow
That rounded all its borders; no hedge
Or wall could separate its space
From a smaller space two blocks away,
The place of one small girl's great pain,
Which still echoes in the stillness that we are.

John Reed

Forgetting

As I get older I find myself
forgetting, waiting for a name's appointment
it won't keep, though it sends excuses:
too little oxygen, too much lead, a tumor
worming like a slug, or just
a minor disfunction, like those that send a t.v.
to the shop. I'm Penelope
bound to her loom, reweaving what my brain
unstrung last night, trying to find
Odysseus' smile again in the colored thread,
but it's just colored thread, a text
of blank parentheses.

You tell me we all forget the nameless
people who never touched us with love or pain,
but can't explain about lost lovers who,
on another day in another mood, would be here
jostled in a crowd of silly, unbidden
faces. And of course you lecture me on Freud,
and how the symbols of our guilt,
or rage, or pain are stowed in tunnels so dark
and far below no bird nor thread
could keep them whole or lead them to the light.
But if that's true, what memory
would ever heel when we call?

Maybe the lost names leave on a dream
of adventure down forgotten streets to shores
past recall where unknown flowers
bloom, filling the night with unnameable passion,
and then return on Lethean seas
here to the bright purlieu that the beacon
of our thoughts has made
on this sharp and stoney coast.

I cannot say, but when I summon
any thing that matters at the time —
a small bird fallen on the lawn,
a woman covering her teacup with her hand,

or a remote star — and it won't come,
I feel the great heron's gigantic wings
battering the nothingness that lifts him
to flight above the lacerating sedge
and insects threading the water's skin,
and nameless life tunneling in the slime,
to turn his ivory beak like a bright auger
drilling into his endlessness of sky.

Paulette Roeske

A Plan to Circumvent the Death of Beauty

Because she thinks it can be bought, she fills
her windows with hibiscus in glamorous pots
to hide the fact of highrise brick.
Some nights she wants to float the magenta blossoms
in shallow dishes on the piano lid,
tie a red-fringed shawl around her waist
and play mazurkas by heart while dreaming of dancing.
But after one season, the perfect blooms are spent
and now, stunted, rootbound, the stems rot from the inside out.

Then she remembers the rows of pet store aquariums,
the stunning neon fish grazing above miniature divers.
(This is almost the same story.) Only one of them lives, a black
angel with tattered wings treading the algae-dark water.
In her dreams it grows enormous, amorous, more
dangerous than flesh. As a child, her least favorite
uncle, a farmer, watched her swing on the gate to the sty.
He said, "A sow like that'll take a man's leg off."

Enticed by the pale filaments of its expressive crest,
seduced by the enviable dark pools of its eyes that see out
both sides at once, its sexual tongue, she buys
a cockatoo in an elegant wrought-iron cage.
When she dreams she can fly beyond the steep faces
of the brick buildings, the exhausting air,
the corridors of winter trees, she looks down
and sees her mother, only thirty,
framed by the doorway of the family home,
the trellises alive with blooms. Her mother
is beautiful, black hair fanned by the breeze.
Shading her eyes, she tilts back her head
and crows at the flying girl who drops
her arms, all the light dissolving around her.

William Pitt Root

Newswalkers of Swidnik

1.
Flattened again for an alien impression,
the wild terrain of Poland

repeatedly erupts with fresh black starts
pushing up cautiously, delicately driven,

impossible to weed out: an old crone
opens her bag, shortens the breadline

reading aloud from Milosz — *On the day
the world ends, a bee circles a clover . . .* —;

workers display the Black Madonna of Czestochwa
for bosses who know it signifies Walsea;

actors refusing to work on official broadcasts
accept hunger instead of official success;

artists rejecting the Ministry of Culture
refuse its invitations, exhibit work for friends;

members of Solidarity, forced underground,
feed their families by swallowing their tongues;

*a bee circles a clover,
a fisherman mends a glimmering net.*

2.
A Pole soon learns how the butter of laughter
improves the bitter crusts of oppression.

Perhaps you dismantle the old radio, pin
a resistor to your worn lapel.

Or you walk barefoot on May Day
in a suit black as a casket,

your protruding bare feet
reminders that the freedoms

buried are still alive. Or maybe you are
a Warsaw University student

forced to attend Military Courses
— at every mention

of the Soviet Union
you applaud, you all applaud

ungovernably.

3.
What happened 100 miles from Warsaw
in the factory town of Swidnik
may have been cued
by the American movie *Network*: One night

during the routine propaganda fix
          of the 7:30 broadcast,
all 30,000 workers turned it off,
          took a walk.

At twilight. A promenade.
Just like the old days.

Promptly: *7 o'clock curfew.*

So they walked out on the 5 o'clock news.

Fines: *two weeks' wages.*
Arrests and expulsions from schools.

A quarter hour work-stoppage at the factory.

Firings and lay-offs, further threats and arrests.

But soon the promenade of the newswalkers
spread to Lublin, Olsztyn, Bialystok,
even to Warsaw itself, making news
no one in Swidnik would see.

4.
To families of the jailed and unemployed
the church passes food and supplies. Surely

the Christian labyrinths under Rome
resonate with strange new names.

And the Experience And Future Group,
an unofficial forum
       of intellectuals and liberal Communists,

describes military rule to General Jaruzelski
so:
    This is an alien and unknown act
    in Polish tradition. It forces

our native citizens to live as if in a strange land.

5.
Such attempts to level the rugged horizon of Poland
invite disruption, paving
the way for the Pope.
                Truly this one is blessed
for blessed means bathed in blood,
and bathed in his own,
he is clean. At just this time,
setting foot in a strange land
no Pope had been in before him,
he knelt down to kiss the earth.

John Paul, on British soil,
knew what song to sing.

*See everything: overlook a great deal:
correct a little. On the day the world ends*

He knelt to kiss the borderless earth.

He arose with a smile.

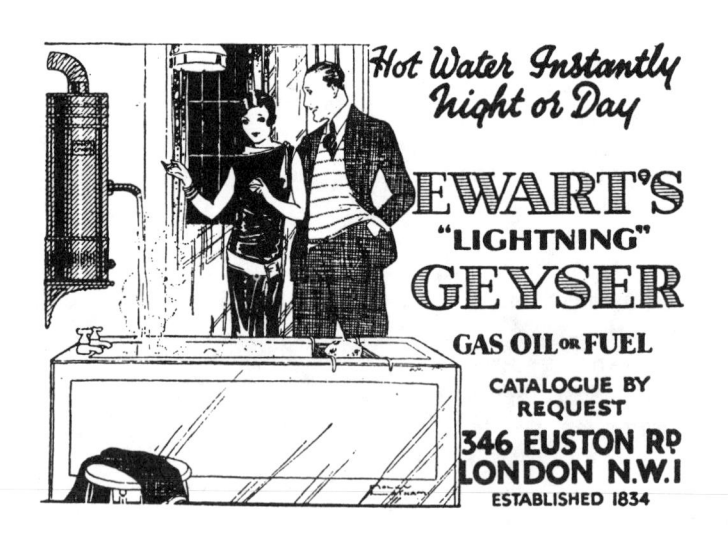

Michael Rosen

Child's Play

Thick as stars within arm's reach,
they clustered three houses down
over the empty lot, flashed
once and gave themselves away:
inexhaustible, sluggish,
more than we could want and more
the next night if we wanted.
We held weddings after dusk.
The boys caught bugs and then girls
to smudge the lights for diamonds
on their ring fingers. We marched
down the walks, all our hands bright
with their bodies, all of us
married and then unmarried
an hour later, when darkness
meant another thing to do.

We collected wood enough
so that it was never dark,
and vowed to stay up all night
reading by lanterns of bugs
till the jars dimmed and the lights
stuck against the sweating glass.
By dawn the campfire smoldered
pink with the sky and I ran
to empty the jars — the bugs
dripped into the coals and flared
in white fires that died before
I slid back inside the tent
where everyone was sleeping.
Breakfast coals, bonfires — summer
those years could burn forever
with everything we fed that fire.

Slowly as constellations
the fireflies define themselves.
September, it's light enough
to catch what looks like shadows
lingering before the flash

that catches the eye. One star
blinks haphazardly across
the bedroom where we're reading
in the dark we hadn't noticed.
I straddle the chairs, swatting;
this starts you laughing. Finally
I cup it between my palms.
As you open the window
it lights inside my fingers,
a red ember in the dark
my hands can't help but make.

Jeff Schiff

Articulating the Familiar

Owning a Chevrolet
is no accident of birth.
Or how could you account

to those close at hand
that you were bound by the womb
to cruise a strip?

That nightly
your life meant something
as moot, perhaps, as pistons —

which follows which,
and who determined the sequence.
There stands, simply, a collective of speed.

Jonah chose the sleekest whale,
and Moses squared off against
the most efficient stone.

The Lord reveals:
the right suspension is
the difference between looking up

and being looked upon.
Truing a valve by eye, revving
through redline

when the oil is nowhere near specs,
dropping a clutch in loose sand,
we go where we want.

Ron Schreiber

Tie
    (var, *Ty, Tighe, Thai*)

Connexion. That which binds
friends, lovers, comrades, or
(2) the result of bondage, as in
being tied — to some object like
a bed or chair, upon which
erotic affections are placed.

Ty. A bar in Greenwich Village,
in the middle of Christopher
Street between Seventh & Hudson,
usually spelled in the
singular possessive, *Ty's,* an
ironic name denoting passages
in the night.

Tighe. The name of a professional
baseball coach & manager, circa
1950's & early 60's, born obese
& chewing tobacco, fattened later
by beer & long evenings listening
to radio, first name, Jack.

Thai. Adjective, once referring
to people living in a country
made popular by Richard Rogers
& Yul Brynner, more recently a
connexion, wrapped in a stick,
sweet smelling & tasting,
powerful; flower tops, laced.

Tie, Ty, Tighe, Thai. What
joins these words together, not
just sound, but soundings. Laced
in the middle of Christopher Street,
playing catch as catch can,
concrete bases, light & high, as in
stickball, Jack, or *tie.*

Bob Shacochis

The Heart's Advantage

Lindy, I said, are you even there? Get up and let me in the door. It was a Saturday morning, not so early. I'd been away in Africa for a month, a hired hand for the government charged with spreading money across the Sahel, the only green they've seen there in generations. The ticket was *appropriate technology,* the words that make clouds of cash wing across oceans to rain change down upon the lives of other men.

I pounded on the door and shouted but it was a full five minutes before I heard her on the other side clawing at the deadbolt. I had been in the air for eight hours. My shirt was like wet celluloid layered to my back, and my intestines gurgled, invaded by microbes. There was a clear joy in me to be back home.

"Lindy?"

"Just a minute. I don't have my contacts in."

"What have you been doing? Were you still asleep?"

Yes, she was. Lindy, a determined early riser, had to be roused. The curtains were still drawn, the house itself in a soporific state. When the door cracked open, I felt an alien proliferation spreading out of the cool dimness beyond. Then she stepped forward and I saw her hair.

For months she had been fussing about a perm, tearing through women's magazines, pricing some of the shops in Coral Gables, pausing in front of mirrors to study herself. I chastised her for being indecisive and said quit whining and just go do it. I don't know, she said. There's no going back once they squirt the gunk on. What if I don't like it? What if *you* don't like it? Take a chance, I advised. You're adventurous. Only stop throwing yourself around and sighing.

"You don't like it, do you?"

She looked like a juju queen. Wrapped in the bars of her yellow blue and green terry robe, she appeared untended, underslept, last night's makeup rendering her face experimental, ghoulish, asymmetrical. Her myopia gave her an intensely dazed stare, and one smudged eye looked a centimeter or so off from its set. She needed a good wipe.

"Dear God, what have you done?"

I could not speak in a calm voice about her once precious hair. Why is the head of a treasonous woman shaved? Why else butcher and abominate those delicate threads if they are not emblematic of her soul? Women used to bundle braid and bind their tresses, let them tumble down at night for their husbands, the first gift of bedtime. They washed their hair lovingly with exotic soaps and rare milks, spiced it with mint extracts and herbs, stroked it over and over into glorious waves, scintillating spills, their proud crop, heavenly curtains parted over the cold fact of the face so that even the ugly could take advantage and be redeemed by exquisite curls. So it is that we soon become estranged from women who allow their hair to depreciate.

Lindy had hair the color of an Irish Setter's, a singular color to be envied, no matter that it is the color of a dog. It was as rich in sight as a brogue in sound, a visual lilt. It crowned her in thick and luscious loops that swayed on small shoulders. You can imagine the pleasure of having it fed to your lips, or seeing it glide strand by strand across the taut cone of a nipple and gather between breasts, watch it open and close the rapture of her face. I smelled long life there in Lindy's hair, good-heartedness and babies. And I felt, as she approached permhood day by day, she will honor her sex.

She did not. To my horror she did not. What I now observed through a dulling shock was a pumpkin-headed debutante of naughtiness, her tresses lopped off inches from her skull and spiked like a guarddog's collar. The spikes were needle-tipped and apparently simonized so they would hold their shape, and there was a hatching grid of distasteful white scalp around the base of the roots.

"You don't like it."

I said That's right. I said You bet I don't. By her tone it was obvious that she knew I didn't — *had known* I wouldn't — and had prepared herself not to be affected by my reaction. She arched her eyebrows defiantly and stepped back to let me in. Her arms were crossed on her chest but when she moved her hands dropped unconsciously and the robe fell open.

"You've slept in your clothes I see."

She glanced down at herself and frowned.

I am a happy witness to the caprice of fashion but I believe each generation identifies itself and marches on, true to its code. Lindy wore one of those crotch-high synthetic knit babydoll dresses — low waisted to a flounced skirt, a loose bodice shaped like a sack, spaghetti strapped, the style popular among tough high school girls who gag at the idea of cute. The fabric was the color of spotted banana peel with broad stripes of tinsel running through it. She had gone beyond vogue, gone a step past the glamor of the magazines.

"You look eighteen and dirty."

She folded her robe closed stoically and tied herself in, the cinch of the belt making the outline of her hips appear. The terry knot bulged with the foretelling of permanence. "Come in," she said. "The air conditioner's on."

There are moments, even days — longer still, phases — when we're not ourselves, when we inhabit foreign moods and obscure desires. We're somebody else for the duration. Blame a planet or odd chemicals in the breakfast cereal. I'm not referring here to such temporary phenomenon. I'm talking about a genuine change of character, like a color television transmuting to black and white without hope of repair, or a nation falling from the grace of its past. What is Persia today, what is Egypt? That's what I mean. Something, from all evidence, irreversible. A cheating, a betrayal.

Lindy's reluctance to let me back in — no hungry kiss, no hug of relief — made me suspect, together with her wretchedly flamboyant hairdo, that she had been unfaithful, not sexually, but to the life we had fabricated as a couple. Decisions with impact had been made that I knew nothing about. Suddenly I was an occupying force, she *le resistance*. It was a flat way to come home from abroad, dragging my absence like a bum who had attached to me.

She whirled toward the bedroom and I tramped straight for the bath where I showered petulantly. Not to be found in its dish was my brand of soap, I scrubbed myself with something similar to a hunk of potter's clay, the lather no more than oily flecks of foam. Searching through the medicine cabinet for a q-tip I discovered a sinister rainbow of nail polish, the shades of Lindy's current fascination — Avocado Whip, Midnight Scream, Angel's Throat, Chocolate Bunny. A bright undented tube of spermicide mystified me. Lindy had been on the pill when I departed in June. In place of her round hairbrush was a rattail comb and a squat jar of gel treatment labelled *Spic n Spike*. Whoa, stop, I said, sliding the mirror back carefully, my breathing shallow.

I emerged fresh, clad in navy running shorts, resolved to adjust to Lindy's remarkable appearance now that the shock had withdrawn, diluted by clean pearls of North American public water, the common blessing of comfort. In the Sahel you go unwashed for as long as you can or people object. Lindy was in the kitchen seated at the table, her eyeballs lacquered into focus, her legs crossed once at the knees and again at the ankles, everything otherwise the same. She blew steam off a cup of coffee. A second cup sat waiting for me. I wrapped my grateful fingers around it, thinking nothing had really changed after all. I lowered my head, waiting for the resolution and the nerve to look at her once again, this time honestly, prepared for kindness. She tapped one foot and sniffed.

"So how'd it go?" she asked.

"I now have seven native wives." I diverted a cruel thought — each less garish than you.

"I bet you do."

"Actually, it went well. Nobody believed in the windmills. We drilled deeper and I designed a prop that generated more rpms. They now have a few drops of water to fight over, and we have more money for the boat. So goes the division of wealth in the world."

She sipped her coffee, her expression unchanged. I kept staring at her, the familiar core. Somewhere there beneath the trendy masquerade was my personal historian and bookkeeper, my partner in escape from various numbing realities, the only person on the globe whose ear I dare whisper into, my night-stilled companion, my arm crooked on the future. Nostalgia took its gummy bite. But then I thought, *thrill to this, thrill to this, man,* she's a strange presence that bears your mark.

"So how was it for you? Did you miss me?"

"A month's a long time," she answered cryptically.

"I missed you. I did. Really." The emotion stalled in my voice and the words blanched. I regretted opening my mouth — no songbird had flown out, only the processed warbling of mealy notes. I wanted to hear an appetite in her voice. I wanted the distance reconciled, the love more splendid for all the anticipation absence had forged. I want it, I thought, battling resentment, like the last time I came home from who knows where.

She cocked her head. The spikes rotated like a satellite positioning itself to fire laser beams. She grimaced, her eyes showing a small impatience for what I had said or how I had said it. I had been standing, hesitant, but now I sat down next to her at the table.

"I meant what I said."

"I know."

"We can do better than this," I clucked.

"It takes a while to get used to you again. I haven't even brushed my teeth."

Her lips looked like a brittle red lariat slipping off the rim of the coffee cup. The gold chain around her neck I hadn't seen before. It encircled the tendons that arched from her collarbone, an aristocratic sweep of lines that had become more pronounced since we first met, she an auditor sent over to our department to punch holes in our budgetary exuberance. A bead of amber dangled from the center of the chain, what looked like a baby cockroach embedded within, an ancient pest that proved the high alchemic value of whatever is stolen from time.

"So," I said, fishing for anything wonderfully nice to say. "So."

She watched me expectantly, her headdress bobbing with each of my *sos*. I had nothing more to say about her hair. That was to be treated in the same manner as if she had wrecked the car — don't worry about it, it's only the fender, we can have it knocked out. But I wanted somehow to reach into her month alone, to extract the thorns she had accumulated deprived of the shield togetherness provides. So I said with all the earnestness of a half-wit priest, "Lindy, I'm sorry I had to be gone so long. I know it must have been terrible for you."

I leaned forward on my elbows, pushing aside my mug, ready for her sad account of life without me.

"Of course it wasn't," she laughed in girlish eighth notes, like a piccolo, a silvery confident melody that made me first ashamed, then defensive. "Oh Lord, don't be mad, Sims. It's nice to have you back, but I have fun, too, when you're gone. I don't dry up, you know."

"Oh." I swallowed my coffee like a frog. The cries of the hadjis echoed in my ears. *What!?* windmills in the desert. Water sucked forth from barrenness? No, *monsieur*. No no.

"Well don't be so surprised," she said.

"Actually I'm not," I sputtered. "This is in fact good news. I worry about you being lonely."

We had struggled through elaborate discussions before I chose to quit the department and join the press of part-time consultants feeding off the huge carcass of foreign policy. It was for the best, we concurred, if we were ever going to get the boat in shape and one day sail off to what we dreamed could happen in our lives. The gaps that would separate us would be no more than the slight blips, the blind spots, encountered on a dial between one level of intensity and the next, like a furnace building heat, a light increasing wattage. I would fly off, a return ticket in my pocket, and then I would retract like the wandering leg of John Donne's compass to the center of the circle, the geometric conceit of love well-architected.

"No need to worry about me," she insisted, giving a cheery toss to the ghost of her hair, a pang of loss sent into my blood.

She had picked up three new accounts in her freelancing work, read a dozen books, started an aerobics class at Miami-Dade. We were edging back into our rhythm as we talked. I felt better all the time. Her hair impressed me as less angry and ominous than when I first saw it, a loud game that would soon stop. Yet I felt on the verge of unwanted discovery. She saw my look and forced it. Her mouth puckered, her eyebrows plumed. She nailed a finger into my arm.

"Well go ahead," she snapped. "Don't hedge, it's not like you. You're dying to say something."

"It's just that I didn't expect to find you quite like this."

"Quite like what?"

"Asleep, for one thing. In your clothes, *those* clothes. Was it wrong of me to expect something else. Now come on, be honest."

She was. "I forgot you were coming today," Lindy said.

I pretended unsuccessfully that this failure was of no importance.

"Don't lock up," she said, tugging my arm, taking my hand in hers. "I was out too late. I was drunk."

I pulled my hand away. "What do you mean you were drunk?" I said stupidly. She crossed her eyes to reinforce my stupidity.

"I had too much to drink. I was dancing and worked up a sweat. The drinks felt like they ran right through me."

"You never sweat," I reminded her.

"I do when I dance."

I was astounded by the implication of this news. "You don't sweat when you dance with me."

"You haven't asked me in ages. Besides, the dances are different today."

I slammed my coffee mug on the table. I seemed to have been invalidated. "Today?" I said loudly. "Today?"

"Look, we've talked enough for now," she proclaimed. "You're just getting mad. I'm going to go shower."

I retrieved my luggage and trudged into the bedroom, disoriented from the moment I set foot in there. Our platform bed had completed a 180 degree turn and now faced south, underneath the double windows, instead of north, underneath the full security of a heartpine wall. On the wall the batik had disappeared, replaced by a chrome-framed abstraction, pink paint splashed and dribbled on a beige background, the impression that of a muffled scream. The curtains had turned white as had the comforter on the bed. My antique oak bookcase was gone. Glass shelves climbed the walls. White gladioli thrust from large raku vases with pinched necks, one in each corner. I flopped down onto the mattress and lit a cigarette. Lindy returned from the shower, a black towel wrapped like a sari around her, a black plastic bathcap pulled over her scalp. Her face is pretty, I thought, no matter what she does to herself. She stopped abruptly, scrinching her nose, her finger aimed and lowered, flashing an oval of Angel's Throat.

"Please don't smoke in the bedroom, okay."

"Why not?" I said, becoming annoyed again. She knew I liked to lay in bed and smoke, think.

"No stinking up the bedroom. Smoke somewhere else."

"Christ." I reared up from the bed and stamped out, looking for an ashtray. When I came back she was stretched out naked on the sheets, her legs raised and bent, the knees splayed, pelvis tilted. The image I got was of a baby about to have her diaper changed. In a second I realized she was inserting her diaphragm. I regarded her position, her exposure, her assumption. Her hands dipped downward between her thighs, one wrist flipped under, pushing up. She rolled her head and looked over at me.

"I think you should keep your mouth closed and come here, boy."

She had never stooped to such strategy and blatent intent before.

"It's different in here. Why have you done this?" I demanded.

"I was bored with the way things were."

"That new canvas on the wall, I hate it. Where's the batik?"

"In the garage. Why don't you climb over here?"

"Whose rain slicker is that on the couch in the living room?

321

It's not mine."

"It must be Champ's. He left it in the car."

"Who?"

"Champ Ransome, this guy."

"That's a preposterous, awful, ridiculous name."

"I think his name is perfect," she said, propping herself on her elbows to stare guileless at me.

"For what?" I bitched. A gigolo, a failed actor, a racehorse. "I suppose now you're going to tell me that you slept with him." I ripped out of my shorts and pitched them toward the closet where the wicker hamper had been relocated and waited, the scorned man, hands on my hips, unadorned before my fate.

"My dear Sims," she said, her eyes inspecting the ceiling, bored with my accusation. "I haven't slept with anybody but you, believe it or not."

I slouched into bed on all fours and hovered above her, sniffing like a bear for the scent of a stranger on the body beneath me, eyeing the sheets for the stains of carnal labor. She held out her arms for me to collapse into and then, thank God, she smiled, cracking the hard red candy of her lips.

"What'd you bring me from Africa?"

"Disease," I answered, colliding with her bones.

Our life. The plural possessive pronoun, the singular noun. What a pair they can be. Lindy slowly accepted me back into it, yet it seemed more hers than mine or ours. I felt I wasn't all the way home, I felt I had missed it by a house or two. There was something going on, as if the woman now worshipped strange idols. Meals were more planned and formal. She wanted us to eat at the table instead of the back porch or crosslegged in front of the news on television. Where before there was serendipity, now there were cookbooks. Vegetables became suddenly exciting, artichokes prepared as feasts, vinagrette splashed on anything. Pasta in drab colors filled the freezer. Coffee beans arrived UPS from New Orleans. Wine was ordered by the case from a store in Pompano. She subscribed to magazines that glorified people whose only talent appeared to be hanging out, the street elite. Jewelry achieved some vague level of meaning. Besides the gold and amber, she took to wearing an elephant's hair ring, a baroque pearl, a poptop from a beer can, and a tiny emerald cluster, all on her left hand, a band of studded leather above on her wrist. A ladder of holes was pierced into each ear, small gems descended to plastic or enamel hardware, household objects, pen caps, and on one occasion, tea spoons. Jogging was also important and she braved the roads at dawn and dusk in wine colored briefs and a lemon danskin, a walkman delivering ska to her brain. In the bathroom you could browse the *New York Review of Books* or *Vanity Fair*. For the first time since I knew her she had a girlfriend, a Cuban woman of carbonated personality. The woman would pick her up in a black Firebird to go shopping over at South Beach.

Here is what I thought I understood, that Lindy was having one last fling with the dazzling, addictive fraud of American culture. She was revving up speed to hurl herself off the edge of the continent, to land with twenty four dollars worth of trinkets on an unknown shore, a parody of the urban frontier, a treat for savages she imagined out there.

I met up with Lindy's Champ Ransome down at the boatyard where our ketch had been sitting for two years, riding the dirt while Lindy and I prepared our life. The old ketch was a piece of sea trash I had saved from worms and disaffection. I could see in her lines the boat once had a passion for speed and enterprise. She was almost ready again to flaunt the crushing wallop of seas, the mammoth torque of full sail, Lindy at the wheel as I tuned the ropes until they hummed freedom.

Since I had left for the Sahel, the yard, a noisy cluttered city of boats, had dragged up a more unpromising pail of junk onto the rails down the way from the ketch, a stubby tramp freighter, ninety feet of negligence, a broad grey-hulled pig bleeding rust, a pilothouse on its stern like a whitewashed shanty. The craft resembled, remarkably, a giant high-topped basketball sneaker, the victim of brutal play. This filthy creation was Champ Ransome's ship. I took one look and said There's a vessel that advertises an association with crime, a dire picaroon. Lindy said no, Champ Ransome was certified clean, a purveyor of innocent cargoes, a man who believed in the benefit of trade. You never know, I said. Any bowery bum might be a master captain, any saint a sinner. The ocean's chased by the best and the worst and sometimes you can't tell the difference.

"There, that's him."

Lindy raised her wierd sunglasses and pointed with her chin. The frames of her sunglasses were lavender and shaped like two obese blowfish kissing on the bridge of her nose. I followed the direction of her Celtic jaw. Up on scaffolding, a man attended a swarm of white sparks, welding a steel plate at the waterline of the freighter. I've always admired the concentration of men at work, the ability to calmly direct a tool whether the heavens sink or the doors of hell blow off. I see it as profound intent, the mojo to pull civilization back from the brink. I knew then and there that Champ Ransome was no flea, nor the punk darling I had envisioned, and if he posed a true threat there was no fast remedy for it. If he had cast this change on Lindy, she would stay changed.

Lindy tucked her fingers into the shallow pockets of her polka dot bloomers. Rearing back as if she would spit the distance, she whistled like a longshoreman, a trick of hers I wish I had. When the man on the scaffolding didn't respond, she started to whistle again but I stopped her.

"Let him finish the bead or it's no good. The weld will be weak."

In another minute he cut the flame on his torch and monkeyed to the ground, the welder's mask still hanging from his face, his eyes a blur behind the scratched window.

"Champ Ransome," Lindy said. I suspected her tone would reveal intimacy but it didn't. She stepped forward, hooked a finger under the mask and tilted it up on its hinge, his face revealed. "Meet Sims. Of whom I have spoken."

"Endlessly," Ransome agreed. He nodded in my direction. Just nodded. No handshake, no smile, no wink, no Hey, nothing. He gestured with his head, the mask shovelling air. "She steers like a horse tank," he said, his accent bred in the glades and keys of southern Florida. "We creased her damn hip docking on the river." His moustache drooped off the corners of his mouth like spanish moss, his chin captured underneath, as blunt as the toe of a cowboy boot, and his eyes, clear as they were with anglo blue, seemed perpetually half-lidded, reaching the unseen and far away.

"We'll let you be," Lindy said. She reached up and pulled the black shield over his face again. It shut like a car hood, closing off the flat expression that was the beginning and the end of Champ Ransome's social grace.

We rambled back to the ketch. Lindy slipped her hand down into the waist of my cutoffs, her fingertips pressed smoothly against my rear. I believed she had shown me what I wanted to know, that Champ Ransome was a new friend and nothing more, no cause for furtiveness, no source of strain. So Champ became more of a mystery to me than ever. Champ was a crow out on the clothesline that wouldn't fly away, a bird that kept watching the house day after day.

I raised a wooden ladder against the sailboat's deck and climbed aboard. Lindy watched from below, sheltering her eyes against the sun.

Champ Ransome knew. Neither conspirator nor sneak, but another restless man who sweated toward dreams like me, he was around when Lindy needed to unload and he carried the weight of the knowledge on his tongue until two days before he left for good, puttering out the Miami River bound for Haiti, his cargo 3,000 cases of German beer. The hull repaired, auxillary fuel tanks installed in the bow, Champ was itching to go. He took us aboard for an inaugural cruise, a cocktail chug out to the continental shelf to determine how the plugs behaved before he stacked the hold with pallets, a bon voyage party for all of us, Lindy and I due to set sail ourselves within the month.

We drove down to the yard late on a Friday morning, the top up on the Volkswagen at Lindy's request. She had been avoiding sunlight, I noticed, her fair skin fairer by the day. She wore pegged jeans, plastic sandals, a camouflage spandex tube top that squeezed her breasts back to prepubescent nubs, those same fish-kissing sunglasses and a Yankee baseball cap, the bill tugged so far down her face that she had to lift her head to see in front of her. I was better dressed for the squalor of Ransome's ship — topsiders, khaki workpants and work shirt with epaulets, the young lieutenant look. We brought along a cooler of ice cold beer, a jug of red wine, steak sandwiches from the deli. And I would not go without my fishing rod and tackle, for I was a man anxious to rob the sea of all its many pleasures.

Overnight the yard had eased the freighter back into the water, Champ's ship the *Southern Wind,* which he had rechristened inscrutably, *Sea-Bop-A-Baby,* I can't guess why. There she wallowed, lashed to the capstans on the dock, looking less malignant with most of her bulk submerged, the Stars and Stripes topping a white triangle imprinted with a martini glass, olive included, stirred by cool zephyrs on the flagpole off the stern. The hatchcovers were piled one on top of the other, revealing the grim cavern of the hold. Champ stepped from the wheelhouse, his skull bound in a red bandana, his stringy pirate's body bare except for cutoff jeans and oversized workboots.

"Permission to come aboard," I called out, a good fellow.

Champ clomped up to midships, brandishing a wrench which he pointed at my stomach. We were several feet above him on the dock. "You like to fish?" he said, examining my pole with an unconcealed lack of esteem.

"You like to breathe?" I answered back.

"I don't give a damn about breathing," Champ said, squaring his shoulders. "I like to fish."

"You coming up?"

"Only if you need me," she said. From my new perspective her head was a cocklebur.

"No, not really. Unless you feel like getting dirty."

"I don't. Not today."

She had done enough anyway, two years at my side in the industry of the yard. The payback wasn't so far off. The diesel would get an overhaul and the main mast, stepped before the Sahel, would be rigged and fitted. The lease on the house expired in seven weeks. Our forwarding address would be as thick as an atlas.

She unfolded a beach chair in the shady lee of the hull and kicked off her pumps, a magazine in her lap, instantly remote. The breeze snuck in off Biscayne Bay and licked the propellor of my wind generator into a lazy spin. I went below, flicking on the cabin lights, inhaling the powerful aromas of canvas, turpentine, machine oil and mold, these sweet smells of moition. I crawled into the engine space and dug for gaskets, breaking for the surface after a couple of hours, greased like a cold water diver. Lindy had abandoned her chair. I saw her down at the freighter, she and Ransome leaning on their elbows into the steel, face to face, their palms against their ears as if they were chatting on the telephone. She in her clownish polka dots and electric jersey, he in black T-shirt, black jeans blushed with rust smears and dark burns. When she wandered back I was on the ground, scrubbing my forearms with a rag soaked in gasoline.

"He doesn't eat well," she said. "Cocoa Puffs and Coca-Cola and hot dogs, crap like that. I invited him for dinner."

Champ moved through the house as if it were a fragile affair and he couldn't quite trust himself under its roof. We drank rum together, spectating from the table while Lindy chucked things into a wok. He had a long brown neck, hands that weren't easily cleaned. I knew he didn't want to be my friend. He was taken by Lindy, a boyish infatuation, eager for her words, wary of mine. I only blamed him for the atmosphere of competition he sent through the room, the soft drumming of a have-not. Yet I don't deny he was a good enough man for me and the evening passed without great event under the dome of Lindy's fantasy — she would feed us and entertain us, we would love her, perhaps a community would be built upon such rocks. She would be modern, we would be rugged, so that the three of us together might balance the world on our toes like a circus ball.

Frankly, I don't know what Lindy thought.

We gathered in the wheelhouse and stowed the gear and provisions. The short-wave radio buzzed non-stop, spoke to us in tongues. Champ rammed a tape, an untalented imitation of Fifties rock and roll, into a cassette player mounted above the chart table. The music was so loud I couldn't see. Lindy plopped down on the bare blue-striped mattress in the lower bunk, her feet bouncing to the concussive rhythm. We were a party that had not yet found its mood though anticipation waxed second by second toward the exhilerated moment of leavetaking. A speedboat passed in the channel beyond our berth, transmitting a pattern of waves toward us that nudged and tickled *Sea-Bop-A-Baby*. My blood paced quickly in a happier heart, heated by rum Champ had harvested from an unpainted plywood cupboard in the narrow galley. I turned the music down so I could speak.

"I hear this is a sea-going vessel," I said to Champ.

"Those who say she is are not wrong."

"Well," I piped. "Let's plow the dreadful deeps. Toot out around the yonder."

"Aye," he answered. "Prepare to blow port."

Lindy marked the two of us jawing this way and seemed pleased, I suppose, though I make no claim to reading her right. For all her transformations, she didn't act the way she looked, at least in my presence, and didn't look the way I thought of her.

Champ opened the single door inside the pilothouse and descended the stairs to the engine room. Out on deck Lindy helped me replace the heavy hatchcovers which we then tarped to keep any maverick sea from bathing the hold. Below deck the big diesel cranked like a helicopter. A black cloud puffed out of the stack that impaled the wheelhouse, followed at intervals by a steady emission of round balls of smoke. The steel deck vibrated under our feet. Champ's head appeared out the port window, ordering me to cast off the lines. We fell away from the dock in slow motion, opalescent mud churned in the blue space widening between us and land. Then we were in deeper water, clear of pilings and other craft, tracing the channel with vigilance out through the calm flats.

Lindy and I took position in the bow, shoulder to shoulder, our arms resting on the flaked surface of the bulwarks, the water below us divided with a gliding hiss. Off starboard we passed the Port of Miami, the wharves crammed with big tankers and cruise liners like captured factories. Behind us the skyline of the city radiated in the sun, a fantast's vision, a hummock where bears once pawed the sand for turtle eggs. We entered Government Cut.

On the north side of the breakwater spray exploded skyward, its white fingers suspended and then crashing down, settling pelicans to flight. I saw the last channel marker ahead of us, the clang of its bell intensifying as we approached — *bong bong* do you know what you're doing? *Bong Bong* you're on your own *BONG BONG* have faith have faith. The water was darker but no less translucent, the mouth of the cut bleached with whitecaps. We passed from shelter into the fluid gleaming hill country of the seas, the bow where we stood a bastion above the almighty sweep of the Atlantic, rising and falling as the ship cantered onward, an old sow lunging again and again for the trough.

"Wonderful," I shouted. I turned to Lindy with a wide grin. "Do you have a better word? I want a better word."

"Yes," she said. "Reckless." She watched me for a time behind her sunglasses before she drew then down an inch and allowed her eyes to linger with mine. "What do we do now?"

I didn't like her attitude, I didn't like the slate green reproach on her face. "We jig atop the pilothouse," I said with an exasperated flourish of my hand, "while your Champ Ransome chauffers us to New Guinea. We get drunk and fall overboard, never to be seen again. What do you mean, *what do we do?* Isn't this enough?"

As I finished my lecture *Sea-Bop-A-Baby* dipped with a force that bent our knees. A fan of water spread at eye level, held utterly still for a second, close enough to touch, broken glass in unreal suspension. Then it swashed down onto our heads, draining through Lindy's baseball cap.

"Oh, ugh! God," Lindy complained, flapping her arms uselessly. "I'm all wet. I'm going back and sit with Champ out of the glare."

She walked the lifeline aft to the wheelhouse. Straight on, its construction resembled an old-fashioned gunner's turret, the corners beveled off octagonally, ringed with windows tinted green like coke bottles. Champ Ransome was a half-shadow behind the glass, mastering the wheel, a beer in one hand. Strung between the staff and boom of the cargo crane was a hammock. I stretched open its edges and climbed into it, elementally secure in its hug, a friend to the world. I dozed off and awoke with Lindy standing watch over me, a sad and tender smile on her lips. I smiled back, in love. The wave had washed out her spikes. She was Peter Pan. A jungle version in a one-piece, one strap leopardskin bathing suit.

"You look pretty," I said, swaying with the roll of the ship.

"That's the first nice thing you've said to me in ages."

"Is that right. I'm sorry."

"That's right," she sulked. "And you ought to be."

I dragged her down into the hammock and kissed her. "Why aren't you having fun?" I asked.

Her teeth nipped into the flesh of my shoulder. The shell earrings she wore scratched my neck. "Oh I am," she said quietly. "Really."

"It will be better on our own boat," I assured her. "Much much better. *Sea-Bop-A-Baby* is like taking a gymnasium out on the ocean."

She pushed herself up off my chest. "Hey," she said. "Champ wants you back there. I think something's wrong."

We lurched and yawed, skating over a sequence of hard knolls that were in opposition to the easy cadence the ship had settled into, renegade thoughts bombarding the flow of meditation. Champ was spreadeagled at the helm, throwing the wheel left and right like a race car driver. His bandana was soaked in perspiration but he seemed well-placed to the task. He had a brave start on a collection of empty beer cans along the window ledges.

"What's wrong?" I said, stepping through the doorway.

"Nothing." He grunted as he adjusted the wheel to the buck of a wave. I went to the cooler and opened a beer. On the radar screen the fading shore was an outline of foxfire. "I'm going below to have a look-see," he reported. "Take the wheel."

Had I taken some long beast by the horns and tried to push it backward through an imaginary gate, the job would have been no different. The bow overswung to the north, overswung to the south, overswung to the north again as I steered twenty degrees past our heading in each direction until I got used to the slack in the linkage. This was Champ's idea of funny.

"Told you," he laughed hoarsely. "She's a straying bitch."

I steered for an hour while Champ played below and let me tell you, it's a fine feeling to captain a ship, a liberation to power it over the depths, surely a magic, like flight. The horizon writhes. You go on and on. The horizon writhes, now brassed with daybreak, now colorless and baleful with the coming of night, and the distance irons out in your wake.

I followed the compass due east. Lindy, a slender pod, hung in the hammock in possession of a magazine. There was a change in the water ahead, a friction, like the line where a meadow ends and the scrub takes over. This was the Gulf Stream pouring northward through the Florida Straits, a wilder current than the one we hitched. Out there beyond the Stream, unseen, were the islands, some as fragrant as cardamom, some with histories hidden like fat beneath a girdle, some as crummy as headaches, some with treasure so abundant it has no value, some only phantasms, some with the power to close on you like Ahab's whale. I wanted to discover each of them, to drive Lindy there on the wind. I never imagined such places, she'd say.

For its greeting the Gulf Stream echoed thunder into us. The old sow dug her snout into the ocean and shook, tossing blue water over the deck that flooded under Lindy and out the scuppers. Champ emerged from the belly of the ship, a man at home with grime and knucklebusting. He clomped on deck and perched over the rail, his nose inches away from the highest rising swells. He clomped back in.

"Stay out of the Stream," he said in passing. The machinery roared when he reopened the engine room door.

"What's up?" I yelled out.

"Not much," he said before disappearing again. "Bilge pump —." He pointed toward Cuba. "Fall off to the south. Take it easy."

I jacked the wheel just as Lindy timed her dash back to the cabin. The change of direction threw her across the room in a stagger.

"*What is going on?*" she inquired breathlessly, grabbing my waist for support. "I'm getting sick."

"We're leveling off for the cocktail hour," I explained. "Eat one of those sandwiches. It'll settle your stomach."

She chewed a few bites and threw up out the lowered port window.

"Feel better now?"

"No."

"You will," I promised. I dropped the throttle one-third.

She crawled into the bottom bunk and lay on her stomach, moaning piteously, her arms draped over her head. Champ came up wiping his hands on a dirty rag, every crease in his skin penciled black.

"What's wrong with her?" he said.

"She feels bad."

"Hunh. Can't have that." But Champ did not come to Lindy's aid. He forgot about her immediately and opened another beer, wolfed down one of the sandwiches.

"How's that bilge pump?"

"What?" he said, distracted. He peered out the windows in each direction. "Where are we? You know?"

I tapped the chart in front of me. "About three miles northeast of Eliot Key."

"Yeah?" he said, not willing to commit himself to this information. He squinted at the water, tipped his beer can out toward the port bow. "Nice weed line out there."

"I've been looking at it," I said. "Why don't you take the helm back?"

"All right," he said, instinctively stepping forward, wiping mayonaisse on his shorts.

I took a direct path to my tackle box and pole. "I'm going to fish," I said.

Champ's eyes bulged. "*Fish?*" He grumbled as if I had tricked him. "Why, damn you."

"Take me right to them, pal," I said and walked back to the stern. Our wake was a tail of smoky suds, the water we had passed over subdued, as if a gloved hand had smoothed it out. Champ must have fixed the bilge because I could hear it over the side, a mushed, sputtery *th-th-th* ending in a gurgle each time the ship dug in her heel. The water line was about four feet down, adding or subtracting two feet with each change in gravity. I tied on a five-inch spoon with a yellow feather and sent it arcing into the air, the line dragging out fifty yards until it dropped the lure under golden patches of sargasso weed shrugged off by the Stream, a gleaming irresistable whisk through the shade where dolphin schooled.

The line wasn't out five minutes before it jerked taut, a false strike that left a faint resistance. I reeled in twenty feet and a clump of grass levitated up, scooning across the surface. I brought it in so I could pick the spoon clean again. Our wake had taken on the aspect of doodling. This was Ransome's spite, I assumed, a maneuvering that would compel me frequently to adjust the tension on the line. Champ came running back to disprove this theory, swiping the air with his own pole. He saw me reeling in and glared.

"Whatcha got there?" he demanded to know.

"Nothing," I said. "Weed."

My poor luck cheered him. "Now we'll see what's what. You step back when I start hauling them in."

"We'll see about that," I said. Even square-fingered he could tie a leader with dexterity. He scoffed at my spoon and chose for himself a black and white jitterbug plug that was out in the water before I realized it.

"You won't catch anything with that," I said, but I didn't care to improve on his judgment.

"You ever fished before?" he said. "In the ocean, I mean." He

331

feigned a rabid concentration as if that would make a difference.

If I took one step backward I could send Champ Ransome overboard with my foot. These impulses are better ignored, the sting of hormones suffered, or you throw yourself into nothing less than war. "Who's at the helm?" I asked, although I already had the picture.

"Why, who do you think?"

"She's sick," I said.

"No she ain't. I gave her a pill."

Champ scouted the vista of sea, rubbing his unshaven cheeks, an angry, underfed osprey. Goodbye crow. He whipped his pole impetuously on the spur of wishful thinking. He whipped his pole again and spit at his lack of success, looking over at me, his eyes squeezed in an outlaw version of a smile. "She wanted that wheel. I told her she could turn the tub around and head for port."

"It's early," I said.

"It won't be." Champ nodded at our crazy wake. "She wants land but she's running a slalom to get there."

We both knew that wheel was a lot of trouble. I suppose if I had another minute to think about it I would have reeled in my line and gone to help her. Maybe it was cruel of us to leave her up there by herself. Maybe it wasn't, since self-sufficiency is a virtue that must be tested. But as soon as Champ shut his mouth, my rod bent double, the drag whirring like a hand-cranked siren. I was occupied thereafter.

"Goddamnit," Champ howled, wounded by my good fortune.

"Slow her down," I shouted back. The drag continued to burn out and the core of the spool began to appear through the wrap. "I'm out of line. Slow her down."

"Aw, goddamn," Champ muttered, gravely disappointed. "All right. Hold on." He took in his ine with great reluctance. I battled the fish against its dive. Champ moseyed forward and I reeled frantically when the engine cut to a purr and the line slackened. Champ jogged right back.

"What is it?" he asked suspiciously. I tugged and reeled, tugged and reeled. Champ answered himself. "I'll bet it's a damn barracuda."

The water broke about a hundred feet out, a metallic flash as sudden as lightning and gone. The energy discharged, the fish spent itself momentarily in a last plunge that brought it straight under the stern. Champ mounted the bulwarks, watching the water like a tomcat. He had outfitted himself on his visit to the wheelhouse, a leather glove on his left hand, an oak billy club clutched in his right. I brought the fish alongside the hull and let it exhaust its fight with a final thrashing.

"That's a big blue," Champ announced. His body twitched. "A big chopper blue. Damn." He tottered over the side and caught the wire leader in his leather paw. "I've got her," he said. "I've got her. Look out now." He yanked the fish with such force that it sailed above our heads and smacked down on the decking behind us. "Look out now," Champ said with high excitement and fell on the fish, beating it repeatedly on its fat nose with the club. The tailfin quivered violently and then relaxed.

"That's enough, Champ," I said. "Let's get the hook out." He had battered an eye from its socket and exposed brain with his hard strokes.

"Jesus," he said, inhaling deeply. "That's a nice one."

"One good rap between the eyes will do it," I said. Big fish are dangerous once you haul them aboard and must be subdued in short order. The common style though is not to pulverize or mutilate beyond recognition.

"Let's get moving," Champ said. "I want mine."

I hoisted the blue under the beautiful span of its tail and trotted to the wheelhouse door. Lindy was crucified to the wheel, in loose control. I held the fish out for her approval.

"We're going back," she said between clenched teeth, an overzealous fire in her eyes.

"Look," I said beaming. "I caught the first fish."

"Get it out of here, man. It's dripping blood all over."

In the galley I exchanged the fish for the bottle of rum. I was shamelessly pleased with myself. "Push her back up to trolling speed, honey," I said. Immediately the engine rumbled and throbbed. "Ho ho," I said. "Old Champ's pissed."

"Hey, can you give me a hand here, Sims?" Lindy said, trying to wrestle the wheel. "My arms are going to break off."

"Yeah, in a minute," I said and took off for the stern, leaving her alone again. Champ's line threaded out into the water. I noticed the black and white plug resting on top of his tacklebox. "What are you using now," I asked him, nudging the lure with my toe.

"You'll see before you want to," he said, "when you remove it from the jaw of a big yellowfin tuna." No sooner had he said that than he obliged himself with a rebel yell. I didn't even bother to pick up my pole.

"Oh yes," he proclaimed with lust. "Oh yes oh yes." When his rod went u-shaped he reclined away from it, employing muscle and weight against the strike. I was sure the line would snap but it held. No one had to tell me what to do next. I sprinted to the wheelhouse and stuck my face in the doorway.

"Slow her down, honey."

Lindy turned to me and snarled. "No."

Champ and I were aroused now and such talk was mutinous. "What do you mean, *no*?" I said, charging forward. I cuffed the throttle back. "*Slow her down*."

I quickly retreated to the stern. Champ collected his line inch by inch, grinding it in. In our wake I spotted a grey torpedo in tow.

"It's a barracuda," I said.

"The hell it is," Champ insisted. "It's a big king mackeral."

I sighted it again. "Naw," I said. "Only a barra plays dead like that."

"You can go farm in Nebraska," Champ said. "It's a big king mackeral." I donned the leather glove and stood ready. "If it's a barracuda I'll shove it up my ass."

"Pull down your pants," I told him, leaning over the rail. I grabbed the leader and raised the fish. It was big but a barracuda nevertheless. "This is how you do it," I said, holding the wire with my left hand and slipping the thumb second and third fingers of my other hand into the gill opening, then wrenching the hook from the wicked grin of the jaws.

"You fool," Champ observed. "You'll lose a finger doing that." The fish shook against my grip, the twist and squirm of a thick snake. I laid it on deck, placed my foot behind its head and clobbered it once with the billyclub. Champ threw his pole down and stomped away. *Sea-Bop-A-Baby* came back to speed.

One more fish to go and it was my catch more or less. Our two lines out dragging their temptations, both of us not disinclined to knife the other in the back, Champ and I sat watch on the froth, the bottle of rum passed between us and emptied before the strike. It occurs to me now that Lindy must have thrown up her hands in disgust and frustration when Champ hustled into the wheelhouse for the third time to choke the throttle. At the time I was acutely aware that *Sea-Bop-A-Baby*, apparently unpiloted, had begun a lazy clockwise circle, batted by the waves, that threatened to cross my line and slice the dolphin free.

There was a split second when neither of us, or both of us, could claim the fish. The dolphin struck on a head-on run, hitting the lure at top velocity and springing into the air upright, an iridescence. Dolphins are bull-nosed, elite warriors, potent and brawny, their vivid colors, a greenish-blue and yellow, unpresent in the same living hues in the world above the surface. When you land one you feel you have ripped the sea's own muscle from the water.

At the strike neither pole reacted. We watched the fish dance and fall, each one of us declaring ownership. But I understood what was happening. I could sense the spirit of the fish like a heating coil in the butt of my rod, confirmed in a violent instant as my line erupted from its spool and I set my strength against the pure unyielding weight of the dolphin. Champ cursed until his tongue turned white.

The fish pierced the atmosphere once again, nearer the ship, its great size more evident, its resistance a ferocity. Bringing the beauty back up took a long time. Each attempt to haul it closer than twenty feet from the stern was denied with fresh power. I had to slack off or lose. The dolphin stayed out there just below the surface sweeping back and forth, a hot electric current, a blue curling form, flashing between the arc circumscribed by the limit of the line I allowed. My will and the will of the fish — this is a tired thought but true, the forces so precisely opposite and therefore exquisite, no chance for sentimentality, for hapless negotiation. Nothing was given. It could go either way — all rare joys are as simple as that.

To land the fish I knew would take good work and patience. It paced the water handsomely, back and forth, back and forth, and I took advantage of each turn to ease the fish alongside the hull. When it thought to duck under the ship I jerked its jaws skyward. They gaped at me through the spangled water and then the fish rolled so its huge yellow-ringed eye, a cold defiance, could form its last judgment on me. Each time I brought its blunt head out of the sea, the body still in its own world spasmed, and I would slack off in fear that the line would break.

"You're gonna lose it," Champ said.

"Stand back out of the way," I ordered. "We need a gaff."

"Well of course we do," Champ said derisively, "but we don't have one. You're gonna lose it."

I glanced across my shoulder at him in an unfriendly way. "Now what would you know about it?"

"A fish that big won't take the test of the line."

"You just stand back."

Champ removed himself from my line of vision and I listened to him scuff away. My plan was to wait it out, to let the fish defeat itself, and then try to fling it over the bulwark. The fish would exert its strength again once I committed myself. The line would snap when the fish was in the air, yet if I timed the move right and the momentum was good I had a chance.

I inched the head up through the sea and prepared myself.

"Hold her steady," Champ commanded from behind me. He stepped forward, a shotgun raised to his shoulder. I could not protest before he acted. My ears boomed with the report. The tall forehead of the fish vaporized, disintegrating into crimson molecules, a residue of pinkish foam. The body slipslided back down into the depths like a flourescent leaf until it eventually disappeared.

Champ said, "Well damn, that was a little high."

"Son of a bitch," I shouted. "A little high? *You shot my fish.*"

"You moved it just as I pulled the trigger."

"You shot my fish."

Champ tried a pout but it didn't suit his nature. "It would have been all right if you hadn't moved it."

"You skunk, you shot my fish."

"You were gonna lose it."

I flung down my pole in a rage. "You're nothing but a damn thief," I said and stalked away. What I wanted more than anything was to have my own boat launched to the wind, out of sight to cities, banks and fools, blowing down to Barbados with Lindy. I couldn't endure Champ Ransome a minute more. I stormed into the wheelhouse determined to get us back on shore with all possible speed. Lindy had been waiting for me to show myself, boiling her words before she threw them in my face.

"*You!*" The intensity of her shriek popped the gold studs from her earlobes. I stood dismayed before her wrath. "*You with your toys and games.* What do I have to do to get you to see *me*?"

My mood wasn't right for taking rebuke or faultfinding. "Calm down," I said. "Let's concentrate on getting out of here." I punched the throttle forward. Lindy wasn't finished with me.

"I've told you every way I can," she cried.

"Told me what? What's this all about?" Innocence has always been a fine target and effective as provocation.

"Have you been blinded! My life has changed."

"Well don't think I haven't noticed a difference," I said.

"You're always flying off and leaving me alone. Whenever you go, I learn about myself. Things I didn't know before."

"So what's wrong with that?" Champ had come to stand in the doorway and witness the knowledge arrow into me. I am not a sensitive man, or so I am told. Yet I tried to let Lindy *be herself* when she decided she wasn't. You know, let Vietnam be Vietnam, Lebanon be Lebanon, El Salvador be El Salvador. What plans these were. Let them be themselves and lose them.

"The boat," Lindy said, seething, her hands trembling in front of her. I didn't know what she meant. "*The ketch*."

"What about it?"

"Sell it," she begged. "If you love me and I know you do, sell the boat and stay with me."

Did I bellow and kick the wall? Maybe I did. What I remember is saying, *Not-on-your-life*, each word measured hateful and numbing. The engine gagged and shut down. My voice resonated in silence, the smell of raw fuel and scorched circuitry. We were dead in the water, as if together we had murdered *Sea-Bop-A-Baby* with the splitting of our faith.

Throughout the night we drifted forlornly, Ishmaels on the water, Lindy in the cold solitude of her bunk, Champ banging below decks, correcting a variety of failures I won't go into. To prevent the ship from running aground, we let the anchor dangle over the side but it wasn't necessary. Our electricity had been lost too. It was my responsibility to sit on top the wheelhouse through those loneliest of hours with a flashlight and beam it out into the shimmering darkness whenever I sighted another vessel. Here we are, I'd signal. Down on our luck, a tub of infants in the night. Stay clear. Steer away. For most of the time I had only the void to examine — me, my nose, and zero. I lay back often, my hands pillowing my head, made despondent by the stars. There were too many of them, a cruel fact. Except for the most practical communications, Lindy avoided me until near dawn when the weakest light transmuted space and caused the black atmosphere to ripple and quake as if it were coming apart. Then she joined me up top and we talked.

"It *is* beautiful," she said, stretching out beside me.

"Tell me," I said, selecting my simplest fear. "Who's Champ Ransome?"

"Nobody," she said ruefully. She paused and then modified her answer. "A nice guy, a pretty fair listener. A wanderer, like you."

"Tell me this," I said. "Why'd you ever do that to your hair?"

"Oh." She laughed, a quiet song on the ocean. "I thought you understood." She lifted herself up on an elbow and gazed down on me. "If you could understand that you'd understand a lot."

"Try me," I said. "Give it a go."

"It was a first step," she said haltingly. "I dared myself. It seemed the most bloodless way to begin to tell you I wanted other things. I guess it was the least, um what? —" She searched for a word that she never found.

The sun came up, painting a distant shoreline to the west. "Look," I said, placing my hand on the warm nape of her neck and turning her head. "There are the beaches of Mauritius. Behind the low cloud is Mt. Pele in Martinique, the coast of the Seychelles. Sri Lanka, with elephants in the sand. Bali. The Azores."

"Stop," she said, shrugging off my hand. "It's only Miami. We live there, Sims. It's our home."

She signed a new lease on the house and enrolled in a graphics design program at the University. I have sworn to send her postcards whenever I'm in port. The ketch has been out in the anchorage for a week while I settled last minute business, all the paperwork that appears on the eve of leavetaking. Two days ago I visited the animal shelter and conscripted an overweight, crosseyed cat as a shipmate.

I pulled anchor this morning. She had to go to class so I said goodbye at the house and took a cab to the bay. Everything I have is hers for as long as I'm gone.

Through Government Cut and I'm out at sea. Where Champ Ransome's freighter rolled with the first swell, I nixed the engine and hoisted the sails, celebrating their silent powering ahead out to the ancient routes and mains, the currents that ushered men to new worlds. And now I've been talking to myself like an old salt, my voice returned to my mouth by the headwind I'm beating into. The cat dashes after imaginary mice, content as far as I can tell. Lindy, I said, honey you should see this. You would be seeing this, had you shunned the lesser patriotisms, chose instead the outward passage, the heart's adventure. I suppose I'm still rather stunned, I can't get over it, I still can't believe she's not coming with me.

Charles Siebert

The Lament of the Air Traffic Controller

Grave instances surround the tower tonight.
I admit or dismiss them evenly;
blinking back all thoughts of who I am
aligns the tentative ground lights again.

Ground lies in all directions from a port
of air. I fall back on it frequently
in thought, one bell-ringing buoy over
the long course of a night, and trace a line

from the city's dense, inland glare over
brittle strands of suburbs to this outer ring
where lights touch briefly down, a new city
trying to take hold in the thin, vacuous

dark. I must think like Ptolemy — his
is the right universe, my dark screen
of concentric rings and base earth, to which
I guide everyone, at the unholy center.

I can't bear to think of us here, how we
go this far into night and walk gangplanks
over runways to meet loved ones. My wife
thinks I'm distant, but I keep everyone

in the sphere of my affections, guiding
flashes of light across a screened sky.
At times, I think of letting a few fly free,
allowing some, as God has in history,

to deviate from the safe course and die;
with each night, I fear I'm passing
through the outwardly diminishing rings
of remorse to become more like Him.

Last winter, one small plane in my sights plunged
into the Detroit River, but it was lost
when I thought of those behind the green flashes —
if God ever thought of us, He'd see

the earth tonight the way I do this screen,
a dark circle of scattered sympathies.
Outside the tower windows, dense air
propelled to night's ceiling, whines,

curdling the low perimeter of trees.
By the deep, bone-blue runway lights, the souls
of the dead given up to stabilize air,
I'm guiding myself from this bad dream.

I'll build a ship, a dream of lifeless things,
with my own hands from the ground,
frame first, as the Greeks built them,
the skeleton of the idea, then the flesh,

each board soaked in salt water, conditioned
to its destiny, shaped to the keel,
and then sail until the dark is free of lights,
and night yields me ground to walk on again.

Jim Simmerman

Rock 'n' Roll

Four elements
to the season,
each season
gets a beat:
a raucous rendition
of *The Four Quartets.*
Bass is wind
and winter,
a blunt Northeastern
huffing up the frets.
And we bow our heads
in the direction of work,
puffing and slipping
on the icy steps.
Percussion is earth
and autumn,
everything yearning
for home and bed.
Who has not
heard a branch
tapping at a window:
let me in and
let me in.
Which returns us
to summer,
the fulgent licks
of electric guitar.
Sheet lightning
flashing on the horizon,
and everywhere
the smell of rain.
Which is the residue
of spring, the voice
of the crooner
flooding the room —
a dry creek bed
the last time
you looked;
now a torrent,

a turgid brew.
It is electric
as we are electric,
as Whitman
and Edison knew:
everyone dancing
for mere life,
who'd forgotten why
and that we could.

What a pity he doesn't take

a laxative which preserves his normal good-humour instead of making him surly and out-of-sorts. What a pity he doesn't take Lixen! For Lixen is thorough without being harsh. Non-griping and non-habit-forming, it is so completely *natural* that children, adults and invalids can take it with equal confidence and safety. From chemists only. LIXEN LOZENGES (fruit-flavoured) 8½d. & 1/2. LIXEN ELIXIR. (in bottles) 1/2, 2/-, 3/6.

MADE BY
ALLEN &
HANBURYS LTD.,
LONDON, E.C.3.

LIXEN

THE *good-natured* LAXATIVE

Jim Simmerman

The reluctant angels

New York City is one place you find them,
huddled in stairwells, frayed sweaters crammed
with yesterday's news. Hope, Arizona

another, meandering its lone street
long after dark, sifting the desert
through tattered boots. Or

threading the interstate through some failed town
or another, you'll spot one standing
in a thicket of weeds — a scarecrow

left standing one too many seasons,
a monosyllable of stunted speech.
In Coos Bay, in interminable rain,

you'll see them sweeping at flooded gutters.
In Starkville, in Carthage, in Union Church,
remanded to benches in public parks

and muttering to whatever it is
won't mind: squirrel, elm, dead brother.
They are like ghosts with permission to haunt

themselves feckless. They are like deities
in which no one any longer believes.
They are like the indelible crosses

on the windows of condemned tenements.
Like a train wreck they go on and on:
in Muleshoe, in Man, in Zion, in Clay,

in the ward no one visits, in trouble,
in the ice-fringed shawl of winter, insane,
in the paupers' graves of their own shadows . . .

They are always lost, always cold
and hugging themselves like distraught lovers.
They are the reluctant angels of hell

on earth — untouchably near, inviolable.

Jim Simmerman

Daedalus aground

You were all I had.
You were nothing.
You were the sun
drowning in the sea —
before clouds gathered,
before night fell.
You were my echo
trying to warn me.

*

Too late, Icarus,
too late for wings.
Too late for feathers
lighter than faith.
Too late for candles
you might have lit,
and wished on,
and snuffed with a breath.

*

Because no voice
is true enough,
I hum these words
until their absence
keens to grief.
Because no hand
is clever enough,
I place one burned match
on each black piano key.

*

Loss is a labyrinth
no one can solve,
is a dimple
on the face
of the sea.

Then comes the ship
with its lifeboat of ash.
Then the rest of my life
like an empty sleeve.

Charlie Smith

White and Scarlet

As I climb into my mistress's yard
I am thinking about how large the world is
and about how I have been lost in it
and maybe am no more. The sky is the color left
when a hand wipes purple off a windshield. It is a yard
of flowers: bumptious roses, day lilies, and hysterical white blossoms
of apricot, a patch of mustard greens bolted
into blooms the color and shape of ten dollar gold pieces.
Through the lighted window I see her moving, carrying
her pregnancy across the kitchen. A child cries in the house
next door, is hushed, cries again, I hear the sound
of a slap and notice the smudge of smoke and the coals
of a used-up fire under the cherry trees. I sink down
and crawl across the rank sweet grass like a commando.
Her husband is in the kitchen; he sits at the table, reaches
up as she places a plate of french toast before him and draws
her breast down like a fruit, tastes the nipple through the cloth.
I am fascinated and in love with them both; she is not sure
who has fathered the child. I sit down with my back against the house,
listen to the murmur of their speech — how cool and loving it is! —
and watch the evening slink into the yard, settling
its dark nets over the camphor tree, over the white and scarlet
blossoms of the peonies, over what is living and dying, until
it pools at my feet, banked against the light falling from the windows.
The next door child cries again, the mother speaks sharply,
there is silence and then the soft hiss and rustle
of a breeze finding itself caught in the new leaves of the red oaks.
The light falling over me, their voices drifting (*Do you like . . . ?*
Yes. Do you? Yes.) — the breast of the evening opens
and I can picture the world sinking into a clear pool,
the slow rise of water like a gentling hand, element of love,
breathing the original fluid
of our creation: the world still though moving, descending
as life itself is a descent, a breeze moving
through the clothes of God, wind in the hair of God,
a wisp of cherry smoke and the cry of a child
abruptly stopped and the voice of a woman from a lighted kitchen:
I will love you forever, yes, yes,
I will love you . . . ,

and then silence and time to rise as I hear her husband, my friend,
get up and cross the kitchen, pass up the hall,
gather hat and coat, unlatch, open and latch the front door,
descend the steps, then the opening and closing of a car door,
the starting of the engine, reving *whing, whing,* and then
the car moving slowly away, crunching last year's acorns, following
the pale beam of headlights under the arches of the oaks —
it is time now, for this is my body rising
from the mulched bed of **alyssum and wild sweet william;**
I get up and climb the three crooked back steps,
the light falls upon me, indelible and distinct,
and she turns from the sink with soapy hands
and smiles and I kneel before her to press my face
against the vigorous, kinetic ripeness of her, body
within a body, life enclosing life, and as the unrepentant night
takes the house in its arms we sink down
onto the cool board floor and, softly, amid the unimaginable presence
of our lives and our deaths
whisper words that are as lovely and passing
as my hand caressing the long shallow curve of her back —
softness of skin, the descent into night, into night, into night.

Judith Steinbergh

Past Time

> *And then my heart with pleasure fills*
> *And dances with the daffodils.*
> W. Wordsworth

Now that we're middle aged, we're reciting Wordsworth
on the front porch on a Sunday afternoon finally
savoring the words like the strawberries in the
collander between us, letting the words bypass our
minds and slip into our hearts so that even the most
innocent phrase catches at our feelings like a thorn
and makes us weep. It's odd when a friend or even worse
a stranger arrives and we're on the verge of tears
over a line that once bored us.

There is no explaining the impact of words. The kids
are half grown, some of our parents have died,
we have lived half our lives and in that time, enough
has happened to strip daffodils down to their truth.
Perhaps we should hide poems from the children
until words take on the power of memory or hope,
until they darken like storm clouds or glitter like
the face of the sea under the moon. Then the poems
are spoken with the import of weather, of celebration
and defeat, then words swell like silk banners far
above the page, and simple conversation is as tender
as a hand stroking your hair.

Stephanie Strickland

In April

Stones hit the glass like gunshot,
sheets of rain run up my windshield in ridges of ice,
hail, forcing branches down,

at the same time mist rises
— Could we have stopped you? —
from warm ground near the parkway.

As it rises in Rome,
through the Borghese, at dawn, a caul of silver
holding the trees like bluegreen

spears, exposing the torsos
of young prostitutes: not flaunted now.
Boys; going home. Blossoms

smashed against the car, the curb, flood the pool
that widens from the sewer.
Dogwood. Forsythia. Why, John?

Your brothers, silent. As they were. I too
have said nothing. I leave your death
unopened. Alone. This year

I left a fetus
with so little mention, the surgeon's knife
still feels cold

between my legs. I left a woman
whose sobbing, swollen
face I deny.

She skids in my body.
The way the car
went wild when you pulled.

Robyn Supraner

The Nannies

There was one who called her *Shooshy*
who, when her mother was out,
took the cardboards from her sleeves
and gave her back
the simple comfort of her thumb.

And one who sang of death
letters edged in black —
who scrubbed the nursery floor and sobbed
her wild despair
into the sloshing bucket
until the child at her side
wept. Then she gathered her
into her soapy arms, stroking her hair
whispering
not you, not you.

But there was one who knew her.
One who told her every bone in her
was a bad one. Who reached down
into her throat, scraped out
the greed with a wooden spoon, and then
dished up the bile
so she could taste her bitter sin.
Who snapped her arm
(for a very good reason
though she's forgotten, precisely) then
dragged her, *fussing all the way,*
to stand before her mother
and father, dangling
her imperfection and watching,
speechless, her parents falling
asleep on their feet
listening to a fairy tale
about a little girl who wouldn't listen
and fell down
and broke.

And that one she believed
even after, one summer, she was gone
and the bruises, like a movie
of a gathering storm played backwards
on its reel, disappeared . . .
and new hair sprouted
where the old clumps were torn out.
She never got it right.

They said it was some nervous disorder,
or other, which made her shed
like a sick canary
and left her pale skin marred
with strange, dark fingerprints.

Arthur Sze

Crush an Apple

Crush an apple, crush a possibility.
No single method can describe the world;
therein is the pleasure
of chaos, of leaps in the mind.
A man slumped over a desk in an attorney's office
is a parrot fish caught in a seaweed mass.
A man who turns to the conversation in a bar
is a bluefish hooked on a cigarette.
Is the desire and collapse of desire in an unemployed carpenter
the instinct of salmon to leap upstream?
The smell of eucalyptus can be incorporated
into a theory of aggression.
The pattern of interference in a hologram
replicates the apple, knife, horsetails on the table,
but misses the sense of chaos, distorts
in its singular view. Then
touch, shine, dance, sing, be, becoming, be.

James Tate

The Chaste Stranger

All the sexually active people in Westport
look so clean and certain, I wonder
if they're dead. Their lives are tennis
without end, the avocado-green Mercedes
waiting calm as you please. Perhaps it is
my brain that is unplugged, and these
shadow-people don't know how to drink
martinis anymore. They are suddenly and
mysteriously not in the least interested
in fornicating with strangers. Well,
there are a lot of unanswered questions
here, and certainly no dinner invitations
where a fella could probe Buffy's inner-
mush, a really complicated adventure,
in a 1930-ish train station, outlandish
bouquets, a poisonous insect found
burrowing its way through the walls
of the special restaurant and into one
of her perfect nostrils — she was reading
Meetings with Remarkable Men, needing
succor, dreaming of a village near Bosnia,
when a clattering of carts broke her thoughts —
"Those billy goats and piglets, they are
all so ephemeral . . ." But now, in Westport
Connecticut, a boy, a young man really,
looking as if he had just come through
a carwash, and dressed for the kind of success
that made her girlfriends froth and lather,
can be overheard speaking to no one
in particular: "That *Paris Review* crowd,
I couldn't tell if they were bright or
just overbred." Whereupon Buffy swings
into action, pinning him to the floor:
"I will unglue your very being from this
planet, if ever . . ." He could appreciate
her sincerity, not to mention her spiffy togs.
Didymus the Blind has put three dollars
on Total Departure, and I am tired of pumping

my own gas. I'm Lewis your aluminum man, and
we are whirling in a spangled frenzy toward
a riddle and a doom — here's looking up

your old address.

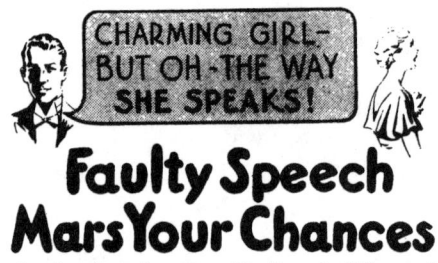

James Tate

The Little Sighs Bite a Sheet

Every day someone walks into the local zoo
and saws off the head of a live moose, drifters
skin random poodles for no reason. I know

more about a certain *ménage à trois* than I
would like. We are here asking these questions,
I am writing this in the middle of nowhere,

coaxing myself into this embarrassing photograph
with ten thousand dolls I never met before . . .
Eighteen exploding possums covered with prayer rugs.

The quotidian melancholy lulls me into dreamless sleep.
Given the supposed diversity of life, the daring
post-parakeet rendevous is made to parade because

I could detect the cross moss of a cello after
the last candle had withdrawn its nose from the world.
Everything's a dream when you're alone with the hollow

bones of a bird. His name is so familiar it's pathetic,
the riddle of his voice, where the deepest sighs congregate
to piss off the masters of the little sighs.

James Tate

No Rest for the Gambler

I am sitting quietly on the verandah, an instrument
for the composition of replies is smoking next to me,
a decoy with a frown.

These are the kinds of details that exhaust me — pine
needles, a fly in a web, seashells — the details
you can never forget for noticing — Sophia's slowly

gliding ducks, her cleavage, her gum . . . . I have questions
that take the form of whippings with fronds, of idleness,
unhappy ancestors fanning the dawn. I predict the destruction

of the temples of Hucumba, and the election of Slick Jones.
Something once terribly important has been lost,
like an island, an embroidered blouse, a colleague

in the parallel world. A swindler's victory, a fly
I had once known. I disapprove, I don't remember!
Beyond the reef are sharks and the dainty frippery

of childhood, and, once there, there is no filching.
I was premature on the beach, like algae at lunchtime
sleepwalking with a harp proscribed by hawks.

One looks backward and one looks forward.
Dust is watching life's talk show.
I plunge like danger into the sea.

My mother stands, facing the wind.

James Tate

The Sadness of My Neighbors

Somehow, one expects
all that food
to rise up
out of the canning jars
and off the dinner plates
and *do* something,
mean something.

But, alas, it's all
just stuff and more
stuff, without pausing
for an interval
of transformation.

Even family
relationships
go begging
for any illumination.

And yet, there is competence,
there is some quiet
glitter to the surface,
a certain cleaniness,
which means next to

nothing, unless you want
to eat off the floor.

James Tate

We'll Burn That Bridge When We Come To It

Silhouette of my hieroglyph,
hyena of my foibles,
and even puniness of my astrological endeavor,
I am scolding these shabby shipmates.
One of them can sneer and sing in falsetto
while murdering frogs — he's a green blowfly
not worthy of scratching our curiosity.
Another left the waterworks for a monastery
in an indigo field, terminating
his little income from the face of the earth.
And there I am, a million tons of buffalo bones,
reconnoitering the chalky goldfields,
raven in hand, grunting imperial sulphur belches
beside the wagon where her blouse hangs
in opalescent darkness, grievous spasms.

O abstinence of my corpulent debauches,
and satchel of my chanting,
turbulence of my decimated bandana,
I am celebrating all this forlorn gazing:
the ship stiffens, numbed by an impulse to fly.

James Tate

Short March, Teeny Wall

A quarrel undresses
an impulse, textbooks
are deposited, but aroused.
A tyranny is subdued
while a rabbit examines

his poultry. Many dimensions
are motionless, like a flood
nowadays appeals to the
tiniest birchtrees. There's
a nuance there, palpable

as a railroad in the ozone
where civilians are debris,
autumnal wind battering
the curtains in the buildings.
My spine is humming music

sheets. My neck is in the door
beneath my eyes. My hand
is whore-hunting beside
the theologues in the church
of intrigue, of serpentine

deportations and imbroglios
mutually embedded in the blind
keyhole of our instruments.
Where the cloud is cleft,
and the machinery is suffocating,

a physician is departing, tush, tush.
An expedition of breathing animals
catapults the bank into bronze,
and the operations of my own personal
mechanism recognize the haziness

of boundaries, with deep respect.
I silence the bells at the doorway.

I call the boys home through thick vines
and fermentation of a national crisis.
In a white tuxedo, I am the bouncer in heaven.

Pretty Teeth

You will always be ready to smile if every night and morning you beautify your teeth with the toothpaste that has a guaranteed measured, germ-killing power. If you do not yet know what a delicious clean feeling Euthymol gives to the mouth, send for the seven-day free trial sample and booklet or buy a large 1/3d. tube with the convenient spring-cap from your chemist, and observe the Golden Rule of Dental Health—Visit the dentist twice a year and twice a day, night and morning, use

Euthymol
TOOTH/PASTE
KILLS DENTAL DECAY GERMS IN 30 SECONDS.

TRIAL OFFER Send to Dept. 86/49, Euthymol, 50 Beak St., London, W.1, for a free trial sample tube.

Chase Twichell

The Odds

1.

The maxim "lucky at cards,
unlucky at love" touches
on a truth, but accidentally.
Luck has nothing to do with it.
Luck is a word for ignorance.

Where the river
rushes down to a rocky pool,
boys skinnydip at twilight,
their bodies midsummer brown,
hurling themselves off the high ledge,
plunging into the black,
reflective water.
Driving the back roads
to a poker game,
I've stopped the car
to watch them.
Jackknife, cannonball,
they remind me of twigs
that nearly break
but then unbend
and go on growing.
Also of leaves in early spring
uncrushing in a muscular,
accelerated splurge
heart-set on summer.
Leaves like my heart,
in which the greensickness
of spring fever lingers.

As I drive on,
the sun sleeps like candlelight
on the barns and sloping fields,
and the rock stars on the radio
come almost close enough to love.
Music, like all sensation
and the passionate mind on paper,

contributes to the fierce
deliciousness of every moment,
and when profound enough
and adamant enough,
engenders hope, an element
one can swim in,
sometimes even drown in.

The idea travels inward,
not outward.
It shrinks and is clarified
in one stroke,
so that it gleams
like a fatal microbe
under the lenses,
a tiny cog, a wheel
spinning with the head-on
inaccuracy of human logic.
Meaning that each card,
depending on its context,
is a source of power
or a source of nothing.

Sometimes the heart
refuses to open,
little wishing-well
choked with pennies.
It knows,
the heart in its heart,
that the odds are against it.
But then the cards can flare
some nights with a force
that must be sexual,
a dark directive
powerful enough
to flow through the deck
and change the outcome,
a sort of voodoo unto oneself.
That's instinct,

experience worked over
until it's second nature,
and with it comes something
that looks like recklessness
but is its opposite.

2.

I thought I knew by heart
every euphemism for expense.
So what new loss unfurls
at the sight of small boys
pushing their bicycles one-handed
along the river bank,
carrying their shoes?

I loved him the way I love
whatever seasons
are not this season,
for his presence-in-absence,
his promises.
I loved him for the way
he flinched when I touched him,
suggesting that the first
instant of the future might yield
not just the certainty of pleasure,
but a dose of pain.
In poker,
there's no equivalent for this,
unless it's the innocent
teasing out his final card
in case courtship might help it.
Cards are all clean edges,
and have no memory.

A little awkwardness
equips the soul for love,
and teaches the ear
the faulty music that endures.

The rounded hollow
of the dove's one note,
breath in a bottle,
or wind in water reeds,
played in both
the green wood and the dead.
If God talks to himself
for intimacy's sake,
I've heard him in the papery,
spiritual sound of shuffling.

Would I have thought of it this way
had it been winter, early dark,
snow and taillights
en route to the game?
Would I have pictured
the deck as pure genetics,
the days ahead still crushed
into their earliest forms
like the traits that swim
latent in the blood,
tumor and gift for music alike?
Or listened for the voice
that enters, after the divorce,
a whole new range
inside the old range,
like an injured muscle
learning its new span
as though pain were a fence?
A voice remorseless
in its lust for limits.
But isn't lust
with its formalities
always the driver?
For love and power
and the joyful
transactions of the body?
Not only that.
It rages also,

an appetite for appetites,
disrupting the small
samples of fate
dealt onto the green tablecloth.

3.

I've loved too many times,
and not enough. So what?
I threw the tokens of affection
onto the quieting felt.
They made their own perfection.

The naked boys belong
no more to one world than the other.
They stand for hunger,
which turns the body inward
to feed on itself,
cell cannibalizing cell.
Men love carelessly when young,
women when they're older.
Guilt is a stupid hammer.

Love, money, music, water.
The night blesses them all
equally as it falls,
and does not distinguish between them.
The verb *abandon*
tips on the fulcrum
of its double meaning.

All lives flash and spark,
trailing a lit fuse.
A boy jumps,
and as his small hard body
enters the water,
the ace of hearts
falls onto the green cloth.
I know exactly what it's worth to me

at this moment, which is
the only moment that exists.
The odds are antibodies,
river stones, the leaves
noisy with changing numbers.
Whatever it cost to understand this,
I would pay again.
I pay for my history with my history.
And so I own the rocky pool,
the blue tattoo of love that died,
music from the radio
that is the world.
They are not a part
of what I have agreed to lose.

Chase Twichell

Translations from the Rational

The roofless houses by the roadside drown
in sky the color of mercurochrome.
Greener than snow, the acres of limestone
force new beauty from a simple noun,
the last of the five elements: bone.
Without a place to rest, the remnant sounds
of aftermath pray to the empty towns
for resurrection of the chromosome.
The distant roses of plutonium
make of the sky a staggering bouquet
turned in upon itself, a cranium
packed with scenes from life, a matinee
of dreams for the millennium,
the lit terrain we called the Milky Way.

Across the bulging, dust-dark summer storm,
lightning prints a jagged, branching track.
Nostalgia's not a longing to go back,
nor love of the world a love of form.
Not quite. We glimpse another paradise
obscured by its protective colorations,
but lose it to a flux of short durations.
All that we love, we try to memorize.
Time undermines that love. Each tense collides,
a broken storm of many blossomings.
The nets we throw out drag the wayward tides
for things lost long ago to the water's rings.
We watch the speckled, paling undersides
of those quick fish, the vanishing evenings.

Chase Twichell

The Moon in the Pines

I do not remember
exactly how the moth
disclosed the blueprint
abridged on its wings,
except that it was August
and the moon fell from a century
unlike the twentieth
into the pines.
This happened on the outskirts
of a town I don't remember.
Starlings drilled for grubs
beneath the deepening neon
of the motel's name
until the moon
cast them back into the shadows.
The air cooled to a resinous perfume,
and a moth made of dark dust
pressed briefly to the screen
a map of unknown regions
now familiar, though
where the heart's grave is,
no one knows.

Chase Twichell

Meteor Showers, August, 1968

A night in August,
in my adolescence,
perseveres intact.
An isolated night,
muscular with cold,
pinned open to reveal
a darkened gulf
filled with the talc
of disembodied minerals.

Part of the mind still lies
on a splintery wooden bench,
hostage to the sparks
that brightened
at their moment of extinction.
Pressed to the glassy barrier,
I was exposed to an austerity
that pleased me.
Embers turning inward
to blueblackness.
A kiss imploding.

Meteors raked the atmosphere,
each one a struck match,
a cat's scratch of light.

Words also fall
across enormous blackness,
small spilled baskets.
Abandoned in that wilderness,
they turn toward one another
and marry, mid-sentence,
becoming in effect
a paradigm of the mind's decorum,
the balance it requires
to hold its illusion of stillness.

It seems that the mind
must renounce

the form that contains it
to swim in the deep,
directionless waters,
or that it must stand
as a stockade or a dam,
opposed to the
starry, immortal flood.

Constance Urdang

Returning to the Port of Authority: A Picaresque

> Some New Yorkers refer to the Port Authority
> Building, where all buses enter and leave New
> York, as the Port of Authority

Where are they going, the crowds that pass in the street?
I had not thought life had undone so many,
So many men and women, seeking the port of authority,
Safe anchorage, harbor, asylum.
                          Late at night
They are the voices on the radio, asking the hard questions;
Or they don't ask. The homeless, the hunted,
The haunted, the night-watchers
Who can't wait any longer for morning,
                                   where are they going?

Returning, revenant, I see Eighth Avenue is a poem,
Seventh and Broadway are epics, Fifth an extravaganza
From the winos and freaks at its feet in Washington Square
(Past once-white buildings, long-ago sidewalk cafes
Behind grimy privet, Fourteenth Street's brash interruption)
To the crossover at Twenty-third.
                              At Thirty-fourth
The mammoth parade of department stores begins,
And, on the pavement, a cacophony of hawkers
That stretches beyond the stone lions, the bravura
Of Forty-second, to a kind of apotheosis
At Fifty-ninth.
                  O prevalence of pinnacles!
O persistence of uniformed doormen sounding, in the rain,
Your peremptory whistles! On Madison and Third
I am assaulted by florists' windows
Bursting with tropical blooms, I'm magnetized
By the windows of jewelry shops, by vegetables
Displayed like jewels, I'm buffeted
By the turbulence of this stream
Of life, this lyric, this mystery,
This daily miracle-play.
                          What impossible collaborations
Are being consummated in cloud-high offices!
How many sweaty love-acrobatics are being performed

Behind a thousand windows
In the tall imperturbable hotels!
                                      And all day long
The restless crowds pass in the street,
Eddying and flowing like the tidal rivers,
And I am carried along, flotsam like the rest,
Riding the crest of the flood down to the sea.

The Empty Chair

means a heartache to the child who has lost his Father; but it means much more. Father's advice and influence will be missing. Mother cannot look after the children whilst she is out at work. A happy home awaits fatherless and motherless boys and girls at the **ALEXANDRA ORPHANAGE**, Maitland Park, Haverstock Hill, London, N.W.3. They are trained to be useful self-reliant citizens. Will you send a gift towards the £10,000 needed each year from voluntary donations, to Fred. J. Robinson, F.C.I.S., Secretary, Alexandra Orphanage, 34-40 Ludgate Hill, London, E.C.4.

Larkin Warren

Rituals of the Ordinary

All day long I inventory what only lately
I have come to love: silver candlesticks,
the gardenia soap in its dish, the rootbound
and purpling Wandering Jew, the chorus
of clean laundry, worn white cotton you wear
closest to your skin, the order of our things
in drawers and closets and finally, three
brass locks on my side of the door,
pleasing to me as antique jewelry.
"It's snowing on Fifth Avenue!" you announce
from a phone booth at noon, this last day
of March. At the sound of your voice, flowers,
real and unreal,
glow in lunatic abundance here.

After your call, I try to return again
to what comforts: old books that came as gifts,
and food in its reliable perfection. Perhaps
artichoke hearts in a sauce of garlic and cheese,
perhaps strong coffee in a mug so large
I must hold it in both hands.
As the daylight goes, the music comes up
like in old movies, bringing dusk, then dark.

Before sleep I adjust the grandfather clock
and a brass weight slides heavily off its hook
into my hand. Unable to remake the connection
in the hallway's faltering light, I give up.
Moonlight washing over your side of the bed
pulls me to the window where overhead, lacy remains
of a jetstream separate and drift, east to west.

The house, shifting from one corner to the other,
wants to settle in around me and the night, wants
me to make some one thing more important
than all others. But I must sit awhile,
tented by lamplight. And the clockweight,
warm and cylindrical in my hand,
conspires now with your absence, and stops time.

Larkin Warren

Vermont, Triptych, 1978

> "Still a man hears
> what he wants to hear
> and disregards the rest."
>
> Paul Simon, "The Boxer"

It is early November in Saxton's River. A man
and a woman, bulky and separate in their coats,
walk through the cemetery
reading stones out loud. Two marble or granite
stones are down, maybe pushed over, uprooted
somehow in the unreliable ground.
Sarah, consort of . . ., she says to his back.
Philip and Jonathan, belov'd sons & brothers,
he reads, wondering at the heart
that absorbs more than one death at a time.

Later, perhaps, they will share lunch in the car
pulled to the side of a dirt road on Putney Ridge.
There are cows in the grey-brown field, placid
like great-aunts at a wedding shower, waiting
to be herded or only persuaded into a winter barn.
Around them, birches rise clean as large bones
on the floor of some ocean
where it is always November, and cold.
The woman says *Birches in all seasons
remind me of thin girls, dancing.*
If we do not hear the man speak, it is because
he cannot, mute and afraid suddenly of winter.
He thinks the air on this mountain
is so clear, so absent of matter, he might drift up
and up and never reach the top of it.

Then the woman sleeps, her coat slightly open
to her red sweater, buttons undone at the neck.
The man, who needs to banish the thing gone hollow
in him, tries to imagine their room at the inn:
perhaps it is yellow, like the inside of birthday cake,
with the last of the cider left cooling on the sill,
three Comice pears in a blue bowl. And the steam
is hissing, clanking as it begins to push heat
up through the silver fingers of the radiator.

Bruce Weigl

The Act

To cold sulfur mornings I want to take us back
Before light, before everything had come to loss.
I close my eyes and waves of dark settle
And I hear my mother and father's
Hushed talk in the kitchen.
He's off to work in the mill and their
Fingers circle the white mugs of coffee
And blowing steam that rises between them they
Talk quietly about nothing in particular,
About nothing lovely at all. Lives later

I still tear sheets and blankets from my bed
To dig away from the dream shadow of jungle
Closing in on me, drowning in the tropical air
I can only travel backwards
To those cold sulfur mornings,
My father shoveling coal,
Stoking the furnace for his sleeping children,
And his holy footsteps in the snow
And the engine turning barely over
And the headlight beam
Swinging across the walls and ceiling of my room
In a great arch I feel pass through me, still.
I didn't have a name for it
But it seems like love to me now, it
Feels a lot like love.

By the strain and the sleeplessness and the gritty air
Of our coming and our going we are worn away.
What we had when we had nothing
But enough coal for most of winter
You could hold in your hands like the heavy mugs of coffee.
What we had when we had nothing
But enough change to count out on the butcher's counter
Was a bond that lashed us to the world,
That held us from tumbling out
Into the cold puzzled times of our lives.

It depends upon a belief that says

I am tethered to those mornings only drifting,
Each rise of wave the coastline smaller.
It depends upon a belief that says
You can go back to the cold morning's sulfur air
When hope was as simple as saying the names of the loved
Into the bare walls of the dream of a life
That will never be true.

Bruce Weigl

To the Dog Dying

In her eyes there is a longing to not move.
She shivers in the warm room,
Old enough so the deaths overlap,
So the numbers of years begin to add up
Long past coincidence
Grows into something more tangible
Like disease.

The light is short.
Into our path the trees' shadows fall
On our cruise around the block
Sniffing sex, pissing where we please
On the neighbor's lawns.
Seven times how many years she is
Is her dumb fate
And she is not full of the human things
To keep her
When the scents fade.
Human things cannot keep her
Alive as we had imagined all these years.

Roger Weingarten

Water Music

There lived a man who suffocated
the mouth of a tobacco jar with a clean
handkerchief, then tipped the corpse, leaving
his wife for another and other lands. This red-eyed
pilgrim was only a little bald, not
that tall, drunk, or that fair
to look upon. He had better things to do

like open a can of deviled ham,
fry an egg over it, and call it supper, coveting
fine instruments, not for the way
they mitered a corner or tightened the string
of a gold lute — life was brandy
soaked tobacco smoke. Red snapper whickered
and swam into his hands. Coconuts

fell and split on his machete, silver and by his side
like a wolfhound or a new bride. Bathed
in sunlight, the wind purred through the turquoise
threads of his hammock, palm fronds
and jasmine strewn across his path.
He stole a boat and whispered
across waves slapping that he couldn't survive

without the blue-smoking tongue of a wife
to tell him this or that or where to put it. Rolling
off the kitchen table, his children
loved him as children love to cool their feet
in a tidepool or tall grass. One morning
in the season of thick moss, pine
needles and ferns steaming, another

and even younger man, without consulting
the knowhow of his old crony, folded a sausage
and cheese into the inner life of a napkin
tied to a stick and left *his* wife. What kind of a general
delivery how-do-you-do do you think he received
months later and out of the blue from his mentor
his old friend — I could end it here.

You could have a beer, unfasten your belt, look
to the title, think the worst or wonder
what kind of a primrose cul de sac is this
bardic fool giving us this time. Keep
your pants on. Such an enterprise
has two purposes: You enter the war zone
of your own contrary forces, searching

the swampy regions to better understand
your own defenses; then, once you've reconnoitered
this terrain (its arbors and mists) and found a familiar
patch of jack-in-the-pulpit and stinkhorns, fall back
and roll around and reminisce about
that cold marriage or kiss
that changed your life. It's here in a relentless

pursuit of pain or pleasure that you
can easily get a purchase on what it's like
to brag to another, turn her over, complain,
keep it to yourself or pass it on. My tale
is done. I like a reader who sits
on his wristwatch and it relaxes me
to imagine him opening the zipper of his purse

after he's finished without being asked. Bless him
for his hearty wine and may his enemies
kiss both cheeks, on the run and after
a preacher after a poacher — whosoever
catches their drift will marry my daughter
or make himself scarce forever, wherever
the morning after is rancid milk

on a thick tongue and the wind
tattoos rain against the windowpane.

Don Welch

First Book Apocrypha

Contrary to all reports, I made you first.

Before one word had closed,
Eve, you were the germ in my broad urge,
the love that quickened me to form.

Shall I tell you how it was before you were?
Black snowflakes fell,
darkness was my only circumstance.

And after this dark had bruised my head,
I saw you coming toward me,

holding my diminished head in your white hands.

Ruth Whitman

Basic Training, 1942

I lay stifling on the sheets
    in a rundown rooming house
        in Miami Beach, Florida.

You, buttoned up in stiff khaki,
    your curly head shaved
        close as a convict's,

were marching a mile away
    with the typewriter brigade —
        artists, actors, pianists.

You were the only poet.
    You held your gun awkwardly
        while the sergeant

barked and snapped at your heels.
    On Sunday we swam among the palms
        in an ocean tepid as a bathtub.

The night sky looked upside down.
    Your friends wept on my shoulder
        for their lost music, their wrenched lives.

Before I left, I ran along
    beside your platoon, shouting
        Look at the sunset, darling!

and every head turned to see
    the sun collapsing
        behind a bloody horizon.

Joy Williams

Health

Pammy is in an unpleasant Texas city, the city where she was born, in the month of her twelfth birthday. It is cold and cloudy. Soon it will rain. The rain will wash the film of ash off the car she is travelling in, volcanic ash that has drifted across the Gulf of Mexico, all the way from the Yucatan. Pammy is a stocky grey-eyed blonde, a daughter, travelling in her father's car, being taken to her tanning lesson.

This is her father's joke. She is being taken to a tanning session, twenty-five minutes long. She had requested this for her birthday, ten tanning sessions in a health spa. She had also asked for and received, new wheels for her skates. They are purple Rannalli's. She had dyed her stoppers to match although the match was not perfect. The stoppers were a duller, cruder purple. Pammy wants to be a speed skater but she worries that she doesn't have the personality for it. "You've gotta have gravel in your gut to be in speed," her coach said. Pammy has mastered the duck walk but still doesn't have a good, smooth cross-over, and sometimes she fears that she never will.

Pammy and her father, Morris, are following a truck which is carrying a jumble of television sets. There is a twenty-four inch console facing them on the open tailgate, restrained by rope, with a bullet hole in the exact center of the screen.

Morris drinks coffee from a plastic-lidded cup that fits into a bracket mounted just beneath the car's radio. Pammy has a friend, Wanda, whose step-father has the same kind of plastic cup in his car, but he drinks bourbon and water from his. Wanda had been adopted when she was two months old. Pammy is relieved that neither her father nor Marge, her mother, drinks. Sometimes they have wine. On her birthday, even Pammy had wine with dinner. Marge and Morris seldom quarrel and she is grateful for this. This morning, however, she had seen them quarrel. Once again, her mother had borrowed her father's hairbrush and left long, brown hairs in it. Her father had taken the brush and cleaned it with a comb over the clean kitchen sink. Her father had left a nest of brown hair in the white sink.

In the car, the radio is playing a song called *Tainted Love,* a song Morris likes to refer to as *Rancid Love.* The radio plays constantly when Pammy and her father drive anywhere. Morris is a good driver. He is fast and doesn't bear grudges. He enjoys driving still, after years and years of it. Pammy looks forward to learning how to drive now, but after a few years, who knows? She can't imagine it being that enjoyable after awhile. Her father is skillful here, on the freeways and streets, and on the terrifying, wide two-lane highways and narrow mountain roads in Mexico, and even on the rutted, soiled beaches of the Gulf Coast. One weekend, earlier that spring, Morris had rented a Jeep in Corpus Christi and he and Pammy and Marge had driven the length of Padre Island. They sped across the sand, the only people for miles and miles. There was plastic everywhere.

"You will see a lot of plastic," the man who rented them the Jeep said, "but it is plastic from all over the world."

Morris had given Pammy a lesson in driving the Jeep. He taught her how to shift smoothly, how to synchronize acceleration with the depression and release of the clutch. "There's a way to do things right," Morris told her and when he said this she was filled with a sort of fear. They were just words, she knew, words that anybody could use, but behind words were always things, sometimes things you could never tell anyone, certainly no one you loved, frightening things that weren't even true.

"I'm sick of being behind this truck," Morris says. The screen of the injured television looks like dirty water. Morris pulls to the curb beside an Oriental market. Pammy stares into the market where shoppers wait in line at a cash register. Many of the women wear scarves on their heads. Pammy is deeply disturbed by Orientals who kill penguins to make gloves and murder whales to make nail polish. In school, in social studies class, she is reading eyewitness accounts of the aftermath of the atomic bombing of Hiroshima. She reads about young girls running from their melting city, their hair burnt off, their burnt skin in loose folds, crying, "Stupid Americans." Morris sips his coffee, then turns the car back onto the street, a street now free from fatally wounded television sets.

Pammy gazes at the backs of her hands which are tan, but, she feels, not tan enough. They are a dusky peach color. This will be her fifth tanning lesson. In the health spa, there are ten colored photographs on the wall showing a woman in a bikini, a pale woman being transformed into a tanned woman. In the last photograph she has plucked the bikini slightly away from her hip-bone to expose a sliver of white skin and she is smiling down at the sliver.

Pammy tans well. Without a tan, her face seems grainy and uneven for she has freckles and rather large pores. Tanning draws her together, completes her. She has had all kinds of tans — golden tans, pool tans, even a Florida tan which seemed yellow back in Texas. She had brought all her friends the same present from Florida — small plywood crates filled with tiny oranges which were actually chewing gum. The finest tan Pammy has ever had, however, was in Mexico six months ago. She had gone there with her parents for two weeks, and she had gotten a truly remarkable tan and she had gotten tuberculosis. This has caused some tension between Morris and Marge as it had been Morris' idea to swim at the spas in the mountains rather than in the pools at the more established hotels. It was believed that Pammy had become infected at one particular public spa just outside the small dusty town where they had gone to buy tiles, tiles of a dusky orange with blue rays flowing from the center, tiles which are now in the kitchen of their home where each morning Pammy drinks her juice and takes three hundred milligrams of isoniazid.

"Here we are," Morris says. The health spa is in a small, concrete block building with white columns, salvaged from the wrecking of a mansion, adorning the front. There are gift shops, palmists and all-night restaurants along the street, as well as an exterminating company that has a huge fiberglass bug with X's for eyes on the roof. This was not the company that had tented Wanda's house for termites. That had been another company. When Pammy was in Mexico getting tuberculosis, Wanda and her parents had gone to San Antonio for a week while their house was being tented. When they returned, they'd found a dead robber in the living room, the things he was stealing piled neatly nearby. He had died from inhaling the deadly gas used by the exterminators.

"Mommy will pick you up," Morris says. "She has a class this afternoon so she might be a little late. Just stay inside until she comes."

Morris kisses her on the cheek. He treats her like a child. He treats Marge like a mother, her mother.

Marge is thirty-five but she is still a student. She takes courses in art history and film at one of the city's universities, the same university where Morris teaches petroleum science. Years ago when Marge had first been a student, before she had met Morris and Pammy had been born, she had been in Spain, in a museum studying a Goya and a piece of the painting had fallen at her feet. She had quickly placed it in her pocket and now has it on her bureau in a small glass box. It is a wedge of greenish-violet paint, as large as a thumb-nail. It is from one of Goya's nudes.

Pammy gets out of the car and goes into the health spa. There is no equipment here except for the tanning beds, twelve tanning beds in eight small rooms. Pammy has never had to share a room with anyone. If asked to, she would probably say no, hoping that she would not hurt the other person's feelings. The receptionist is an old, vigorous woman behind a scratched metal desk, wearing a black jumpsuit and feather earrings. Behind her are shelves of powders and pills in squat brown bottles with names like DY—NAMIC STAMINA BUILDER and DYNAMIC SUPER STRESS-END and LIVER CONCENTRATE ENERGIZER.

The receptionist's name is Aurora. Pammy thinks that the name is magnificent and is surprised that it belongs to such an old woman. Aurora leads her to one of the rooms at the rear of the building. The room has a mirror, a sink, a small stool, a white rotating fan and the bed, a long bronze coffin-like aparatus with a lid. Pammy is always startled when she sees the bed with its frosted ultraviolet tubes, its black vinyl headrest. In the next room, someone coughs. Pammy imagines people lying in all the rooms, wrapped in white light, lying quietly as though they were being rested for a long, long journey. Aurora takes a spray bottle of disinfectant and a scrap of toweling from the counter above the sink and cleans the surface of the bed. She twists the timer and the light leaps out, like an animal in a dream, like a murderer in a movie.

"There you are, honey," Aurora says. She pats Pammy on the shoulder and leaves.

Pammy pushes off her sandals and undresses quickly. She leaves her clothes in a heap, her sweatshirt on top of the pile. Her sweatshirt is white with a transfer of a skater on the back. The skater is a man wearing a helmet and knee-pads, side-surfing goofy-footed. She lies down and with her left hand pulls the lid to within a foot of the bed's cool surface. She can see the closed door and the heap of clothing and her feet. Pammy considers her feet to be her ugliest feature. They are skinny and the toes are too far apart. She and Wanda had painted their toes the same color, but Wanda's feet were pretty and hers were not. Pammy thought her feet looked like they belonged to a dead person and there wasn't anything she could do about them. She closes her eyes.

Wanda, who read a lot, told Pammy that tuberculosis was a very romantic disease, the disease of artists and poets and "highly sensitive individuals."

"Oh yeah," her stepfather had said. "Tuberculosis has mucho cachet."

Wanda's stepfather speaks loudly and his eyes glitter. He is always joking, Pammy thinks. Pammy feels that Wanda's parents are pleasant but she is always a little uncomfortable around them. They had a puppy for awhile, a purebred Doberman which they gave to the SPCA after they discovered it had a slightly over-shot jaw. Wanda's step-father always called the puppy a sissy. "You sissy," he'd say to the puppy. "Hanging around with girls all the time." He was referring to his wife and to Wanda and Pammy. "Oh, you sissy, you sissy," he'd say to the puppy.

There was also the circumstance of Wanda's adoption. There had been another baby adopted, but it was learned that the baby's background had been misrepresented. Or perhaps it had been a boring baby. In any case the baby had been returned and they got Wanda.

Pammy doesn't think Wanda's parents are very steadfast. She is surprised that they don't make Wanda nervous, for Wanda is certainly not perfect. She's a shoplifter and gets C's in Computer Language.

The tanning bed is warm but not uncomfortably so. Pammy lies with her arms straight by her sides, palms down. She hears voices in the hall and footsteps. When she first began coming to the health spa, she was afraid that someone would open the door to the room she was in by mistake. She imagined exactly what it would be like. She would see the door open abruptly out of the corner of her eye, then someone would say, "Sorry," and the door would close again. But this had not happened. The voices pass by.

Pammy thinks of Snow White lying in her glass coffin. The Queen had deceived her how many times? Three? She had been in disguise, but still. And then Snow White had choked on an apple. In the restaurants she sometimes goes to with her parents there are posters on the walls which show a person choking and another person trying to save him. The posters take away Pammy's appetite.

Snow White lay in a glass coffin, not naked of course but in a gown, watched over by dwarfs. But surely they had not been real dwarfs. That had just been a word that had been given to them.

When Pammy had told Morris that tuberculosis was a romantic disease, he had said, "There's nothing romantic about it. Besides, you don't have it."

It seems to be a fact that she both has and doesn't have tuberculosis. Pammy had been given the tuberculin skin test along with her classmates when she began school in the fall and within forty-eight hours had a large swelling on her arm.

"Now that you've come in contact with it, you don't have to worry about getting it," the pediatrician had said in his office, smiling.

"You mean the infection constitutes immunity," Marge said.

"Not exactly," the pediatrician said, shaking his head, still smiling.

Her lungs are clear. She is not ill but has an illness. The germs are in her body, but in a resting state, still alive but rendered powerless, successfully overcome by her healthy body's strong defenses. Outwardly, she is the same, but within, a great drama had taken place and Pammy feels herself in possession of a bright, secret, and unspeakable knowledge.

She knows other things too, things that would break her parents' hearts, common, ugly, easy things. She knows a girl in school who stole her mother's green stamps and bought a personal massager with the books. She knows another girl whose brother likes to wear her clothes. She knows a boy who threw a can of motor oil at his father and knocked him unconscious.

Pammy stretches. Her head tingles. Her body is about a foot and a half off the floor and appears almost grey in the glare from the tubes. She has heard of pills one could take to acquire a tan. One just took two pills a day and after twenty days one had a wonderful tan which could be maintained just by taking two pills a day thereafter. You ordered them from Canada. It was some kind of food-coloring substance. How gross, Pammy thinks. When she had been little she had bought a quarter of an acre of land in Canada by mail for fifty cents. That had been two years ago.

Pammy hears voices from the room next to hers, coming through the thin wall. A woman talking rapidly says,

"Pete went up to Detroit two days ago to visit his brother

who's dying up there in the hospital. Cancer. The brother's always been a nasty type, I mean very unpleasant. Younger than Pete and always mean. Tried to commit suicide twice. Then he learns he has cancer and decides he doesn't want to die. Carries on and on. Is miserable to everyone. Puts the whole family through hell, but nothing can be done about it, he's dying of cancer. So Pete goes up to see him his last days in the hospital and you know what happens? Pete's wallet gets stolen. Right out of a dying man's room. Five hundred dollars in cash and all our credit cards. That was yesterday. What a day."

Another woman says, "If it's not one thing, it's something else."

Pammy coughs. She doesn't want to hear other people's voices. It is as though they are throwing away junk, the way some people use words, as though one word were as good as another.

"Things happen so abruptly any more," the woman says. "You know what I mean?"

Pammy does not listen and she does not open her eyes for if she did she would see this odd bright room with her clothes in a heap and herself lying motionless and naked. She does not open her eyes because she prefers imagining that she is a magician's accomplice, levitating on a stage in a coil of pure energy. If one thought purely enough, one could create one's own truth. That's how people accomplished astral travel, walked over burning coals, cured warts. There was a girl in Pammy's class at school, Bonnie Black, a small owlish looking girl who was a Christian Scientist. She raised rabbits and showed them at fairs, and was always wearing the ribbons they had won to school, pinned to her blouse. She had warts all over her hands, but one day Pammy noticed that the warts were gone and Bonnie Black had told her that the warts disappeared after she had clearly realized that in her true being as God's reflection, she couldn't have warts.

It seemed that people were better off when they could concentrate on something, hold something in their mind for a long time and really believe it. Pammy had once seen a radical skater putting on a show at the opening of a shopping mall. He leapt over cars and pumped up the sides of buildings. He did flips and spins. A disc jockey who was set up for the day in the parking lot interviewed him. "I'm really impressed with your performance," the disc jockey said, "and I'm impressed that you never fall. Why don't you fall?" The skater was a thin boy in baggy cut-off jeans. "I don't fall," the boy said, looking hard at the microphone, "because I've got a deep respect for the concrete surface and because when I make a miscalculation, instead of falling, I turn it into a new trick."

Pammy thinks it is wonderful that the boy was able to say something which would keep him from thinking he might fall.

The door to the room opened. Pammy had heard the turning of the knob. At first she lies without opening her eyes, willing the sound of the door shutting, but she hears nothing, only the ticking of the bed's timer. She swings her head quickly to the side and looks at the door. There is a man standing there, staring at her. She presses her right hand into a fist and lays it between her legs. She puts her left arm across her breasts.

"What?" she says to the figure, frightened. In an instant she is almost panting with fear. She feels the repetition of something painful and known, but she has not known this, not ever. The figure says nothing and pulls the door shut. With a flurry of rapid ticking, the timer stops. The harsh lights of the bed go out.

Pammy pushes the lid back and hurriedly gets up. She dresses hastily and smooths her hair with her fingers. She looks at herself in the mirror, her lips parted. Her teeth are white behind her pale lips. She stares at herself. She can be looked at and not discovered. She can speak and not be known. She opens the door and enters the hall. There is no one there. The hall is so narrow that by spreading her arms she can touch the walls with her fingertips. In the reception area by Aurora's desk, there are three people, a stoop-shouldered young woman and two men. The woman was signing up for a month of unlimited tanning which meant that after the basic monthly fee she only had to pay a dollar a visit. She takes her checkbook out of a soiled handbag, which is made out of some silvery material, and writes a check. The men look comfortable lounging in the chairs, their legs stretched out. They know one another, Pammy guesses, but they do not know the woman. One of them has dark spikey hair like a wet animal's. The other wears a red tight t-shirt. Neither is the man she had seen in the doorway.

"What time do you want to come back tomorrow, honey?" Aurora asks Pammy. "You certainly are coming along nicely. Isn't she coming along nicely?"

"I'd like to come back the same time tomorrow," Pammy says. She raises her hand to her mouth and coughs slightly.

"Not the same time, honey. Can't give you the same time. How about an hour later?"

"All right," Pammy says. The stoop-shouldered woman sits down in a chair. There are no more chairs in the room. Pammy opens the door to the street and steps outside. It has rained and the street is dark and shining. The air smells fresh and feels thick. She stands in it, a little stunned, looking. Her father will teach her how to drive, and she will drive around. Her mother will continue to take classes at the university. Whenever she meets someone new, she will mention the Goya. "I have a small Goya," she will say, and laugh.

Pammy walks slowly down the street. She smells barbequed meat and the rain lingering in the trees. By a store called *IMAGINE*, there's a clump of bamboo with some beer cans glittering in its ragged, grassy center. *IMAGINE* sells neon palm trees and silk clouds and stars. It sells greeting cards and chocolate in shapes children aren't allowed to see and it sells children stickers and shoelaces. Pammy looks in the window at a huge satin pillow in the shape of a heart with a heavy zipper running down the center of it. Pammy turns and walks back to the building that houses the tanning beds. Her mother pulls up in the car. "Pammy!" she calls. She is leaning toward the window on the passenger side which she has rolled down. She unlocks the car's door. Pammy gets in and the door locks again.

Pammy wishes she could tell her mother something, but what can she say? She never wants to see that figure looking at her again, so coldly staring and silent, but she knows she will, for already its features are becoming more indistinct, more general. It could be anything. She coughs, but it is not the cough of a sick person because Pammy is a healthy girl. It is the kind of cough a person might make if they were at a party and there was no one there but strangers.

Marge, driving, says, "You look very nice. That's a very pretty tan, but what will happen when you stop going there? It won't last. You'll lose it right away, won't you?"

She will. And she will grow older, but the world will remain as young as she was once, infinite in its possibilities and uncaring.

Ellen Wittlinger

Blue Murder

1.
For sport the bluefish kills
a thousand other fish a day,
more than it can possibly eat.

So you might say the man
is justified to reel them in
twenty-two in one afternoon

and still throwing the oily meat
up on the beach, a line of thrashing
flesh, breathing, dying.

2.
We're getting older.
The number of people
who remember our names
from one day to another
dwindles: two old friends,
one lifelong enemy, maybe
the landlady. Spouses
are in a different category.
Like mothers and fathers
their names become symbols
even the faultiest memory
cannot help but match.
This is the mistake one makes
by killing in passion.
I would imagine the name
would be written in blood
on your brain.

3.
In the city we circumvent
certain areas: random death
has favorite neighborhoods.

Statistics comfort: most murders
take place in the home. After love
a woman fuels the bedroom

leaves her sleeping husband
to bake and burn,
forgotten meat in the busy

housewife's oven. But the jury
lets her off. Everyone knows
there is more punishment than she

deserves every day she wakes
in the new bed. Sometimes
she could scream bloody murder.

4.
One day when the bluefish were running
you rode your bike to the shore.
"Here! Take a couple home to the wife."
A satisfied fisherman flung two
huge fish into the wire basket.
He made a face: "I don't eat 'em.
Too rich!" I watched you come riding
down the street, the old bike wobbling
under the weight and thought for a moment
the dead thing hanging there
would be a horror: someone's dog, something
wrong. But you were smiling.
For us it was a delicacy.
And as I watched you cut and bone
the great assassin fish,
I wondered if there would be a day
when these small murders
were simply not enough.

Carolyne Wright

Eugenia

> "Arauco tiene una pena
> que no la puedo callar..."
> —Violeta Parra

Where are you now, Eugenia?
Are you still climbing the rain-scarred
road out of Arauco? You're eleven,
carrying water, two cutaway tin buckets
with baling-wire handles —
your head lowered, black hair cropped,
a child of brave words
and shoulders broadened by homespun.

I still see you standing
against the cinder-block wall
of the Save the Children Fund office,
do you remember? You clutch
your printed number card,
trying to make the right face
for the rich ladies, flicker
of disbelief in your eyes
as the shutter-gun flashes, your name
tumbling into hundreds of mail boxes
at the end of the month.

On the Arauco Road, you're yourself
again. At your door, chickens
dart in and out across the lintel,
your grandmother between bean rows
shields her eyes from the watery sun
of the coastland. Mother-of-pearl woman
under a spun-wool sky, gray braids
roped together down her back,
smoke from the cooking fire
on the packed earth floor
working its way through her shadow.

Eleven more years will pass
after you ask me in for supper.
After I watch you hurry back

and forth for kindling and *mate* leaves
as evening takes over the one small window
and I finally catch on: tonight there are
no beans, no bread, no *mate*.

The next day, I sign up for you,
bring apples, cheese and underwear
because today's your birthday.
My friends and I take you to Café Lebu
where the Peace Corps eats. You sit
wordless, shy, concentrating on your hamburger
and homefries and the gauchos in hats
and spurs galloping around borders
of the placemats. You nod yes
to every question, try not to stare
at what we leave on our plates.

Madriña, godmother, you call me
in the seven years of letters —
those construction-paper cards
listing sweaters and shoes and medicines —
and a snapshot of you every Christmas.
Your hair in ribbons, longer now,
arms around schoolbooks or gifts
my money buys. Each year
you're taller, almost a woman,
but your writing never changes —
the same blue copybook scrawl,
and the same question:
When would I return?

I never did, Eugenia, and at eighteen
your letters stopped.
                    Was there a man —
some dark-mantled farmer who rode past you
on his way to town, mustachioed,
lashing his pony, and you whispered
Arbolé, arbolé, seco y verdé, a song
you'd memorized in school, as he waved?

Did you go with some miner's son
who drove his oxcart for you
from the bituminous smoke of Lota?
Do your own lungs blacken
as you wait with the other women
in the ration lines at dawn?

Or were you among those rounded up
in the Coronel strikes, rumors
of *desaparecidos* at the Dawson Island
camp, their names lost and found
and lost again in the headlines?

How do you live, Eugenia?
There is no one I can speak to.
My letters come back unopened,
a 3 x 5 blank in the file
where your picture was.

Have you followed what Violeta Parra
cried for, chanting Arauco's sorrow
that nobody could silence?
Are you still waiting in the rain
and glacial distance for the long train
from the North? In this undecided
season, it's time I came back
as I promised, when you pressed
the *copihue* blooms into my hands,
the national flower of your hunger.

Carolyne Wright

Talking Politics

       (Ouro Preto, Brasil: February 1972)

We walk to the top of Sao Francisco
and huddle under the portico
of the red-tile and soapstone church
while afternoon rain washes away footsteps
of police. "They got my brother
first," you say. "We found him
in the high grass, bound hand and foot
and blindfolded."
         Suicide,
the uniform at the guard post shrugged,
turning up his soccer game.
You look out past crooked streets
where voices through doorways chant
away the thunder, past the damp green
confusion of hills. You push dark hair
from your eyes, one hand covers mine
as if tonight your body could protect me
from the story.
       Your friends all
fled to Chile those days. Marcos
in the trunk of the red VW
Regina drove from Rio. Chico Lopes
locked eight months in a closet
in Leblon, lying flat under Guarani Blankets
at the Paraguayan border. Marisa,
pregnant, sobbing in a rented room
in Santiago,
       and you, Wander Luis,
safe in the School of Mines.
The engineers' pension, a gallery
of blue shuttered doors, constant
trickle of water in the garden.
"What else can I do?" you ask,
three days from anywhere
on the empty highways
of Minas Gerais, between no life
and no other.

You've learned what's precious
in those hills — diamonds and coal
these towns were named for, stress-
tested metals. And occasionally
a glint of sunlight on a thighbone,
last white flash of understanding
in the cells. What is the atomic weight
of loss? You know your subject,
Father, brother, son. Each name
divided by the blood factor.

"Too many of us live in doubt's
shadow," you say. Your uncle
the graveyard-shift printer,
purple smudges of samisdat on his hands
when they came for him.
Your cousin, drilled with M-16 rounds
under the Father of His Country statue.
And you, hitchhiking in Ash Wednesday
rain for the inquest, with drivers
who scarcely knew the language.

How convenient the dead heroes,
after Goulart's and Castelo Brânco's madness,
all the blond families friendly
with Stroessner, running a country
like one big *fazênda*, Pôrto Alegre
full of Klaus Barbie connections.

And *Brasil mulato*, laughing and talking
all night, drinking *cachaça* and slave coffee
to forget the parrot perch, the rubber
truncheon, shaved heads of deportees.
Three thousand a year give themselves
to the knife-samba, the slow fade
of rain, *favêlas* crumbling on hills
in sight of the Sheratons.

That night, while storms
batter the flagstones, I grow
suddenly afraid, ask you to leave —
harsh words on your tongue, in my mouth
only sounds that stumbled forward
for the border guards, their hands
hard and fast for contraband.

Later, I stand outside your door,
listening to your breath come slow
between the shutters, wondering who
would be left to regret us.
Your one letter months from then,
breathless with dashes and wide-open
vowels — the letter I never answered
for fear you'd follow it
or understand the wanderer's
cowardice that filled my body
with your name.
                "Next year
I'll be gone," you said.
"London, Santiago, New York . . ."
You slap your hands in that strange
Brasilian gesture — *não se não,*

who knows? I ask now,
ten years since corpses floated
under the Mapocho River bridges,
and the rich women of Santiago
parked their cars along the bank
to stare at the dark-skinned ones
among them, and all letters out of Chile
stopped? Ten years since Marisa
lay down with the child whose name
never reached us, since Chico
slept with a revolver by his pillow
and Marcos finally won his game

of Russian roulette.
                    Ten years,
Wander Luis, since you sat cross-legged
on a curbstone in the only photo
I have of you, in a white shirt
with its pocketful of cigarettes
and ballpoints, strumming a *frêvo*
rhythm on your dead brother's guitar,
your eyes half-closed, your face,
like his, never getting any older.

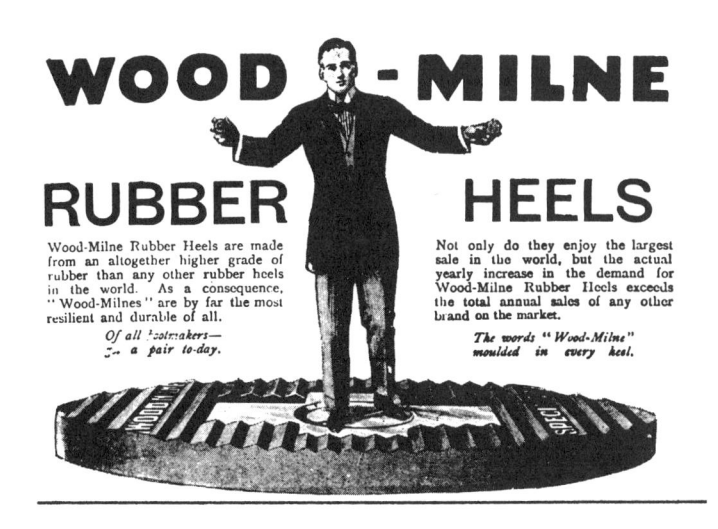

Feature Poet: Raymond Carver

TESS GALLAGHER

Where Water Comes Together With Other Water

I love creeks and the music they make.
And rills, in glades and meadows, before
they have a chance to become creeks.
I may even love them best of all
for their secrecy. I almost forgot
to say something about the source!
Can anything be more wonderful than a spring?
But the big streams have my heart too.
And the places streams flow into rivers.
The open mouths of rivers where they join the sea.
The places where water comes together
with other water. Those places stand out
in my mind like holy places.
But these coastal rivers!
I love them the way some men love horses
and glamorous women. I have a thing
for this cold swift water.
Just looking at it makes my blood run
and my skin tingle. I could sit
and watch these rivers for hours.
Not one of them like any other.
I'm forty-five years old today.
Would anyone believe it if I said
I was once thirty-five?
My heart empty and sere at thirty-five!
Five more years had to pass
before it began to flow again.
I'll take all the time I please this afternoon
before leaving my place alongside this river.
It pleases me, loving rivers.
Loving them all the way back
to their source.
Loving everything that increases me.

The Young Fire Eaters of Mexico City

They fill their mouths with alcohol
and blow it out over a lit candle
at traffic signs. Anyplace, really,
where cars line up and the drivers
are angry and frustrated and looking
for distraction—there you'll find
the young fire eaters. Doing what they do
for a few pesos. If they're lucky.
But within a year their lips
are parched and their throats raw.
They have no voice within a year.
They can't talk or cry out—
these poor children who hunt
through the streets, silently,
with a candle and a beercan filled with alcohol.
They are called "Milusos." Which translates
into "a thousand uses."

Interview

Talking about myself all day.
It brought back
something I thought over
and done with. What I'd felt
for Maryann—Anna, she calls
herself now—all those years.

I went to draw a glass of water.
Stood at the window for a time.
When I came back
we passed easily to the next thing.
Went on with my life. But
that memory entering like a spike.

Away

I had forgotten about the quail that live
on the side of the hill over behind Art and Marilyn's
place. I opened up the house, made a fire,
and then afterwards slept like a dead man.
The next morning there were quail in the drive
and in the bushes outside the front window.
When I talked to you on the phone,
I tried to joke. Don't worry
about me, I said, I have the quail
for company. Well, they took flight
when I opened the door. Been a week now
and they haven't come back. When I look
at the silent telephone I think of quail.
When I think of the quail and how they
went away, I remember talking to you that morning
and how the receiver lay in my hand. My heart—
the blurred things it was doing at the time.

Ask Him

Reluctantly, my son goes with me
through the iron gates of
the cemetery in Montparnasse.
"What a way to spend a day in Paris!"
is what he'd like to say. Did, in fact, say.
He speaks French. Has started a conversation
with a white-haired guard who offers himself
as our informal guide. So we move slowly,
the three of us, along row upon row of graves.
Everyone, it seems, is here.

It's quiet, and hot, and the street sounds
of Paris can't reach. The guard wants to steer us
to the grave of the man who invented the submarine,
and Maurice Chevalier's grave. And the grave
of the 28 year old singer, Nonnie,
covered with a mound of red roses.

I want to see the graves of the writers.
My son sighs. He doesn't want to see any of it.
Has seen enough. He's passed beyond boredom
into resignation. Guy de Maupassant; Sartre; Saint-Beauve;
Gautier, the Goncourts, Paul Verlaine and his old comrade,
Charles Baudelaire. Where we linger.

None of these names, or graves, have anything to do
with the ordered lives of my son, or the guard.
Who can this morning talk and joke together
in the French language under a fine sun.
But there are several names chiseled on Baudelaire's stone,
and I can't understand why.
Charles Baudelaire's name is between that of his mother,
who loaned him money and worried all her life
about his health; and his stepfather, a martinet
he hated and who hated him and everything he stood for.
"Ask your friend," I say. So my son asks.
It's as if he and the guard are old friends now,
and I'm there to be humored.
The guard says something and then lays

one hand over the other. Like that. Does it
again. One hand over the other. Grinning. Shrugging.
My son translates. But I understand.
"Like a sandwich, pop," my son says. "A Baudelaire sandwich."

At which the three of us walk on.
The guard had as soon be doing this as something else.
He lights his pipe. Looks at his watch. It's almost time
for his lunch, and a glass of wine.
"Ask him," I say, "if he wants to be buried
in this cemetery when he dies.
Ask him where he wants to be buried."
My son is capable of saying anything.
I recognize the words *tombeau* and *mort*
in his mouth. The guard stops.
It's clear his thoughts have been elsewhere.
Underwater warfare. The music hall, the cinema.
Something to eat and the glass of wine.
Not corruption, no, and the falling away.
Not annihiliation. Not his death.

He looks from one to the other of us.
Who are we kidding? Are we making a bad joke?
He salutes and walks away.
Heading for a table at an outdoor cafe.
Where he can take off his cap, run his fingers
through his hair. Hear laughter and voices.
The heavy clink of silverware. The ringing
of glasses. Sun on the windows.
Sun on the sidewalk and in the leaves.
Sun finding its way onto his table. His glass. His hands.

The Young Girls

Forget all experiences involving wincing.
And anything to do with chamber music.
Museums on rainy Sunday afternoons, etcetera.
The old masters. All that.
Forget the young girls. Try and forget them.
The young girls. And all that.

The Garden

In the garden, small laughter from years ago.
Lanterns burning in the willows.
The power of those four words, "I loved a woman."
Put *that* on the stone beside his name.
God keep you and be with you.

Those horses coming into the stretch at Ruidoso!
Mist rising from the meadow at dawn.
From the veranda, the blue outlines of the mountains.
What used to be within reach, out of reach.
And in some lesser things, just the opposite is true.

From a break in the wall, I could look down
On the shanty lights in the Valley of Kidron.
Very little sleep under strange roofs. His life far away.
Order anything you want! Then look for the man
With the limp to go by. He'll pay.

Playing checkers with my dad. Then he hunts up
The shaving soap, the brush and bowl, the straight
Razor, and we drive to the county hospital. I watch him
Lather my grandpa's face. Then shave him.
The dying body is a clumsy partner.

The meeting between Goethe and Beethoven
Took place in Leipzig in 1812. They talked into the night
About Lord Byron and Napoleon.
She got off the road, and from then on it was nothing
But hardpan all the way.

Drops of water in your hair.
The dark yellow of the fields, the black and blue rivers.
Going out for a walk means you intend to return, right?
Eventually.
The flame is guttering. Marvelous!

She took a stick and in the dust drew the house where
They'd live and raise their children.
There was a duck pond and a place for horses.

To write about it, one would have to write in a way
That would stop the heart and make one's hair stand on end.

Cervantes lost a hand in the Battle of Lepanto.
This was in 1570, the last great sea battle fought
In ships manned by galley slaves.
In the Unuk River, in Ketchikan, the backs of the salmon
Under the street lights as they come through town.

Redoubtable. There's a word!
It suited him down to the ground.
He fished with the rod that belonged to the deceased.
It seemed like a good idea at the time.
But later, he had his doubts.

Students and young people chanted a requiem
As Tolstoy's coffin was carried across the yard
Of the station master's house at Astapovo and placed
In the freight car. To the accompaniment of singing,
The train slowly moved off.

A hard sail and the same stars everywhere.
But the garden is right outside my window.
Don't worry your heart about me, my darling.
We weave the thread given to us.
And Spring is with me.

Wenas Ridge

The seasons turning. Memory flaring.
Three of us that fall. Young hoodlums—
shoplifters, stealers of hubcaps.
Bozos. Dick Miller, dead now.
Lyle Rousseau, son of the Ford dealer.
And I, who'd just made a girl pregnant.
Hunting late into that gold afternoon
for grouse. Following deer paths,
pushing through undergrowth, stepping over
blow-downs. Reaching out for something to hold onto.

To the top of Wenas Ridge.
Where we walked out of pine trees and could see
down deep ravines, where the wind roared, to the river.
More alive then, I thought, than I'd ever be.
But my whole life, in switchbacks, ahead of me.

Hawks, deer, coons we looked at and let go.
Killed six grouse and should have stopped.
Didn't, though we had limits.

Lyle and I climbing fifty feet or so
above Dick Miller. Who screamed—"Yaaaah!"
Then swore and swore. Legs numbing as I saw what.
That fat, dark snake rising up. Beginning to sing.
And how it sang! A timber rattler thick as my wrist.
It'd struck at Miller, but missed. No other way
to say it—he was paralyzed. Could scream, and swear,
not shoot. Then the snake lowered itself from sight
and went in under rocks. We understood
we'd have to get down. In the same way we'd got up.
Blindly crawling through brush, stepping over blow-downs,
pushing into undergrowth. Shadows falling from trees now.
But flat rocks that held the day's heat. And snakes.
My heart stopped, and then started again.
My hair stood on end. This was the moment
my life had prepared me for. And I wasn't ready.

We started down anyway. Jesus, please help me

out of this, I prayed. I'll believe in you again
and honor you always. But Jesus was crowded out
of my head by the vision of that rearing snake.
That singing. Keep believing in me, snake said,
for I will return. I made an obscure, criminal pact
that day. Praying to Jesus in one breath.
To snake in the other. Snake finally more real
to me. And memory of that day
like a blow to the calf now.

I got out, didn't I? But something happened.
I married the girl I loved, yet poisoned her life.
Lies began to coil in my heart and call it home.
Got used to darkness and its crooked ways.
Since then have always feared rattlesnakes.
Been ambivalent about Jesus.
But someone, something's responsible for this.
Now, as then.

The Juggler

(Or, The Scene to Remember from *Heaven's Gate*)

for Michael Cimino

Behind the dirty table where Kristofferson is having
breakfast, there's a window that looks onto a nineteenth-
century street in Sweetwater, Wyoming. A juggler
is at work out there, wearing a top hat and a frock coat,
a little reed of a fellow keeping three sticks
in the air. Think about this for a minute.
This juggler. This amazing act of the mind and hands.
A man who juggles for a living.
Everyone in his time has known a star,
or a gunfighter. Somebody, anyway, who pushes somebody
around. But a juggler! Blue smoke hangs inside
this awful cafe, and over that dirty table where two
grownup men talk about a woman's future. And something,
something about the Cattlemen's Association.
But the eye keeps going back to that juggler.
That tiny spectacle. At this minute, Ella's plight
or the fate of the landed emigrants
is not nearly so important as this juggler's exploits.
How'd *he* get into the act, anyway? What's his story?
That's the story I want to know. Anybody
can wear a gun and swagger around. Or fall in love
with somebody who loves somebody else. But to *juggle*
for God's sake! To give your life to that.
To go with that. A juggler.

Venice

The gondolier handed you a rose.
Took us up one canal
and then another. We glided
past Casanova's palace, the palace of
the Rossi family, palaces belonging
to the Baglioni, the Pisani, and Rajione.
Flooded. Stinking. What's left
left to rats. Blackness.
The silence total. Or nearly.
The man's breath coming and going
behind my ear. The drip of the oar.
We gliding silently on, and on.
Who would blame me if I fall
to thinking about death?
A shutter opened above our heads.
A little light showed through
before the shutter was closed once
more. There is that, and the rose
in your hand. And history.

The Eve of Battle

There are five of us in the tent, not counting
the batman cleaning my rifle. There's
a lively argument going on amongst my brother
officers. In the cookpot, salt pork turns
alongside some macaroni. But these fine fellows
aren't hungry—and it's a good thing!
All they want is to harrumph about the likes
of Huss and Hegel, anything to pass the time.
Who cares? Tomorrow we fight. Tonight they want
to sit around and chatter about nothing, about
philosophy. Maybe the cookpot isn't there
for them? Nor the stove, or those folding
stools they're sitting on. Maybe there isn't
a battle waiting for them tomorrow morning?
We'd all like that best. Maybe
I'm not there for them, either. Ready
to dish up something to eat. *Un est autre*,
as someone said. I, or another, may as well be
in China. Time to eat, brothers,
I say, handing round the plates. But someone
has just ridden up and dismounted. My batman
moves to the door of the tent, then drops his plate
and steps back. Death walks in without saying
anything. He's dressed in a morning coat and tails,
as if he's on his way to some important function.
At first I think he must be looking for the Emperor
who's old and ailing anyway. That would explain
it. Death's lost his way. What else could it be?
He has a slip of paper in his hand, looks us over
quickly, consults some names.
He raises his eyes. I turn to the stove.
When I turn back, everyone has gone. Everyone
except Death. He's still there, unmoving.
I give him his plate. He's come a long
way. He is hungry, I think, and will eat anything.

Extirpation

A little quietly outstanding uptown
piano music played in the background,
as we sat at the bar in the lounge.

Discussing the fate of the last caribou herd in the U.S.
Thirty animals who roam a small corner
of the Idaho Panhandle. Thirty animals

just north of Bonner's Ferry,
this guy said. Then called for another round.
But I had to go. We never saw one another again.

Never spoke another word to each other,
or did anything worth getting excited about
the rest of our lives.

The Hat

Walking around on our first day
in Mexico City, we come to a sidwealk café
on Reforma Avenue where a man in a hat
sits drinking a beer.
At first the man seems just like any
other man, wearing a hat, drinking a beer
in the middle of the day. But next to this man,
asleep on the broad sidewalk, is a bear
with its head on its paws. The bear's
eyes are closed, but not closed. As if
it were there, but not there. Everyone

is giving the bear a wide berth.
But a crowd is gathering, too, bulging
out onto the Avenue. The man has
a chain around his waist. The chain
goes from his lap to the bear's collar,
which is a band of steel. On the table
in front of the man rests an iron bar
with a leather handle. And as if this
were not enough, the man drains the last
of his beer and picks up his bar.
Gets up from the table and hauls
on the chain. The bear stirs, opens its
mouth—old brown and yellow fangs.
But fangs. The man jerks on the chain,
hard. The bear rises to all fours now
and growls. The man slaps the bear on
its shoulder with the bar, bringing
a tiny cloud of dust. Growls something
himself. The bear waits while the man takes
another swing. Slowly, the bear rises
onto its hind legs, swings at air and at
that goddamned bar. Begins to shuffle
then, begins to snap its jaws as the man
slugs it again, and, yes, again

with that bar. There's a tamborine.
I nearly forgot that. The man shakes

it as he chants, as he strikes the bear
who weaves on its hind legs. Growls
and snaps and weaves in a poor dance.
This scene lasts forever. Whole seasons
come and go before it's over and the bear
drops to all fours. Sits down on its
haunches, gives a low, sad growl.
The man puts the tamborine on the table.
Puts the iron bar on the table, too.

Then he takes off his hat. No one
applauds. A few people see
what's coming and walk away. But not
before the hat appears at the edge
of the crowd and begins to make its
way from hand to hand
through the throng. The hat
comes to me and stops. I'm holding
the hat, and I can't believe it.
Everybody staring at it.
I stare right along with them.
You say my name, and in the same breath
hiss, "For God's sake, pass it along."
I toss in the money I have. Then
we leave and go on to the next thing.

Hours later, in bed, I touch you
and wait, and then touch you again.
Whereupon, you uncurl your fingers.
I put my hands all over you then—
your limbs, your long hair even, hair
that I touch and cover my face with,
and draw salt from. But later,
when I close my eyes, the hat
appears. Then the tamborine. The chain.

In the Lobby of the Hotel Del Mayo

The girl in the lobby reading a leather-bound book.
The man in the lobby using a broom.
The boy in the lobby watering plants.
The desk clerk looking at his nails.
The woman in the lobby writing a letter.
The old man in the lobby sleeping in his chair.
The fan in the lobby revolving slowly overhead.
Another hot Sunday afternoon.

Suddenly, the girl lays her finger between the pages of her book.
The man leans on his broom and looks too.
The boy stops in his tracks.
The desk clerk raises his eyes and stares.
The woman quits writing.
The old man stirs and wakes up.
What is it?

Someone is running up from the harbor.
Someone who has the sun behind him.
Someone who is barechested.
Someone waving his arms.

It's clear something terrible has happened.
The man is running straight for the hotel.
His lips are working themselves into a scream.
Everyone in the lobby will be able to recall their terror.
Everyone will remember this moment the rest of their lives.

Next Door

The woman asked us in for pie. Started
telling about her husband, the man who
used to live there. How he had to be carted
off to the nursing home. He wanted
to cover this fine oak ceiling
with cheap insulation, she said. That was the first
sign of anything being wrong. Then he had
a stroke. Is a vegetable now. Anyway,
next, the game warden stuck the barrel
of his pistol into her son's ear.
And cocked the hammer. But the kid
wasn't doing that much wrong, and the game
warden is the kid's uncle, don't you see?
So everybody's on the outs. Everybody's
nuts and nobody's speaking to anybody
these days. Here's a big bone the son
found at the mouth of the river.
Maybe it's a human bone? An arm bone
or something? She puts it back on the window
sill next to a bowl of flowers.
The daughter stays in her room all day,
writing poems about her attempted suicide.
That's why we don't see her. Nobody sees
her anymore. She tears up the poems
and writes them over again. But one of these
days she'll get it right. Would you believe it—
their car threw a rod? That black car
that stands like a hearse
in the yard next door. The engine winched out,
swinging from a tree.

Late Night With Fog and Horses

They were in the living room. Saying their
goodbyes. Loss ringing in their ears.
They'd been through a lot together, but now
they couldn't go it another step. Besides, for him
there was someone else. Tears were falling.
When a horse stepped out of the fog
into the front yard. Then another, and
another. She went outside and said,
"Where did you come from, you sweet horses?"
and moved in amongst them, weeping,
touching their flanks. The horses began
to graze in the front yard.
He made two calls: one call went straight
to the sheriff—"someone's horses are out."
But there was that other call, too.
Then he joined his wife in the front
yard. Where they talked and murmured
to the horses together. (Whatever was
happening now was happening in another time.)
Horses cropped the grass in the yard
that night. A red emergency light
flashed as a sedan crept in out of fog.
Voices carried out of the fog.
At the end of that long night,
when they finally put their arms around
each other, their embrace was full of
passion and memory. Each recalled
the other's youth. Now, something had ended.
Something else rushing in to take its place.
Came the moment of leave-taking itself.
"Goodbye, go on," she said.
And the pulling away.
    Much later,
he remembered making a disastrous phone call.
One that had hung on and hung on,
like a malediction. It's boiled down
to that. The rest of his life.
Malediction.

Elk Camp

Everyone else sleeping when I step
to the door of our tent. Overhead,
stars brighter than stars ever
in my life. And farther away.
The November moon driving
a few dark clouds over the valley.
The Olympic Range beyond.

I believed I could smell the snow that was coming!
Our horses feeding inside
the little rope corral we'd put together.
From the side of the hill the sound
of spring water. Our spring water.
Wind passing in the tops of the fir trees.
I'd never smelled a forest before that
night, either. Remembered reading how
Henry Hudson and his sailors smelled
the forests of the New World
from miles out at sea. And then the next thought—
I could gladly live the rest of my life
and never pick up another book.
I looked at my hands in the moonlight
and understood there wasn't a man,
woman, or child I could lift a finger
for that night. I turned back and lay
down then in my sleeping bag.
But my eyes wouldn't close.

The next day I found cougar scat
and elk droppings. But though I rode
a horse all over that country,
up and down hills, through clouds
and along old logging roads,
I never saw an elk. Which was
fine by me. Still, I was ready.
Lost to everyone, a rifle strapped
to my shoulder. I think maybe
I could have killed one.
Would have shot at one, anyway.

Aimed just where I'd been told—
behind the shoulder where the heart
and lungs are located. "They might
run, but they won't run far. Look
at it this way," my friend said.
"How far would you run with a piece
of lead in your heart?" That depends,
my friend. That depends. But that day
I could have pulled the trigger
on anything. Or not.
Nothing mattered any more
except getting back to camp
before dark. Wonderful
to live this way! Where nothing
mattered more than anything else.
I saw myself through and through.
And I understood something too
as my life flew back to me there in the woods.

And then we packed out. Where the first
thing I did was take a hot bath.
And then reach for this book.
Grow cold and unrelenting once more.
Heartless. Every nerve alert.
Ready to kill, or not.

In Switzerland

First thing to do in Zurich
is take the No. 5 "Zoo" trolley
to the end of the track,
and get off. Been warned about
the lions. How their roars
carry over from the zoo compound
to the Flutern Cemetery.
Where I walk along
the very beautiful path
to James Joyce's grave.
Always the family man, he's here
with his wife, Nora, of course.
And his son, Giorgio,
who died a few years ago.
Lucia, his daughter, his sorrow,
still alive, still confined
in an institution for the insane.
When she was brought the news
of her father's death, she said:
>   What is he doing under the ground, that idiot?
>   When will he decide to come out?
>   He's watching us all the time.
I lingered a while. I think
I said something aloud to Mr. Joyce.
I must have. I know I must have.
But I don't recall what,
now, and I'll have to leave it at that.

A week later to the day, we depart
Zurich by train for Lucerne.
But early that morning I take
the No. 5 trolley once more
to the end of the line.
The roar of the lions falls over
the cemetery, as before.
The grass has been cut.
I sit on it for a while and smoke.
Just feels good to be there,

close to the grave. I didn't
have to say anything this time.

That night we gambled at the tables
at the Grand Hotel-Casino
on the very shore of Lake Lucerne.
Took in a strip show later.
But what to do with the memory
of that grave that came to me
in the midst of the show,
under the muted, pink stage light?
Nothing to do about it.
Or about the desire that came later,
crowding everything else out,
like a wave.
Still later, we sit on a bench
under some linden trees, under stars.
Made love with each other.
Reaching into each other's clothes for it.
The lake a few steps away.
Afterwards, dipped our hands
into the cold water.
Then walked back to our hotel,
happy and tired, ready to sleep
for eight hours.

All of us, all of us, all of us
trying to save
our immortal souls, some ways
seemingly more round-
about, and mysterious
than others. We're having
a good time here. But hope
all will be revealed soon.

Anathema

The entire household suffered.
My wife, myself, the two children, and the dog
whose puppies were born dead.
Our affairs, such as they were, withered.
My wife was dropped by her lover,
the one-armed teacher of music who was
her only contact with the outside world
and the things of the mind.
My own girlfriend said she couldn't stand it
anymore, and went back to her husband.
The water was shut off.
All that summer the house baked.
The peach trees were blasted.
Our little flower bed lay trampled.
The brakes went out on the car, and the battery
failed. The neighbors quit speaking
to us and closed their doors in our faces.
Checks flew back at us from merchants—
and then mail stopped being delivered
altogether. Only the sheriff got through
from time to time—with one or the other
of our children in the back seat,
pleading to be taken anywhere but here.
And then mice entered the house by the droves.
Followed by a bull snake. My wife
found it sunning itself in the living room
next to the dead TV. How she dealt with it
is another matter. Chopped its head off
right there on the floor.
And then chopped it in two when it continued
to writhe. We saw we couldn't hold out
any longer. We were beaten.
We wanted to get down on our knees
and say forgive us our sins, forgive us
our lives. But it was too late.
Too late. No one around would listen.
We had to watch as the house was pulled down,
the ground plowed up, and then
we were dispersed in four directions.

Energy

Last night at my daughter's, near Blaine,
she did her best to tell me
what went wrong
between her mother and me.
"Energy. You two's energy was all wrong."
She looks like her mother
when her mother was young.
Laughs like her.
Moves the drift of hair
from her forehead, like her mother.
Can take a cigarette down
to the filter in three draws,
just like her mother. I thought
this visit would be easy. Wrong.
This is hard, brother. Those years
spilling over into my sleep when I try
to sleep. To wake to find a thousand
cigarettes in the ashtray and every
light in the house burning. I can't
pretend to understand anything:
today I'll be carried
three thousand miles away into
the loving arms of another woman, not
her mother. No. She's caught
in the flywheel of a new love.
I turn off the last light
and close the door.
Moving toward whatever ancient thing
it is that works the chains
and pulls us so remorselessly on.

The Fishing Pole of the Drowned Man

I didn't want to use it at first.
Then I thought, no, it would
give up secrets and bring me luck—
that's what I needed then.
Besides, he'd left it behind for me
to use when he went swimming that time.
Shortly afterwards, I met two women.
One of them loved opera and the other
was a drunk who'd done time
in jail. I took up with one
and began to drink and fight a lot.
The way this woman could sing and carry on!
We went straight to the bottom.

CONTRIBUTORS

Joan Aleshire is presently working as interum director of the MFA Writing Program at Warren Wilson College. She is the author of *Cloud Train* (U. of Texas Tech Press).

Keith Althus is a member of the Writing Committee for the Fine Arts Work Center in Provincetown, MA.

Barbara Anderson has held a Stegner Fellowship from Stanford and currently teaches at the University of Arizona. Her chapbook, *Ordinary Days*, is available from Porch Press.

Phillip Appleman, Distinguished Professor of English at Indiana University, has published three volumes of poetry, the latest being *Open Doorways* (W.W. Norton). A new volume, *Darwin's Ark*, has just been published by Indiana University Press.

Jennifer Atkinson has just completed an MFA in Poetry at the University of Iowa Writers' Workshop. She recently spent six months living and working in the Kathmandu Valley in Nepal.

Wendy Battin's *In The Solar Wind* has just been published by Doubleday as a selection of the 1984 National Poetry Series.

Charles Baxter's stories have appeared in *Atlantic*, and *Triquarterly*, among others and have been selected for *The Best American Short Stories of 1983*. He was the winner of this year's AWP Fiction Award and his collection of stories, *The Harmony of the World*, has just been published by the U. of Missouri Press. A second collection will be published in 1985 by Viking.

Ann Beattie's most recent books are *The Burning House* and *Falling in Place*. She lives in New York City.

Robin Behn's poems have appeared in *APR, Antioch Review, Crazyhorse, Field, Missouri Review*, and others. She teaches in Iowa City.

Ted Bettinen is an oceanographer on the staff of the U. of Rhode Island. His work has appeared in *Mother Jones, The Massachusetts Review*, and others.

Jane Birdsall lives in St. Louis and is currently working on a children's book about potato farming in Michigan.

W. Bishop works at Navajo Community College in Tsaile, AZ. Her work has appeared in *Mississippi Review, Denver Quarterly*, and *The Southern Review*.

Jane Blue lives in Sacramento, CA.

Deborah Boe has recently published poems in *Kayak, Nantucket Review*, and other journals. She has received writers' grants from the NEA and the New Jersey State Council on the Arts.

mR

MISSISSIPPI REVIEW
SOUTHERN STATION
BOX 5144
HATTIESBURG, MS 39406
$10/$18/$26   1/2/3 YRS

Philip Booth was recently elected a Fellow of the Academy of American Poets. He is at work on his seventh book.

Charles Bukowski is the author of a number of books of poetry and fiction, including *Women* and *Ham on Rye*, both from Black Sparrow Press.

Teresa Cader lives in Cambridge, MA. Her poems have appeared in *Tendril* and *Triquarterly*.

Hayden Carruth's most recent books are *If You Call This Cry a Song* (poems) and *Effluences from the Sacred Caves* (criticism), both published in 1983.

Raymond Carver is the author of four books of short stories, *Will You Please Be Quiet, Please?*, *Furious Seasons*, *What We Talk About When We Talk About Love*, and *Cathedral* (Knopf, 1983), which was nominated for the National Book Critics Circle Award, was a runner up for the Pulitzer Prize, and has been translated into 20 languages. He has taught at the University of California at Berkeley and at Santa Cruz, at the University of Iowa, the University of Texas, and at Syracuse University. He has been awarded Fellowships from the Guggenheim Foundation and from the National Endowment for the Arts in both poetry and fiction. He is also currently a recipient of the American Academy of Arts & Letters' Strauss Living Award. His fourth book of poems, *Where Water Comes Together With Other Water*, will be published in April by Random House.

David Citino teaches at Ohio State at Marion. His most recent book is *The Appasionata Poems* (Cleveland State U. Press, 1983). This year Texas Review will publish *The Appasionata Lectures*.

Robert Clinton lives in Rochester, MA., and works as a carpenter.

Judith Ortiz Cofer's poems have appeared in *New Letters, Prairie Schooner*, and *Southern Poetry Review* among others. Her first book of poems, *Reaching for the Mainland*, is forthcoming from Bi-Lingual Review Press/ SUNY Binghampton. She teaches at the U. of Georgia.

Gillian Connoley, who was born and raised in Texas, now lives in New Orleans. Her chapbook, *Woman Speaking Inside Film Noir*, has just been published by Lynx House Press.

Kenneth Zamora Damacion's poems have appeared in *Croton Review, MSS, Columbia*, and *Tendril*.

Charles Darling has published poems recently in *Poets On*, and *Samisdat*, among others.

Jon Davis is in the MFA program at the University of Montana, Missoula, where he edits *Cutbank* Magazine. His chapbook, *West of New England*, won the 1982 Morriam Frontier Award, and he has publshed in such magazines as *Missouri Review, Poetry Now*, and *Another Chicago Magazine*.

40th Anniversary

DAVID SCHUBERT
Works and Days

Collected POEMS

These poems that "poets keep... to remind them of what poetry can be."—JOHN ASHBERY

They "speak out with an Orphic voice."—DAVID IGNATOW

He is "the rightful heir of Stevens, Eliot and Crane."
—IRVIN EHRENPREIS

Multi-Auto BIOGRAPHY

Composed by Renée Karol Weiss.

Schubert's life in its world and time— New York in the 30's and 40's.

"An inspired collage..."—JAMES MERRILL
of letters, poems, news, memoirs, interviews.

"A remarkable document: haunting, suspenseful, original, deeply moving. As a tribute to a gifted poet who died tragically young, it attains the dignity and clarity of poetry itself."
—JOYCE CAROL OATES

ESSAYS

on Schubert by Ashbery, Ehrenpreis, Galler, Gibbons, Gregory, Ignatow, Wright.

QRL 2 volume subscription $15
Single paper $10, cloth $20

Joseph Deumer teaches creative writing at San Diego State. A chapbook, *The Light of Day,* was published this year by Windhover Press.

Jond Devol is an undergraduate at Ohio University. These are her first published poems.

Deborah Diggs is a teaching-writing fellow at UI. Her poems have appeared in *Antaeus, APR, Georgia Review,* and *Antioch Review,* among others.

Carol Dine's poems have appeared in such magazines as *Harbor Review* and *The Writer.* Her manuscript, *Naming the Sky,* is in search of a publisher.

Patricia Dobler's poetry was included in last year's Pushcart Prize anthology. She teaches at Carnegie Mellon University and at the University of Pittsburgh. Her work has recently appeared in *Kayak, Ohio Review,* and *Prairie Schooner.*

Elizabeth Dodd teaches Introductory Creative Writing at Indiana University where she is an MFA candidate.

Susan Dodd is the winner of the 1984 Iowa School of Letters Award for Short Fiction. Her collection of stories, *Old Wives Tales,* has just been published by the University of Iowa. She is on the Faculty of the MFA Writing Program at Vermont College. She lives in Connecticut.

Denis Dorney lives in Venice, CA. Recent poems have appeared in *Cutbank, Cimarron Review, West Branch,* and *Pequod.*

Charles Edward Eaton has published eight collections of poetry, three collections of short stories, and a book of art criticism. His ninth book of poems, *The Work of the Wrench,* will be published by Cornwall Books in 1985.

Jane Eklund's poetry has appeared in *The Massachusetts Review* and *The Seattle Review.* She works for the publications Dept. at the University of Iowa.

Kathy Fagan is a winner of the 1985 National Poetry Series. Her book will be published by E.P. Dutton in April.

Donald Finkel is poet-in-residence at Washington U. in St. Louis. His most recent book, *The Detachable Man,* will be published by Atheneum in late 1984.

Caroline Finkelstein lives in Rochester, MA. She is the recipient of an NEA Fellowship for 1984.

Robert Funge's "John/Henry" is a long poem to and about John Berryman, parts of which are appearing in such periodicals as *Cottonwood Review, Kansas Quarterly,* and *Great River Review.*

T. Gertler lives in New York City and is the author of *Elbowing the Seducer* (Random House, 1984) from which "An Affair, I Guess" is taken.

The Coordinating Council of Literary Magazines Announces the Winners of The 1984 General Electric Foundation Awards for Younger Writers:

John Godfrey
for poetry
published in
GANDHABBA
and MAG CITY,
New York.

Paul Hoover
for poetry
published in
ANOTHER
CHICAGO MAGAZINE,
Chicago.

Michelle Huneven
for fiction
published in
WILLOW SPRINGS,
Cheney,
Washington.

Tama Janowitz
for fiction
published in
MISSISSIPPI REVIEW,
Hattiesburg,
Mississippi.

Margo Jefferson
for
a literary essay
published in
GRAND STREET,
New York.

Rudy Wilson
for fiction
published in
THE PARIS
REVIEW,
New York.

The awards recognize excellence in new writers while honoring the significant contribution of America's literary magazines. This year's judges were Doris Grumbach, Elizabeth Hardwick, Kenneth Koch, James Alan McPherson and Gary Soto.
For information about
THE GENERAL ELECTRIC FOUNDATION AWARDS FOR YOUNGER WRITERS, please write to: CCLM, 2 Park Avenue, New York 10016.

Line portraits by David Johnson.

Patricia Goedicke teaches at the University of Montana in Missoula. Her work has appeared in *The New Yorker*, and *Hudson Review*, among others. Her sixth book of poems, *The Wind of Our Going*, has just been published by Copper Canyon Press.

Beckian Fritz Goldberg teaches English and Creative Writing at Arizona State U. Her work has appeared in *New Letters, Antioch Review*, and *Nimrod*, among others. She was a finalist for the 1984 Pablo Neruda Prize.

Raphael Guillen lives in Granada, Spain and has published 10 books of poetry.

Carol Hamilton lives in Berkeley, CA., where she works as an editor.

Amy Hempel lives in New York City and San Francisco. Her stories have appeared in *Vanity Fair* and *Triquarterly*. A collection of her short stories, *Reasons to Live*, will appear in the Spring of 1985 from Alfred A. Knopf.

Carol Henri's work has appeared in *Tendril, Ironwood*, and *Poetry Now*, among others.

John Hildebidle's collection of poems, *The Old Chore*, is available from Alice James Books. He is also the author of *Thoreau: A Naturalist's Liberty* (Harvard U. Press). His poems have appeared in *Poetry Northwest, Ploughshares*, and *Kenyon Review*. He teaches literature at M.I.T.

Art Homer is poet-in-residence at the University of Nebraska at Omaha's Writers' Workshop. His first collection, *What We Did After The Rain*, is forthcoming from Abbattoir Editions.

Jane Hoogestraat is working on a Ph.D. in English at the University of Chicago. Her work has appeared in *North Dakota Quarterly*, and *Kansas Quarterly*.

Lynda Hull is an Associate Editor for *Crazyhorse* Magazine. She lives in Provincetown, MA.

Joseph Hutchison is the author of two collections of poems from Juniper Press, *Thirst*, and *Weathers, Vistas, Houses, Dust*. He is also the author of *Shadow-Light*, the 1982 Colorado Governor's Award volume.

Kit Irwin lives in Langhorn Manor, PA.

Sibyl James lives in Seattle, WA.

Phyllis Janowitz is the author of *Visiting Rites* (U. of Princeton Press, 1982) which was nominated for the National Book Critics Circle Award, and *Rites of Strangers*, the 1978 AWP Award winner. She teaches Creative Writing at Cornell.

Marilyn Kallet teaches writing at the U. of Tennessee in Knoxville. Her most recent book of poems is *In the Great Night* (Ithaca House). In 1985 LSU will publish her critical study, *Honest Simplicity in William Carlos Williams' "Asphodel, That Greeny Flower."*

Writing in a Nuclear Age

Jim Schley, editor

"Anyone concerned for the fate of literature in the U.S. today, which means anyone aware of the impending death of our civilization, *must* read this book. *Writing in a Nuclear Age* is an anthology of our only collective hope."—Hayden Carruth

47 writers, including Denise Levertov, Grace Paley, Robert Penn Warren, Seamus Heaney, Maxine Kumin, William Matthews, Galway Kinnell, William Stafford, and Susan Griffin, explore the multitude of ways contemporary imaginative writing has come to terms with—or sought to evade—the acute sense of danger we all face. Dedicated to the potential for language to expose and comfort, prophesy and inspire, these writers have tried to restore to poetry and fiction their historic role as wellsprings of new thoughts and feelings.

"A resounding reaffirmation of the importance of contemporary writing as a moral force."—*Choice*

"There is little 'protest poetry' in this excellent collection, but much thoughtful consideration of what it means to be living in this unprecedented historic moment . . . This volume should be in every library, public and personal."—*Beloit Poetry Journal*

Reprint of a special issue of *New England Review and Bread Loaf Quarterly*. Paper, $8.95

University Press of New England
3 Lebanon Street
Hanover, New Hampshire 03755

Lawrence Kearney is the author of *Kingdom Come* (Wesleyan, 1980), has received NEA, CAPS, and Massachusetts Artists Foundation Grants. He is currently on a Guggenheim Fellowship. He works as an antique dealer in Cambridge, MA.

Dave Kelly is the author of thirteen books and chapbooks of poetry and prose, including *Filming Assassinations* (Ithaca House, 1982). He is the director of the creative writing program at the State University College in Genesco, NY.

Chuck Kinder teaches in the English Department at the University of Pittsburgh. "Disneyland" is an excerpt from his forthcoming novel, *Honeymooners*.

Phyllis Koestenbaum is the author of four books. Her work has been published in *NER/BLQ*, *Threepenny Review*, and *Northwest Review*, where her work was featured.

Kendra Kopelke is a graduate of the Johns Hopkins Writing Seminars. She is currently writer-in-residence at Washington College in Chestertown, MD.

Judith Kroll's poems are from her manuscript, *Rumors of the Goddess*. She is the author of *In the Temperate Zone* (Scribners) and has had poems published in such magazines as *The New Yorker, Poetry,* and *Antaeus*. Since leaving Vassar in 1975, she has lived mostly in Simla, India, in the lower Himalayas.

Maxine Kumin's *Our Ground Time Here Will Be Brief: New and Selected Poems* was published by Viking in 1982 simultaneously with a collection of short stories, *Why Can't We Live Together Like Civilized Human Beings*. She was the poetry consultant to the Library of Congress in 1981–1982.

James Howard Kunstler's stories have appeared in *Playboy, Penthouse,* and *Cosmopolitan*. He is the author of four novels, the most recent of which, *An Embarrassment of Riches*, an adventure set in the Ohio River Wilderness in 1803, will be published by Dial Press early next year.

Dorianne Laux lives in Berkeley, CA. Her work appeared in *The San Diego Poet's Press*, and the *Suisan Valley Review*.

Sydney Lea is the founding editor of *New England Review/Bread Loaf Quarterly*. He is the author of two books of poems from Illinois: *Searching the Drowned Man* (1980) and *The Floating Candles* (1982). His work has recently appeared in *Atlantic, The New Yorker,* and *The New Republic*.

Lisa Lewis is a Ph.D. student and teaching assistant in literature at the University of Iowa. Her work has appeared in *Poetry, Cutbank,* and *Southern Poetry Review*.

David Long's book of short stories, *Home Fires* (U. of Illinois Press), won the 1983 St. Lawrence Award for short fiction. He lives in Kalispell, MT.

ESSAY ON AIR
Reg Saner

Green Feathers

Five minutes till dawn
and a moist breath of pine resin comes to me
as from across a lake. It smells of wet lumber, naked
 and fragrant,
whose sap is another nostalgia.

In the early air
we keep trying to catch sight of something lost up ahead,
a moment when the light seems to have seen us
exactly as we wish we were.

Like a heap of green feathers poised on the rim of a cliff?
Like a sure thing that hasn't quite happened?
Like a marvelous idea that won't work?

Routinely amazing—
how moss tufts, half mud, keep supposing
almost nothing is hopeless. How even the dimmest potato
grew eyes on faith the light would be there
and it was.

102 pages
$12.95 hardcover
$ 5.95 softcover

A new book of poems by the winner of
the Walt Whitman Award *(Climbing Into the Roots)*
and the
National Poetry Series Open Competition *(So This Is The Map)*.

OHIO REVIEW BOOKS
Ellis Hall
Ohio University
Athens, Ohio 45701
(614) 594-5889

Gary Margolis is director of counseling at Middlebury College. Last year the University of Georgia Press published his book *The Day We Still Stand Here*.

Paul Mariani's most recent book of poems is *Crossing Cocytus* (Grove). He is also the author of *A New World Naked*, a biography of poet William Carlos Williams. He teaches at the University of Massachusetts.

Lynn Martin is a graduate student in the U. of Washington's Writing Program and recently received the Vernon M. Spence Poetry Prize from the University of Washington. She lives in Wauna, WA.

Mekeel McBride is the author of two books of poems, *No Ordinary World* and *The Going Under of the Evening Land*, both from Carnegie-Mellon. She teaches at the University of New Hampshire.

Gardner McFall lives and works in New York City. Her poems have appeared in *The Georgia Review*, *Shenandoah*, and *Ploughshares*.

Martin McGovern is currently a doctoral candidate in the creative writing program at the University of Houston. His poems have appeared in *The North American Review*, *Crazyhorse*, and *The Chicago Review*.

Sandy McKinney is a freelance writer, editor, and translator and has recently returned to the US from Spain, where she was working with Raphael Guillen on a book length selection of his poetry.

Lynn McMahon's poems have appeared in *The Atlantic*, *Iowa Review*, *Missouri Review*, and *Prairie Schooner*, among others. Her chapbook, *White Tablecloths* was the 1983 winner of the Riverstone International Chapbook Competition and has been published by the Foothills Art Center.

Jane Miller's latest book of poems is *The Greater Leisures*, a winner in last year's National Poetry Series. She lives in Provincetown, MA., and is currently writing a novel.

Judson Mitcham is a psychology teacher at Fort Valley State College. His poems have appeared in *Georgia Review*, *Prairie Schooner*, and *Ironwood*, among others.

Greg Moore is working on a Ph.D. at the U. of Colorado. His work has appeared in *Atlantic*, *Mississippi Review*, and others. He is presently completing a book of translations of the Mexican poet, Jose Emilio Pacheco's *Desde Entonces*.

Fred Muratori is a reference librarian at Cornell University and has an MA in Creative Writing from Syracuse U. His poems have appeared in *NER/BLQ* and *Poetry Northwest*, among others.

Bea Opengard teaches at the University of Kentucky in Lexington. A chapbook is forthcoming from The Seamark Press.

Brenda Marie Osbey teaches at Dillard University and is the author of *Ceremony for Minneconjoux* (Callaloo Poetry Series, 1983).

GODDARD MFA WRITING PROGRAM AT VERMONT COLLEGE

Faculty
Joe David Bellamy
Dianne Benedict
Kelly Cherry
Mark Doty
Mekeel McBride
Larry Millman
Jack Myers
Gladys Swan
Leslie Ullman
Roger Weingarten

Visiting Writers
Andre Dubus
George Garrett
Albert Goldbarth
Robert Herz
Richard Howard
Denis Johnson
Howard Norman
Jayne Anne Phillips
Marge Piercy
Susan Fromberg Schaeffer
Laurie Sheck
Jane Shore
Richard Tillinghast
Charles Wright

Intensive 12-Day Residencies
August and January on the Vermont campus

- Workshops, classes, readings
- Planning for 6-month projects

Non-Resident 6-Month Writing Projects
Individually designed during residency

- Direct criticism of manuscripts
- Sustained dialogue with faculty

Degree work in poetry, fiction and non-fiction.

For further information:

**Roger Weingarten
MFA Writing Program
Box 515,
Vermont College
Montpelier
Vermont 05602**

Other opportunities for graduate and undergratuate writing study are also available at the college. Vermont College admits students regardless of race, creed, sex or ethnic origin.

Alicia Ostriker's most recent book of poems is *A Woman Under the Surface* (Princeton). In 1984, she was the recipient of a Guggenheim Foundation grant and is at work on a new book of poems *The Imaginary Lover*.

Robert Pack's new book, *Faces in a Single Tree: A Cycle of Monologues*, has just been published by David Godine.

Eric Pankey's poems have recently appeared in *Kenyon Review, Ironwood,* and *Crazyhorse*. His first book, *For The New Year*, is the 1984 Walt Whitman selection and will be published in November by Atheneum.

Wyatt Prunty's collection of poems, *The Times Between*, was published by Johns Hopkins University Press in 1982. His poems have appeared in *The Georgia Review, Southern Review,* among others.

John R. Reed's book, *A Gallery of Spiders*, was published in 1980 by Ontarion Review Press. His poems have appeared in *Poetry, Triquarterly, the Paris Review,* and are featured in the current issue of *Ontario Review*.

Paulette Roeske recently completed an MFA at Warren Wilson College. She has recently completed a book of poems, *Breathing Under Water*.

William Pitt Root's most recent book is *Invisible Guests* (Confluence, 1984). He is currently writer-in-residence at the U. of Montana.

Michael Rosen's collection, *A Drink at the Mirage*, was recently published by Princeton University Press. He is working on a new collection while on an NEA Fellowship.

Jeff Schiff is presently engaged in postdoctoral work in rhetoric & composition at Purdue University.

Ron Schreiber works as a typist, manuscript marker, & homemaker in Cambridge, MA. His poems have appeared in a number of respectable and fugitive magazines.

Bob Shacochis's stories have appeared in *Esquire, Playboy,* and numerous other magazines. A collection of stories, *Easy in the Islands*, has just been published by Crown, Inc.

Charles Siebert lives in New York City. His work has recently appeared in *The New Yorker* and in the Howard Moss anthology, *New York Poems*. He is currently traveling in Central America, completing a book of poems.

Jim Simmerman's *Home* is available from Dragon Gate, Inc. He is director of the creative writing program at Northern Arizona University.

Charlie Smith is a native of Georgia and a graduate of the Iowa Writers' Workshop. His novel *Canaan*, will be published in February by Simon & Schuster. In 1983 he won the *Paris Review* Aga Khan Prize for Fiction.

Judith Steinbergh lives in Brookline, MA., and is the author of *Lillian Bloom: A Separation* and *Motherwriter*, both from Wampeter Press.

ROBERT PACK

Faces in a Single Tree

A Cycle of Monologues

With this new book of monologues Robert Pack becomes the true heir of his fellow New Englander, Robert Frost. It is a great rarity at any time but I think especially now to find voices so believable and verse so good.
–*Donald Justice*

Robert Pack always is attentive to the music of language and landscape. "What human love allows, we have," a character in the book's concluding poem, "Prayer for Prayer," proclaims, and he could be describing the range of emotions illuminated in this powerful and satisfying collection of dramatic monologues. –*Linda Pastan*

FACES IN A SINGLE TREE by Robert Pack

Please send: to: _____
____ softcovers @ $7.95 each   _____
____ hardcovers @ $13.95 each   _____
(Mass. residents add 5% sales tax)
postage and handling $1.50
TOTAL (enclosed)   _____

DAVID R. GODINE, PUBLISHER, 306 Dartmouth Street, Boston, MA 02116

Wood engraving by Thomas W. Nason, courtesy of the Boston Public Library Print Department

Stephanie Strickland's poems have been published in *Ploughshares, Agni Review, Chowder Review, Ironwood,* and others.

Robyn Supraner is the author of award winning children's books. Her poems have appeared in *Ploughshares, Southern Poetry Review,* and others.

Arthur Sze received an NEA Fellowship in 1982. His third book of poems, *Dazzled,* was published by Floating Island Publications. He lives in Santa Fe.

Margaret Szumowski lives in Western Massachusetts.

James Tate's most recent volume of poems, *Constant Defender,* was published by Ecco Press in 1983. In the Spring of 1984, he occupied the Endowed Chair of Creative Writing at the University of Alabama.

Chase Twichell's first book of poems, *Northern Spy,* was published in 1981 by the University of Pittsburgh Press. Her work has appeared in such journals as *Crazyhorse, Field, Ploughshares,* and *Prairie Schooner.*

Constance Urdang was raised in New York City and now lives in St. Louis. Her latest book, *Only The World,* was published last year by the Pitt Poetry Series.

Larkin Warren is a freelance writer currently living in Brooklyn. She was the recipeint of an NEA Fellowship for 1984.

Bruce Weigl teaches at Old Dominion University in Norfolk. *The Imagination as Glory: Essays on the Poetry of James Dickey* has just been published by the University of Illinois; a book of poems, *Monkey Wars,* is forthcoming from the University of Georgia Press.

Roger Weingarten directs the MFA Writing Program at the University of Vermont. With Jack Myers, he recently edited the *New American Poets of the 80's* anthology from Wampeter Press.

Don Welch lives in Kearney, NE, and was the 1980 winner of the Pablo Neruda Prize.

Joy Williams is the author of two novels, *State of Grace* and *The Changeling.* A collection of short stories, *Taking Care,* was published in 1982 by Random House. She lives in Florida.

Ruth Whitman is the author of seven books of poetry and translation including *Tamsen Donner: A Woman's Journey* and *Permanent Address: New Poems 1973-1980.* She is a senior Fulbright Writer-in-Residence in Jerusalem for 1984-85.

Ellen Whittaker's poems have appeared in *Ploughshares, Pequod,* and *The Antioch Review.*

Carolyn Wright's most recent book was *Premonitions of an Uneasy Guest* (AWP Award Series, 1983). A chapbook, *From a White Woman's Journal,* is forthcoming from Water Mark Press. She is currently Visiting Assistant Professor of Creative Writing at Whitman College.

"Writers who love and create short stories in America today are our purest literary artists, and Robley Wilson, Jr. is a prince among them." —Vance Bourjaily

DANCING FOR MEN

Winner of the Drue Heinz Literature Prize

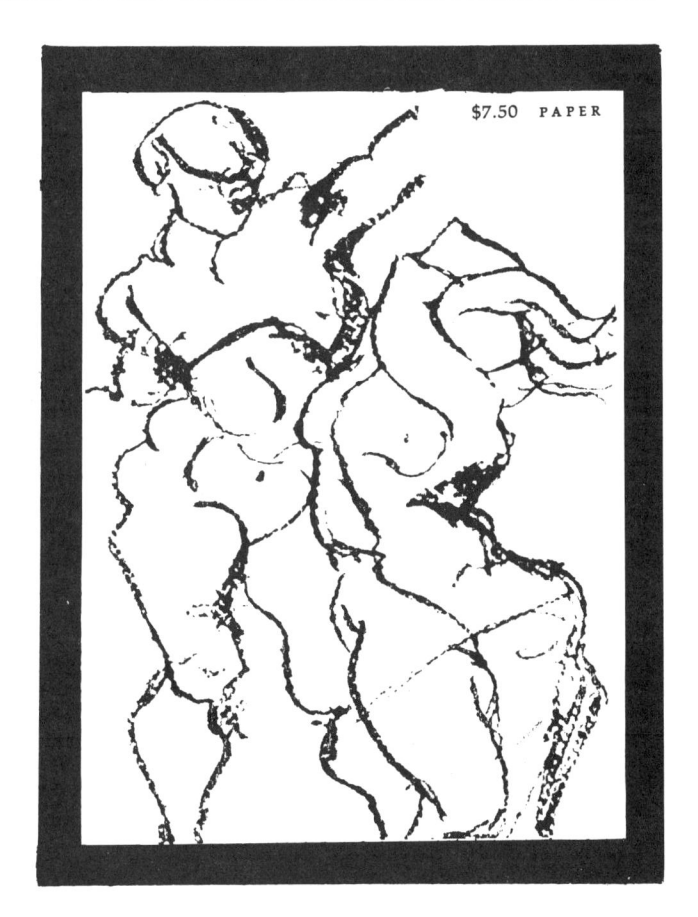

$7.50 PAPER

Robley Wilson, Jr.

The Ecco Press
18 West 30th Street, New York 10001

Ai
John Ashbery
Marvin Bell
Michael Benedikt
Elizabeth Bishop
Robert Bly
James Dickey
Michael S. Harper
Richard Hugo
Donald Justice
Galway Kinnell
Stanley Kunitz
Denise Levertov
W. S. Merwin
Josephine Miles
Adrienne Rich
May Sarton
Charles Simic
W. D. Snodgrass
William Stafford
Mark Strand
James Tate
David Wagoner
Diane Wakoski
Richard Wilbur
James Wright

American Poetry Observed

Poets on Their Work

Edited by

Joe David Bellamy

In *American Poetry Observed* twenty-six major contemporary poets discuss everything from conjuring the muse to breaking a line, from their personal lives to the future of poetry and its relation to politics, religion, and the arts. Throughout, they lead us to a clearer understanding of the elusive craft of poetry and, in the process, reveal a great deal about themselves. "Lively and informed." – *Publishers Weekly*. $19.95

Order toll free 800 / 638-3030.
Maryland residents phone 301 / 824-7300.

UNIVERSITY OF ILLINOIS PRESS
54 E. Gregory Drive / Champaign IL 61820

MATTERS OF LIFE AND DEATH
NEW AMERICAN STORIES
EDITED AND WITH AN INTRODUCTION BY
TOBIAS WOLFF

▶ *"Wonderful stories... This is the sound of today's fiction."*
-Annie Dillard

▶ *"Wolff has impeccable judgement. The variation of vision and voice in this collection is dazzling."*
-Hilma Wolitzer

▶ *"The best collection of recent short fiction I've seen. I read it in one sitting and will continue to read it for a long, long time."*
-Harry Crews

▶ *"Wow! You won't find a more exciting collection of contemporary short fiction."*
-Tim O'Brien

SHORT STORIES BY
ANN BEATTIE • RAYMOND CARVER • STANLEY ELKIN
RICHARD FORD • JOHN GARDNER • BARRY HANNAH
RON HANSEN • WILLIAM KITTREDGE • JOHN L'HEUREUX
LEONARD MICHAELS • JAYNE ANN PHILLIPS • DAVID QUAMMEN
MARY ROBISON • JEAN THOMPSON • STEPHANIE VAUGHN
JOY WILLIAMS • RICHARD YATES

256 pages. $9.95 paperbound, postpaid. ISBN 0-931694-14-0
$14.95 casebound, postpaid. ISBN 0-931694-17-5

WampeterPress   Box 512   Green Harbor. Mass. 02041

Won't You Subscribe?

"What I admire most about *Tendril* is its editorial balance . . . incredibly diverse yet consistently outstanding writing. And the magazine is so beautifully produced."
Scott Walker, Greywolf Press

"Imaginative editing . . . A true treasure for both casual readers and members of literature departments everywhere . . . recommended for Library collections . . . The whole magazine is a delight."
Bill Katz, *Library Journal*

"The editorial basis for accepting poetry for publication in *Tendril* is literary quality and specifically 'eclectic quality.' . . a wide range of subject matter equalled by a variety of cogent themes. Attractive, lively, and readable . . . *Tendril* deserves the support — because it has earned the support — of all those who care about poetry."
James B. Hall
Literary Magazine Review

---

mail to: TENDRIL, Box 512, Green Harbor, Massachusetts 02041

☐ 1 year/$12   ☐ 2 years/$17   ☐ 3 years/$27

Begin with issue No._____

Name _____

Address _____

City _____ State _____ Zip _____